Richard Rorty

Richard Rorty

Critical Dialogues

Edited by

Matthew Festenstein and
Simon Thompson

Polity

Copyright © this collection Polity Press 2001
Chapter 7 © Taylor & Francis Inc.
Chapter 8 © Norman Geras. Chapter 11 © University of Hawaii Press

First published in 2001 by Polity Press in association with Blackwell Publishers Ltd

Editorial office:
Polity Press
65 Bridge Street
Cambridge CB2 1UR, UK

Marketing and production:
Blackwell Publishers Ltd
108 Cowley Road
Oxford OX4 1JF, UK

Published in the USA by
Blackwell Publishers Inc.
350 Main Street,
Malden, MA 02148, USA

A catalogue record for this book is available from the British Library.

Library of Congress Cataloging-in-Publication Data

Richard Rorty : critical dialogues / edited by Matthew Festenstein and Simon Thompson.
   p. cm.
   Includes bibliographical references and index.
   ISBN 0-7456-2165-1 (alk. paper)—ISBN 0-7456-2166-X (pbk. : alk. paper)
   1. Rorty, Richard. I. Festenstein, Matthew. II. Thompson, Simon.

  B945.R24 R55 2001
  191—dc21   2001021498

Typeset in 10.5 on 12 pt Sabon
by Kolam Information Services Pvt Ltd, Pondicherry, India
Printed in Great Britain by MPG Books Ltd, Bodmin, Cornwall

This book is printed on acid-free paper.

031102-5276D8

Contents

Acknowledgements

The editors and publisher would like to thank the following for permission to quote copyrighted material:

'Reason and Aesthetics between Modernity and Postmodernity' by Richard Shusterman, copyright 1997 from *Practicing Philosophy* (1997), reproduced by permission of Taylor and Francis, Inc., *http://www.routledge.ny.com*; 'Justice as a Larger Loyalty', from *Justice and Democracy: Cross-Cultural Perspectives*, edited by Ron Bontekoe and Marietta Stepaniants (1997), reproduced by permission of The University of Hawaii Press.

Norman Geras's chapter, 'Progress without Foundations?' appeared originally in *Res Publica*, II, 2, Deborah Charles Publications (1996) and subsequently in *Contract of Mutual Indifference* (Verso 1998).

Contributors

Molly Cochran is Assistant Professor of International Affairs at the Georgia Institute of Technology. She is the author of *Normative Theory in International Relations* (Cambridge University Press, 1999).

Daniel Conway is Professor of Philosophy at Pennsylvania State University. He is the author of *Nietzsche and the Political* (Routledge, 1996) and *Nietzsche's Dangerous Game* (Cambridge University Press, 1997).

Matthew Festenstein is Lecturer in Politics at the University of Sheffield. He is the author of *Pragmatism and Political Theory* (Polity, 1997).

Norman Geras is Professor of Government at the University of Manchester. He is the author of *The Legacy of Rosa Luxemburg* (Verso, 1976), *Marx and Human Nature* (Verso, 1983), *Literature of Revolution* (Verso, 1986), *Solidarity in the Conversation of Humankind: the ungroundable liberalism of Richard Rorty* (Verso, 1995), and *The Contract of Mutual Indifference: political philosophy after the holocaust* (Verso, 1998).

John Horton is Reader in Political Theory at the University of Keele. He is the author of *Political Obligation* (Macmillan, 1992).

David Owen is Senior Lecturer in Political Theory and Assistant Director of the Centre for Post-Analytic Philosophy at the University of Southampton. He is the author of *Maturity and Modernity*

(Routledge, 1993) and *Nietzsche, Politics and Modernity* (Sage, 1995).

Richard Rorty teaches philosophy in the Comparative Literature Department at Stanford University. His principal books include *Philosophy and the Mirror of Nature* (Princeton University Press, 1979), *Consequences of Pragmatism* (Minnesota University Press, 1982), *Contingency, Irony, and Solidarity* (Cambridge University Press, 1989), *Objectivity, Relativism and Truth, Philosophical Papers*, vol. 1 (Cambridge University Press, 1991), *Essays on Heidegger and Others, Philosophical Papers*, vol. 2 (Cambridge University Press, 1991), *Achieving Our Country: leftist thought in twentieth century America* (Harvard University Press, 1998), *Truth and Progress, Philosophical Papers*, vol. 3 (Cambridge University Press, 1998), *Philosophy and Social Hope* (Penguin, 1999).

Richard Shusterman is Professor and Chair of the Department of Philosophy at Temple University and Directeur de Programme at the Collège Internationale de Philosophie, Paris. His books include *Pragmatist Aesthetics* (Blackwell, 1992), *Practicing Philosophy* (Routledge, 1997), and *Performing Live* (Cornell University Press, 2000).

Kate Soper is Professor in the School of Humanities at the University of North London. She is the author of *Troubled Pleasures* (Verso, 1990) and *What is Nature?* (Blackwell, 1995).

Simon Thompson is Senior Lecturer in Politics at the University of the West of England. He is working on a book about the politics of recognition.

1
Richard Rorty
Pragmatism, Irony and Liberalism

Matthew Festenstein

Since the publication of *Philosophy and the Mirror of Nature* Richard Rorty has become one of the most widely read and controversial of contemporary philosophers. Significant though his previous writing was, this book not only represented an important contribution to a range of key debates in the philosophy of mind and language, but inaugurated a broadening of Rorty's interests, as he developed the ethical, social and political implications of his philosophy. The results have been immensely provocative. Rorty has become perhaps the most extensively referred to of contemporary philosophers, both inside and to an unusual extent outside academia. With this impact, he has attracted vast opprobrium – as a renegade from analytic philosophy, as a frivolous debunker of moral and intellectual standards, and as a complacent American bourgeois.

Our aim in this book is to offer a range of perspectives on Rorty's significance for social and political philosophy. The assumption of the authors is that neither ritual denunciation nor, for that matter, deference is an appropriate response to his work. In offering a more nuanced engagement they traverse a wide array of topics, including liberalism, socialism, irony, humanism, aesthetics, modernity and postmodernity, pragmatism, international relations, and the moral significance of the Holocaust, a breadth which itself indicates the scope and suggestiveness of Rorty's writings. But taking Rorty seriously is not the same as accepting all his beliefs, and the essays collected here offer in various ways critical perspectives on this *oeuvre*. The purpose of this introduction is to set the scene for the essays and for Rorty's responses, by blocking out in broad outline the themes and concerns of his work, and relating them to the contributions which follow.

Philosophy without mirrors

Rorty trained as a philosopher at Chicago and Yale, although for nearly twenty years he has taught outside academic departments of philosophy. His earlier writing included important papers on transcendental arguments, reductionism, incorrigibility, and the mind–body problem. While influential on its own terms, this work did not attract much attention outside the circle of philosophers concerned with these particular problems. This changed with the publication of *Philosophy and the Mirror of Nature* in 1979, a book which imposed itself not only on philosophers but also more widely on the intellectual scene. In an engaging autobiographical essay, Rorty describes himself as having 'spent forty years looking for a coherent and convincing way of formulating my worries about what, if anything, philosophy is good for'.[1] This worry is not near the surface of much of his earlier philosophical writing, although the latter is characterized by methodological self-consciousness, notably in the anthology *The Linguistic Turn*.[2] In the preface to that text, he confronted the thought that the differences between competing approaches to analytic philosophy could not be resolved with reference to criteria which were uncontroversial from the point of view of one or other approach. For example, 'ordinary language' philosophers such as J. L. Austin addressed issues through the inherited wisdom embodied in everyday speech, where the tradition descending from Bertrand Russell and Rudolf Carnap aimed at more rigorous forms of logical expression. But these differences could only be addressed through the commitment to an ongoing dialogue, Rorty argued, rather than through the quest for criteria of validity which would settle such differences once and for all. But if philosophy does not aim at such criteria, what does it do?

Rorty's worries emerge as central to *Philosophy and the Mirror of Nature*, in the form of a critical narrative of modern Western philosophy. The work sets out to deconstruct this tradition's purported demonstrations of grounds for knowledge and rationality which reach beneath the wilfulness and contingency of actual human thought. The terminus of this account, Rorty's pragmatism, addresses the problems and dilemmas encountered along the way, not by specifying solutions, but by setting them aside, as the products of a misconception of philosophy as the supreme arbiter of all human knowledge, 'knowing something about knowing which nobody else knows so well'.[3]

In an essay on the historiography of philosophy, published five years after *Philosophy and the Mirror of Nature*, Rorty distinguishes several genres, as he calls them, in which this history may be written. Historical reconstruction is the detailed presentation of the ideas of a past thinker, on her own terms, which attempts to show the meaning of that thinker's utterances in the specific social, cultural and linguistic context in which she lived. Rational reconstruction, by contrast, is an effort to mine the past for ideas and arguments relevant to current philosophical concerns. This usually involves reworking the original thinker's ideas in ways he or she could not have recognized, transplanting those ideas to quite other contexts; for example, we may understand Hobbes's account of the state of nature as a contribution to the efforts of recent game theory to describe how cooperation among humans is possible. Rorty's own narrative in *Philosophy and the Mirror of Nature* belongs to a third genre, which he calls *Geistesgeschichte*. Like rational reconstructions, these accounts are written in the light of current concerns and problems. However, unlike a rational reconstruction, a *geistesgeschichtlich* account operates at the more general level of problematics rather than of solutions to particular problems. It 'spends more of its time asking "Why should anyone have made the question of——central to his thought?" or "Why did anyone take the problem of——seriously?" than in asking in what respect the great dead philosopher's answer or solution accords with that of contemporary philosophers'.[4] This aims to sweep away a current but, in the view of the narrator, outmoded or pernicious way of understanding philosophy by tracing back current practice to its origins in order to diagnose the source of the error. In doing so it tells a story which tries to recast what constitutes the basic subject matter, problems, and canon of philosophy. The paradigm of such an account, in Rorty's opinion, is Hegel's *Phenomenology of Spirit*, but his work may also be affiliated with the diagnostic attempts of contemporaries such as Alasdair MacIntyre, Ian Hacking, and Michel Foucault to illuminate and criticize prevalent modes of thinking (about ethics, in MacIntyre's case, about probability and statistical reasoning, in Hacking's, and about penology and sexuality (among other matters), in Foucault's) by tracing them back to their origins.[5] As with these other authors, Rorty's narrative is an assault on the alleged timelessness of philosophical problems and concepts.

Rorty holds with Wittgenstein that 'a *picture* held us captive': the picture is that of the mind as the mirror of nature and of philosophy as the custodian and caretaker of this mirror.[6] The tradition that Rorty rejects is structured around the discipline of epistemology, understood as the ultimate arbiter of the grounds on which a belief may be found true or false. The idea of this arbiter, in Rorty's narrative, was constructed around the complementary fantasies of nature, envisaged as wholly independent of the categories through which humans come to understand it, and of the human subject, whose own essential nature drives it to gain an increasingly complete and accurate view of nature. This vision encouraged the belief that in order to achieve knowledge of nature, and to know that we have achieved it, we require

> a special privileged class of representations so compelling that their accuracy cannot be doubted... The theory of knowledge will be the search for that which compels the mind to belief as soon as it is unveiled. Philosophy-as-epistemology will be the search for the immutable structures within which knowledge, life and culture must be contained – structures set by the privileged representations which it studies.[7]

Candidates for this privileged class of representations have included sense impressions and innate ideas; the role of epistemology is to discern the best candidates. The picture of the 'mirror of nature' is vague enough to be interpreted in different ways: for empiricists, the mind passively reflects reality, while idealists envisage the mind as more actively moulding reality. These differences are relatively unimportant in comparison with what is shared: the goal of 'finding some permanent neutral framework of inquiry, an understanding of which will enable us to see, for example, why neither Aristotle nor Bellarmine was justified in believing what he believed', a framework that can act as a touchstone for sorting justified from unjustified beliefs.[8] We avoid a regress in justifying a belief only by virtue of the fact that there exist some beliefs which possess unconditional justification: their acceptability does not depend on their relation to other beliefs.

However, he argues, the picture is fundamentally flawed, since the idea of a privileged representation, or an unconditionally justified belief, is incoherent. The central contention is that there are no entities which possess any justificatory force prior to human interpretation, and that the necessity for such interpretation means that there can be no intrinsically veridical relationship between mind or language and the world. Simple perceptual beliefs, for example, may appear to have some 'phenomenological' claim to be uninferred from other beliefs and thus to be plausible candidates for the status of unconditionally justified. But even simple perceptual reports presuppose abilities and presuppositions on the part of the reporter, and possess justificatory weight only against that background; that is, conditionally. There is no privileged grid of concepts or categories against which the variety of human practices and beliefs can be judged in order to determine their rationality.[9]

The justification of beliefs is instead understood as intelligible only within particular social practices of reason-giving; rationality is not the product of a privileged relationship between mind and nature, but is contingent on 'what our peers, *ceteris paribus*, will let us get away with saying'.[10] Adopting pragmatism for Rorty is a matter of accepting that 'there are no constraints on inquiry save conversational ones – no wholesale constraints derived from the nature of the objects, or of the mind, or of language, but only those retail constraints provided by the remarks of our fellow inquirers'.[11] This is not to say that we cannot make judgements about whether some description is accurate. But the criteria by which we judge accuracy in description are given sociologically, by the language game or vocabulary in which we are making the judgement. As he puts this point, in *Contingency, Irony, and Solidarity*:

> We often let the world decide the competition between alternative sentences (e.g. between 'Red wins' and 'Black wins' or between 'The butler did it' and 'The doctor did it')... But it is not so easy when we turn from individual sentences to vocabularies as wholes. When we consider examples of alternative language games – ancient Athenian politics versus Jefferson's, the moral vocabulary of Saint Paul versus Freud's, the jargon of Newton versus that of Aristotle, the idiom of Blake versus that of Dryden – it is difficult to think of the world as making one of these better than another, of the world as deciding between them. When the notion of 'description of the world' is moved from the level of criterion-governed sentences within language games to language games as wholes, games which we do not choose between by reference to criteria, the idea that the world decides which descriptions are true can no longer be given a clear sense.[12]

Conceptions of truth and falsity, rationality and irrationality, are constituted within particular vocabularies. For entire vocabularies, the ideas of truth, rationality and correspondence lose their grip. There is no view of the world *sub specie aeternitatis* against which particular human versions may be judged. The role of philosophy is not to adjudicate among different vocabularies but only to offer a conversational rapprochement or mediation, which helps us to illuminate our commitments and beliefs in the light of very different vocabularies.

In accordance with the conception of *Geistesgeschichte*, Rorty's account reconfigures the philosophical canon. Important influences on the assault on the epistemological tradition and on the defence of the idea of rationality as a matter of 'conversational' rather than intrinsic relations include W. V. Quine, Wilfrid Sellars and Thomas Kuhn.[13] More famously, in *Philosophy and the Mirror of Nature*, Rorty enlists a more heterogeneous and striking trio as figureheads for his counter-tradition, Martin Heidegger, Ludwig Wittgenstein and John Dewey.[14] The pre-eminence for Rorty of Dewey in this list quickly became apparent.[15] This is not because Dewey offered the purest account of a philosophy which rejects neutral standpoints and underlying essences – there was, Rorty concedes, a 'bad' or 'backsliding' element in Dewey's thought which had not wholly shaken off the grip of this tradition.[16] Yet Dewey also tethered his critique of the epistemological tradition to the 'social hope' for a liberal and egalitarian society, rather than to despair at the absence of epistemological foundations. The assault on tradition also opened up a continuing dialogue in Rorty's work with contemporary Continental philosophy – with Derrida, Foucault, Lyotard, Habermas and others.[17] Yet this engagement for Rorty is framed by the presumption that what is valid in their work overlaps with his pragmatism; that (as he wrote in 1982): 'James and Dewey were not only waiting at the end of the dialectical road which analytic philosophy traveled, but are waiting at the end of the road which, for example, Foucault and Deleuze are currently traveling.'[18]

There is no need to emphasize the controversial character of Rorty's claims about the character of epistemology and of the historical analysis which he offers: 'the very obscurity of the suggestion that we should abandon the epistemological enterprise', as Ian Hacking has argued, 'makes one insist quite vigorously on the obligation to tell the history right'. [19] And Rorty's account has been contested at each step of the way. At the same time Rorty's interpretation of those figures whom he casts as fellow-travellers, such as Kuhn, Foucault and even Dewey, has been sharply criticized. These concerns are not central to this volume, but are touched on particularly in the essays by Kate Soper, Richard Shusterman and Matthew Festenstein.

More centrally at issue here is the meaning of this account for social and political theory. To paraphrase Rorty's worry, what is political theory good for? The clearest conclusion is negative: Rorty's philosophy intends to rid us of 'theory-guilt', the belief that there exist uncontroversial rational criteria by which we should judge particular beliefs and desires.[20] Yet his writing after *Philosophy and the Mirror of Nature* is replete with more positive ideas and suggestions about the meaning of his pragmatism for social and political thought, and it is to this that I now turn.

The primacy of practice

In a series of essays published in the 1980s such as 'Postmodernist Bourgeois Liberalism' and 'The Priority of Democracy to Philosophy', Rorty rejects the idea that moral views, and specifically his own preferred liberalism, require philosophical foundations. Justificatory accounts of liberal (or other) political practice embody a version of the systematic mistake of the epistemological tradition: they strive to hook up the particular beliefs, desires, institutions and practices which people have to a general and authoritative framework, which will justify them. By contrast, Rorty argues, we should reject the myth of such a framework: this is something philosophy is *not* good for. My belief that a person ought to be free to worship whatever deity she pleases, or none at all, should be viewed as the product of my particular background, not as a response to an underlying truth about human beings which everyone ought to recognize, or at which everyone would arrive, if they reflected hard enough.

Yet Rorty holds on to the thought that someone who fails to have this belief is wrong, and not, as a relativist may argue, 'right within the context of her culture or her system of beliefs'. There is no neutral standpoint outside particular evaluative schemes or world-views from which to assess those schemes. But it does not follow that it is impossible or inappropriate to appraise other world-views; indeed, part of what it means to be a liberal is that one appraise other world-views in particular ways. If one is asked 'Why be a liberal?', then this should not be treated as the occasion to construct a justificatory framework which aspires to be authoritative for all rational agents (an 'Archimedean point', in John Rawls's well-known image), but as a particular sort of dialectical challenge, which requires the liberal only to come up with enough concrete examples of the

superiority of liberal proposals and practices to persuade her interlocutor. If the latter remains immune to such persuasion, he is eventually written off as 'mad'.[21]

The primacy Rorty accords to practice over theoretical articulation
has attracted flak from both left and right. From the right he has been
criticized for cynicism, nihilism, and for mobilizing students to mind-
lessness.[22] From the left authors such as Richard Bernstein and Norman Geras have censured him for complacency.[23] Rorty's bold
statements on these themes furnish the starting point for Simon
Thompson's essay in this volume on truth and justification. Rorty's
conception of reason and practice is also an issue in the contributions
from Richard Shusterman (who compares Rorty's conception to
Habermas's) and Matthew Festenstein (who examines Rorty's relationship to Dewey).

In rejecting the myth of the neutral justificatory framework, Rorty
wants to hang on to the idea that forms of human organization,
including science, art and politics, may progress, but he does not
want to view this as a process of 'getting the world right' or of
'more accurately expressing human nature'. The latter are only
empty compliments, or generic descriptions of what particular
forms of organization hope to achieve, but not a justification from a
neutral standpoint of why one language game should have replaced
another (e.g. why Galilean mechanics replaced Aristotelian physics).
Instead progress is understood to occur through a radical redescription of some subject matter until 'a pattern of linguistic behavior [is
created] which will tempt the rising generation to adopt it, thereby
causing them to look for appropriate new forms of nonlinguistic
behavior, for example, the adoption of new scientific equipment or
new social institutions...[A]nything can be made to look good or
bad, important or unimportant, useful or useless by being redescribed.'[24] Rorty's conception of progress is grounded in a romantic
interpretation of Kuhn's famous account of scientific revolutions.[25]
We do not test theories according to how well they fit with the facts,
since the facts are themselves filtered through our existing paradigms.
One can compare paradigms and theories but not from an objective
position outside any theory or paradigm; in this sense differing paradigms are incommensurable, and (in Kuhn's notorious formulation)
scientists working in one operate in a different world from those in
the other.[26] Where Rorty is more romantic than Kuhn (or Promethean, as Kate Soper puts it, in her essay) is in his belief that we
should try to launch new paradigms or languages into the world in a
self-conscious effort to improve the human condition, 'to respond to
the needs of ever more inclusive groups of people.'[27]

Irony and cruelty

Yet this is not the only implication of the rejection of philosophical foundations and the importance granted to powerful redescriptions. In Rorty's view the rejection of foundations removes the metaphysical and theological glue which binds together two distinct sorts of human motivation, the drive to individual self-fulfilment and the impetus towards ameliorating the lot of others:

> The attempt to fuse public and private lies behind both Plato's attempt to answer the question 'Why is it in one's interest to be just?' and Christianity's claim that perfect self-realization can be attained through service to others. Such metaphysical or theological attempts to unite a striving for perfection with a sense of community require us to acknowledge a common human nature. They ask us to believe that...the springs of private fulfillment and of human solidarity are the same.[28]

But they are not. Or, at least, there is no presumption of a common human nature which unites individual self-realization and social obligation: 'one should abjure the temptation to tie in one's moral responsibilities to other people with one's relation to whatever idiosyncratic things or persons one loves with all one's heart and soul and mind.'[29]

Rorty's view of this relationship is explored in *Contingency, Irony, and Solidarity* (1989). If one accepts the contingency of language which Rorty presses on us, one finds oneself in the position of an 'ironist', someone whose fundamental values and commitments (what Rorty calls a 'final vocabulary') become problematic in a particular way. Ironists'

> realization that anything can be made to look good or bad by being redescribed, and their renunciation of the attempt to formulate criteria of choice between final vocabularies, puts them in a position which Sartre called 'meta-stable': never quite able to take themselves seriously because always aware that the terms in which they describe themselves are subject to change, always aware of the contingency and fragility of their final vocabularies, and thus of their selves.[30]

For the ironist this is a liberating revelation, unleashing powers of self-creation. Most people, however, are not ironists, and distrust the powers of redescription. For the rest of us there is 'something potentially very cruel' about the claim that their final vocabularies are 'up for grabs'; for the 'best way to cause people long-lasting pain is to humiliate them by making the things that seemed most important to them look futile, obsolete, and powerless.'[31] Fortunately, the *liberal* ironist's commitment *qua* liberal to eschew cruelty squares this circle: in public at least, she will refrain from humiliating redescription of her fellow citizens; in private, of course, she may describe them as she pleases.

Rorty's account of the relationship between irony, liberalism and cruelty has been the subject of fierce critical onslaught. He has been accused of reinforcing the gendered and oppressive distinction between a political public sphere and an allegedly depoliticized realm of personal relations. The commitment to avoid cruelty has been considered too bland as a view of the content of liberal political morality. At the same time, contingency on the favourable dispositions of individuals has been thought too precarious a basis for this political morality. The interest in self-creation and private redescription has been attacked as narcissistic, and the ironist's moral psychology as unstable.[32] The essays here by John Horton, Daniel Conway and David Owen engage in these debates from different perspectives, although each combines a detailed critical understanding of Rorty's concerns with a degree of sympathy for his arguments.

Enlarging community

An obvious item of evidence to establish that Rorty is not merely concerned with elaborating an apologia for private fantasy is the emphasis in his work on community and solidarity. If we can create ourselves in any way that we wish through redescription, what becomes of our obligations to, and the entitlements of, others? The absence of a common human essence and the licence to redescribe ourselves freely means that it is not the case that we *must* view ourselves as obliged to respect the needs and interests of others – or even to notice that they have needs and interests, or that they are human. Nor are we restrained from any actions on the grounds that they violate our essential nature: '[o]ur insistence on contingency, and our consequent opposition to ideas like "essence", "nature", and "foundation", makes it impossible for us to retain the notion that some actions and attitudes are naturally "inhuman".'[33] Obligations flow not from the recognition of such a foundation but from particular loyalties.

To the extent that community is possible it is as an achievement not a presumption, and best promoted through detailed imaginative identification with the lives of others. In Rorty's opinion, the intensity of solidarity is stronger the more parochial the attachment is in scope. In the absence of any general grounds for identifying with the universal human community, we should acknowledge that the most potent identities are particular: fellow Americans, fellow Sikhs, or fellow Glaswegians constitute the groups whose lives we understand and to whom we may feel sympathy and obligation.[34] Conscious that this argument may appear to endorse a complacent or vicious ethical chauvinism, Rorty emphasizes that the burden of liberal political morality is to extend the sense of community in order to include hitherto neglected or despised social groups: it is 'a form of life which is constantly extending psuedopods and adapting itself to what it encounters. Its sense of its own moral worth is founded on its tolerance of diversity'.[35] Justice aims at a larger loyalty than the narrowly parochial. The achievement of this sense of expanded obligation proceeds through radical redescription, the telling of stories which alter our self-understandings so that we come to see ourselves as sharing a common predicament with those whom we had thought of as strangers. This does not boil down to a banal injunction to respect difference, reducing morality and politics to niceness: 'some cultures, like some people are no damn good . . . they cause too much pain and so have to be resisted (and perhaps eradicated) rather than respected'.[36] But the respect and loyalty which we can extend is not the product of ahistorical standards but of the particular sympathies and motivations which we possess already.

Kate Soper in her essay builds on her work on humanism in order to tease out what she sees as a residual commitment on Rorty's part to some of the conceptions of human nature which he officially rejects. Richard Shusterman and Norman Geras, writing from different perspectives and sympathies, find too much contingency remaining in Rorty's conception of human nature. In his wide-ranging study, Shusterman taxes Rorty with possessing an excessively linguistic conception of the self. Geras discusses the grounds for moral community through the exploration of a stark limit case for ethical thinking, the Holocaust. The essays by Molly Cochran and by Matthew Festenstein discuss the political meanings of Rorty's account of community. Cochran takes as her cue Rorty's Amnesty lecture, 'Human Rights, Rationality and Sentimentality', in order to explore the lessons Rorty's work holds for the theory of international relations.[37] Festenstein discusses his narrative of the American left, *Achieving Our Country*, and particularly his relationship to Dewey's rather different account of liberal individuality and community.[38] Rorty speaks for himself in reply to each of the contributors, and in the closing essay on justice. Our hope is that the conversation which results deepens the reader's understanding of Rorty's work and of its repercussions for social and political thought. This body of work is full of possibilities, as well as pitfalls, and deserves continued serious attention.

Notes

1 Richard Rorty, 'Trotsky and the Wild Orchids', *Philosophy and Social Hope* (Penguin, Harmondsworth, 1999), p. 11.
2 Richard Rorty (ed.), *The Linguistic Turn* (University of Chicago Press, Chicago, 1967).
3 Richard Rorty, *Philosophy and the Mirror of Nature* (Princeton University Press, Princeton, 1979), p. 392.
4 Richard Rorty, 'The Historiography of Philosophy: Four Genres', in *Truth and Progress, Philosophical Papers*, vol. 3 (Cambridge University Press, Cambridge, 1998), p. 256.
5 See, for example, Alasdair MacIntyre, *After Virtue: A Study in Moral Theory*, 2nd edn (Duckworth, London, 1985); Ian Hacking, *The Emergence of Probability* (Cambridge University Press, Cambridge, 1975); Michel Foucault, *Discipline and Punish*, trans. Alan Sheridan (Penguin, Harmondsworth, 1991); Michel Foucault, *The History of Sexuality*, vol. 1, trans. Robert Hurley (Penguin, Harmondsworth, 1984). For Rorty's own account see Rorty, 'Trotsky and the Wild Orchids', pp. 11–12.
6 Ludwig Wittgenstein, *Philosophical Investigations*, trans. G. E. M. Anscombe (Basil Blackwell, Oxford), s. 115; Rorty, *Philosophy and the Mirror of Nature*, p. 12.
7 Rorty, *Philosophy and the Mirror of Nature*, p. 163.
8 Ibid., p. 211.
9 Ibid., p. 330.
10 Ibid., p. 176.
11 Richard Rorty, *Consequences of Pragmatism* (University of Minnesota, Minneapolis, 1982), p. 165. See Rorty, *Philosophy and the Mirror of Nature*, p. 389.
12 Richard Rorty, *Contingency, Irony, and Solidarity* (Cambridge University Press, Cambridge, 1989), p. 5.
13 See W. V. Quine, *From a Logical Point of View* (Harper Torchbooks, New York, 1963), esp. pp. 20–46; Wilfrid Sellars, *Empiricism and the Philosophy of Mind* (Harvard University Press, Cambridge, Mass., 1997); Thomas S. Kuhn, *The Structure of Scientific Revolutions*, 2nd edn (University of Chicago Press, Chicago, 1970).
14 Rorty, *Philosophy and the Mirror of Nature*, pp. 5–7, 365–72, 392–3.

15 See Rorty, 'Overcoming the Tradition: Heidegger and Dewey', in *Consequences of Pragmatism*, pp. 37–59, and the essays in Part I of Richard Rorty, *Essays on Heidegger and Others, Philosophical Papers*, vol. 2 (Cambridge University Press, Cambridge, 1991), pp. 9–82.

16 Rorty, 'Dewey's Metaphysics', in *Consequences of Pragmatism*, pp. 72–89; Richard Rorty, 'Reply to Sleeper and Edel', *Transactions of the Charles S. Peirce Society*, 21 (1985), pp. 38–48; Rorty, 'Dewey between Hegel and Darwin', in *Truth and Progress*, pp. 290–306.

17 See Rorty, 'Philosophy as a Kind of Writing: An Essay on Derrida', in *Consequences of Pragmatism*, pp. 90–109; Rorty, *Contingency, Irony, and Solidarity*, pp. 122–39; Rorty, 'Cosmopolitanism without Emancipation: A Reply to Jean-François Lyotard', *Objectivity, Relativism, and Truth, Philosophical Papers*, vol 1 (Cambridge University Press, Cambridge, 1991), pp. 211–22; Rorty, *Essays on Heidegger and Others*, pp. 85–198; Chantal Mouffe (ed.), *Deconstruction and Pragmatism* (Routledge, London, 1996).

18 Rorty, *Consequences of Pragmatism*, p. xviii.

19 Ian Hacking, 'Is the End in Sight for Epistemology?', *Journal of Philosophy*, 77 (1980), pp. 579–88, at pp. 580–1. The best places to start for a sense of how these criticisms have been elaborated are A. Malachowski (ed.), *Reading Rorty* (Blackwell Publishers, Oxford, 1990) and Robert B. Brandom (ed.), *Rorty and his Critics* (Blackwell Publishers, Oxford, 2000).

20 Rorty, *Philosophy and Social Hope*, p. 96.

21 Richard Rorty, 'The Priority of Democracy to Philosophy', in *Objectivity, Relativism and Truth*, p. 187.

22 Neal Kozody, cited by Rorty, *Philosophy and Social Hope*, p. 3.

23 See, for example, Richard Bernstein, *The New Constellation* (Polity, Cambridge, 1991), pp. 230–92, and see Rorty's reply, 'Thugs and Theorists', *Political Theory*, 15 (1987), 564–80; Norman Geras, *Solidarity in the Conversation of Humankind: The Ungroundable Liberalism of Richard Rorty* (Verso, London, 1995); Christopher Norris, *The Contest of Faculties* (Methuen, London, 1985), pp. 139–66; Terry Eagleton, 'Defending the Free World', in Ralph Miliband and Leo Panitch (eds), *The Socialist Register 1990: The Retreat of the Intellectuals* (Merlin, London), pp. 85–94.

24 Rorty, *Contingency, Irony, and Solidarity*, p. 9.

25 Cf. Rorty, *Philosophy and the Mirror of Nature*, pp. 322–42.

26 Kuhn, *Structure of Scientific Revolutions*, pp. 134–5.

27 Rorty, *Philosophy and Social Hope*, p. 81.

28 Rorty, *Contingency, Irony, and Solidarity*, p. xiii.

29 Rorty, *Philosophy and Social Hope*, p. 13.

30 Rorty, *Contingency Irony, and Solidarity*, pp. 73–4.

31 Ibid., p. 89.

32 See, for example, Thomas McCarthy, 'Private Irony and Public Decency', *Critical Inquiry*, 16 (1990), pp. 355–70; Charles B. Guignon and David

R. Hiley, 'Biting the Bullet', in Malachowski, *Reading Rorty*, pp. 339–64; Bernstein, *New Constellation*, pp. 258–92; Simon Critchley, 'Deconstruction and Pragmatism: Is Derrida a Private Ironist or a Public Liberal?', in Mouffe, *Deconstruction and Pragmatism*, pp. 19–40.

33 Rorty, *Contingency, Irony and Solidarity*, p. 189.
34 Cf. ibid., pp. 190–1.
35 Richard Rorty, 'On Ethnocentrism: A Reply to Clifford Geertz', *Objectivity*, p. 204.
36 Richard Rorty, 'In a Flattened World: Review of Charles Taylor, *The Ethics of Authenticity*', *London Review of Books*, 8 April 1993, p. 3.
37 Richard Rorty, 'Human Rights, Rationality and Sentimentality', in Susan Hurley and Stephen Shute (eds), *On Human Rights: The 1993 Oxford Amnesty Lectures* (Basic Books, New York, 1993), reprinted in *Truth and Progress*, pp. 167–85.
38 Richard Rorty, *Achieving Our Country: Leftist Thought in Twentieth Century America* (Harvard University Press, Cambridge, Mass., 1998).
39 I would like to thank Simon Thompson and Mike Kenny for some helpful comments on an earlier draft.

2
Irony and Commitment
An Irreconcilable Dualism of Modernity

John Horton

Over the last twenty years Richard Rorty's writings have constituted a continuous and radical challenge to the assumptions which inform much of contemporary academic philosophy. His iconoclasm has met with a wide variety of reactions but, perhaps predictably, these have mostly been negative. Although his critics sometimes write as if he were the leader of a large and dangerous band of disciples, the truth is much closer to his being everybody's whipping boy. Conservatives demonize him as a threat to civilization as we know it; Marxists and other political radicals deplore what they see as his complacent and uncritical defence of American capitalism; postmodernists disdain his shallowness compared with the arcane profundities of their European gurus; analytical philosophers shake their heads sadly at a good man gone to the bad; and the leading liberal political theorists for the most part studiedly ignore him. Moreover, the intensity of the hostility which has often been directed towards him is unusual in contemporary philosophy.[1] To give only one example, a recent critic variously describes Rorty as like the sophists of ancient Athens, as engaging in an 'exercise in bad faith', as propounding 'a philosophy appropriate to the shallow narcissism of our era', and of adopting a position which is merely 'a de facto glorification of the world as it is'.[2] This is not the sort of language which simple error, no matter how serious, would normally elicit.

Confronted by his capacity to annoy so many thinkers of differing persuasions and to elicit such personal invective it is hard to resist the thought that Rorty must have hit a sensitive nerve in contemporary philosophical discourse. Of course, it would also be surprising if such a widespread reaction was entirely without some legitimate justification, and Rorty's later writings are, indeed, uneven: at times he can be an exasperating and frustrating writer to read. Partly, and much to his credit, this is because he writes in such a plain, non-technical, straightforward, almost folksy prose that the tensions, inconsistencies, contradictions and even occasional ill-considered remarks in his works are readily apparent. He refuses to make his ideas more 'sophisticated' either by lapsing into abstruse technicalities or by employing the mystificatory style which sometimes passes as profundity in philosophy. But this is only part of the explanation. Another is that Rorty seems at times to be trying to say something which it is not obvious can be coherently stated.[3] This is a point I shall touch on later but it does give rise to a certain problem – a problem of how to read Rorty.

There are, it seems to me, broadly two ways of approaching Rorty's work in the light of these tensions, inconsistencies and contradictions. First, we can ruthlessly seek them out and use them as a stick with which to beat Rorty: we can make him an easy target for finely honed analytical and argumentative skills. If one adopts this approach, I believe, it is not too hard to bring out the internal difficulties in the way in which he has articulated the views he has sought to advance. Not surprisingly, this approach is popular with those who are unsympathetic to those views. It is of course an entirely legitimate approach and one which in sharp but less than totally hostile hands can be illuminating.[4] However, if we are to derive most value from Rorty's writings, I suggest we should adopt a rather different strategy. This second approach involves treating Rorty in a more receptive spirit, one which involves giving him the benefit of the doubt and which genuinely seeks to understand what it is that he is trying to say and why. It means treating Rorty in the spirit in which he often treats others – taking up what is useful, pursuing what looks promising and rejecting or passing over what look to be his less impressive lines of thought. To be clear, this does not require one to abandon all critical standards or simply to ignore the internal difficulties of his work, and any serious reflective engagement with his work cannot eschew criticism. But it does mean not making refutation the immediate objective of one's engagement. It also means not trying to assemble all of Rorty's scattered remarks into a comprehensive and coherent system. Rather, I suggest it is more profitable to see Rorty's latter writings as essentially experimental or exploratory; as initial, sometimes faltering, attempts to think through what it would be to take seriously the implications of his critique of philosophy – how one might think about the world and our place within it once one gives up a particular picture of truth, rationality and objectivity.

Whether or not this is the most profitable way to read Rorty's writings, it is the approach I propose to adopt here in exploring one broad strand of that work. I find much in Rorty's critique of epistemology, of the correspondence theory of truth and of the more ambitious claims of many philosophers which resonates with my own views about these matters. I shall not be concerned, however, to defend or even set out that critique although, it must be conceded, there is a very large issue here about the adequacy of Rorty's account of the epistemological tradition he criticizes.[5] However, whatever the precise weaknesses of that account and of the way in which he articulates his critique, he seems to me to be onto something. In the long term one would hope that some of those weaknesses could be eliminated; that better, more perspicuous, even fairer, ways of presenting that critique can be found, if not by Rorty himself then by others. But I do start from the assumption – and assumption is all it can be for the purpose of this discussion – that there is something persuasive in the story Rorty has to tell and in the lessons which he draws from it. Of course, this assumption is ultimately defeasible. It may be that after much effort to explore the problems to which Rorty's reconstruction gives rise nothing can be made of it; that the internal difficulties simply multiply and that what, for want of a better expression, might be called Rorty's 'vision' is found to be irredeemably confused and unsustainable. But this will come, if it comes at all, a lot further down the line. Most attempts radically to alter the way we think about the world, including ourselves, whether philosophical or scientific, initially seem unpersuasive and easy to refute. It is only by allowing such views the time and space in which to develop that we can see whether or not they have the resources to overcome their apparent weaknesses.

In this essay, therefore, I want to begin in this spirit to explore one issue to which Rorty's work gives rise. This issue concerns the relationship between irony and commitment. It can be expressed through a cluster of closely related questions: How far is it possible to live the life of a consistent ironist in Rorty's sense? Is it almost inevitable that irony will undermine moral and political commitment? Could there be a society of thoroughgoing ironists? If not, is this significant? Are deep moral and political commitments compatible with an ironical disposition? These are not questions which have escaped Rorty's own attention. Quite the contrary, he mostly takes them very seriously. However, I do not think his treatment of them is satisfactory. In what follows, therefore, I want to pursue further those answers and explore what it would mean to take seriously Rorty's idea of the ironist, and more particularly his attempt to combine irony with solidarity; at the level of the individual through his picture of the liberal ironist and politically through his sketch of the ideal liberal society.

Roughly, my aim is to discuss some of the difficulties with what Rorty has to say about these matters. The tentative conclusion towards which this discussion leads is that Rorty's attempt to reconcile, or at least amicably accommodate, irony and commitment at both the individual and the social level is more deeply flawed than he allows. However, I do not infer from such a conclusion that the anti-foundationalism which lies at the heart of Rorty's conception of the ironist is therefore mistaken. On the contrary, as has already been indicated, I believe that anti-foundationalism captures something very central to modern secular Western culture. What I want to suggest, however, is that this anti-foundationalism simply does not fit with our sense of what it is to have deep moral and political commitments, and why they matter in the way that they do. We are torn between two largely opposed perspectives – the anti-foundationalism of the ironist and the anti-ironical, non-historicist impulse which informs our sense of what it is to have deep moral and political commitments. At a social and political level it seems very difficult, as Rorty himself is aware, to imagine a society of ironists. A sense of solidarity is indeed necessary, but it is likely to be undermined by the ironist outlook.

However, this is to get ahead of ourselves; we need to begin by looking at Rorty's conception of the ironist. This is someone who self-consciously accepts Rorty's anti-foundationalism. The ironist meets three conditions:

(1) She has radical and continuing doubts about the final vocabulary she currently uses, because she has been impressed by other vocabularies, vocabularies taken as final by people or books she has encountered; (2) she realizes that argument phrased in her present vocabulary can neither underwrite nor resolve these doubts; (3) in so far as she philosophizes about her situation, she does not think that her vocabulary is closer to reality than others, that is in touch with a power not herself. Ironists who are inclined to philosophize see the choice between vocabularies as made neither within a neutral and universal metavocabulary nor by an attempt to fight one's way past appearances to the real but simply by playing the new off against the old.[6]

Ironists realize, in a phrase recurrent in Rorty's writings, that 'anything can be made to look good or bad by being redescribed'. The ironist is someone who is able to take up a certain kind of attitude to her own beliefs and values, an attitude which distances the ironist from the beliefs and values she holds. Ironists understand their final vocabularies – that is, their most fundamental beliefs and convictions – as contingent, in the sense that they are a social and historical product and that they have no more claims to truth or rationality than other final vocabularies. The ironist 'is a nominalist and a historicist' who thinks that terms like justice and rationality have no independent, critical force.[7]

However, Rorty claims that this way of thinking about our relationship to our final vocabulary does not mean that we cannot be critical of that vocabulary, or indeed that we cannot judge some to be better or worse than others. In a typical, but I shall argue perplexing, comment he writes:

> The ironist spends her time worrying about the possibility that she has been initiated into the wrong tribe, taught to play the wrong language game. She worries that the process of socialization which turned her into a human being by giving her a language may have given her the wrong language, and so turned her into the wrong sort of human being. But she cannot give a criterion of wrongness. So, the more she is driven to articulate her situation in philosophical terms, the more she reminds herself of her rootlessness by constantly using terms like 'Weltanschaung', 'perspective', 'dialectic', 'conceptual framework', 'historical epoch', 'language game', 'redescription', 'vocabulary' and 'irony'.[8]

Now one important puzzle here concerns what it is that the ironist is worrying *about* when she worries about being initiated into the wrong tribe or taught to play the wrong language game. The ironist has no criteria of wrongness and, therefore, no criteria of rightness either. A little later Rorty adds that ironists 'do not see the search for a final vocabulary as (even in part) a way of getting something distinct from this vocabulary right'.[9] This may suggest that there is a sense of getting the vocabulary right but that this does not depend upon anything *distinct* from the vocabulary. But what can this mean and do we still not need *some* criteria? How can terms like 'rightness' or 'wrongness', 'better' or 'worse' function without *something* in terms of which this judgement is made?

Rorty's eschewal of anything distinct from language as a criterion may suggest a strong and a weak reading of the claim that the ironist has no criteria of wrongness. On the strong interpretation this means just what it appears to say. But, as I have suggested, if we do read it in this way, it is entirely mysterious what one would be doing worrying about whether one was playing the wrong language game. Indeed, in the absence of *any* criteria it is difficult to see what sense can be given to right or wrong. So I think we have to assume that this is not what Rorty means.[10] What then of the weaker interpretation? On this reading what Rorty is denying is that the ironist invokes anything external to some vocabulary. One danger here is that the claim may be so weak as to be uninteresting and acceptable to almost anyone. If the claim is only that criteria of wrongness have to be formulated in some vocabulary, then this will not be widely disputed. But it seems clear that Rorty is intending to say something stronger than that. He is claiming more than that criteria of wrongness have to be expressed in language but less than that we have no criteria of wrongness; rather criteria of wrongness are no more stable, secure or immune from criticism than what they are being used to evaluate. There is no Archimedean point, no bedrock, no foundation, no indisputable method which can serve as a basis for rightness or wrongness. However, this is not merely because we cannot be certain that they are right. Rather, it is because the very idea of 'rightness' in this sense is illusory. There is nothing to which being right corresponds, other than the mutable criteria contained in our vocabularies. And when we put our final vocabularies in question, there is nothing further to which appeal can be made.

Unfortunately, this is still a less than perspicuous answer to the question of what the ironist is doing when she worries, for example, about whether she is playing the wrong language game. On Rorty's account this worry still cannot be given a cognitive content. For if the worry is about the criteria as well as the final vocabulary – indeed there is no categorical distinction between them – this seems to be the manifestation of a psychological state rather than a matter for cognitive inquiry. Rorty wants to preclude us from asking a question such as 'Why does the ironist worry?' precisely because it seems to be structured by the epistemological picture he rejects; but, if like Rorty we still think these worries intelligible, we remain in need of *some* account of this activity which will make sense of it. We need an account which will bring out the point of such worry. For in the absence of such a point the ironist's worry is likely to seem merely neurotic. Rorty, however, is surely correct that people, or at least some of them, do worry about their final vocabularies. But what they often actually worry about is precisely what Rorty says the ironist does not – that is, the possibility of their being in error. In short, what gives point to this worry is the possibility of being mistaken. The puzzle is what is to take the place of the object of worry for the ironist?

Rorty claims that the ironist worries about having been 'initiated into the wrong tribe', 'taught to play the wrong language game' and turned 'into the wrong sort of human being'. But once we dispense with there being something which answers to the description 'the right tribe', 'the right language game' and 'the right sort of human being', what is there for the ironist to worry *about*? It is true that I may wish I had been born into some other tribe, learnt to play some other language game, turned into some other human being but for Rorty's ironist these seem to be no more than the expressions of the preferences or desires I happen to have. The worry, therefore, amounts only to doubts about whether I (or perhaps others) would have been happier, more content or whatever if I had been born into a different tribe, learnt a different language game, been a different sort of human being. In so far as it is in my power to do anything about these, then there may be point to the worry. If I can learn another language game, if I can turn myself into a different human being, then I may worry about whether I should do so (although since I cannot alter what tribe I was born into, worry about that seems peculiarly pointless for the ironist). Of course people do worry in these ways but they miss what people take to be their deepest worry, that is, they fail to capture the moral concerns that people have.

Important parts of people's final vocabulary are their moral values and commitments. In regarding them as moral, people do not understand them simply as reducible to their preferences or to what makes them happy or content. And in so far as they worry about them, whether or not they make them happy or content is not the only, or even the deepest, worry that they have. This is because people view moral demands as making claims on them, independently of their contribution to their personal happiness or contentment. Indeed it is precisely because morality is not reducible to self-interest that we often feel ourselves tempted to do wrong. But it is far from clear what the ironist can make of this way of thinking. If it is just a matter of redescribing what is bad to make it look good, then why not so redescribe it, especially if it will make one happier or bring about other things one wants?

The difficulty for the ironist is that she is self-consciously aware that good and bad, right and wrong are just the contingent descriptions of a particular group in a particular place at a particular time. Once the ironist comes to see things in this way – good is merely another description of bad and vice versa – then it seems hard to distinguish this view from one in which there is no sense of there being anything of fundamental importance to the distinction between good and bad. The perspective of the ironist appears less one of redescribing the difference between good and bad, right and wrong, than of dissolving it. The trouble is that this whole way of thinking about morality seems to imply the kind of contrast which Rorty's anti-foundationalism under-mines. It seems (as in fact one might expect) that dropping the foun-dationalist picture does create problems for our understanding of our deepest moral commitments. Moreover, it not only gives rise to pro-blems within the individual who tries to combine irony with such commitments; it also generates problems at a social level. Standards of right and wrong in a community are seen as not only a contingent historical product but also as having no special claims on people beyond their happening to accept such standards.

If morality is one of the constituents of the glue of social solidarity, then the ironist's relationship to the wider society looks problematic. Her questioning of final vocabularies, and Rorty's rather romantic portrait of her as engaged in an almost continuous process of self-creation, suggests both a high degree of detachment from the final vocabularies of any particular society and a potentially worrying self-absorption. In short, the ironist seems suspiciously close to the alie-nated intellectual who stands outside the society observing the assumptions and aspirations of its denizens with at best benign amuse-ment and at worst malign contempt. It is extremely difficult to see how the ironist can genuinely share in the sense of solidarity of those people whose attachment to their values is unironical. Moreover, the idea of a society composed entirely of ironists is, as Rorty accepts, deeply implausible. Rorty himself denies 'that there could or ought to be a culture whose public rhetoric is ironist'; and even he 'cannot imagine a culture which socialized its youth in such a way as to make them continually dubious about their own process of socialization'.[11] So the question for someone like Rorty, who values liberal institutions and practices, is whether these can be combined with ironism in a viable liberal political community.

One way Rorty has of trying to deal with this question is by distinguishing ironism and historicism, and making a consequent distinction between intellectuals who are ironists and everyone else who is not. He says:

In the ideal liberal society, the intellectuals would still be ironists, although the non-intellectuals would not. The latter would, however, be commonsensically nominalist and historicist. So they would see themselves as contingent through and through, without feeling any particular doubts about the contingencies they happened to be ... They would feel no more need to answer the questions 'Why are you a liberal? Why do you care about the humiliation of strangers?' than the average sixteenth-century Christian felt to answer the question 'Why are you a Christian?'[12]

The public culture of a liberal society would not be ironist and people generally would accept liberal values because they were brought up to do so. When doubts were raised about liberal values, they would want to know what the alternatives were rather than what was the philosophical or principled justification of those liberal values and practices.

Now there are several features of what Rorty is saying which are either worrying or puzzling. For instance, the elitism implicit in Rorty's distinction between intellectuals and non-intellectuals does not seem to fit well with the requirements of a democratic culture. However, I want to focus on the plausibility of this sharp distinction between ironist intellectuals and commonsensical nominalist and historicist non-intellectuals, and how far the latter can be insulated from being infected by irony. To begin, Rorty's comparison of non-intellectuals' attitude to their liberalism to the average sixteenth-century Christians' attitude to their religion seems misconceived precisely because the latter most likely did think that Christianity was true in the kind of way that Rorty rejects. They may not have been able to provide theological justifications for their beliefs but they almost certainly will have believed that there were such justifications. It is most unlikely that 'average sixteenth-century Christians' were 'commonsensically nominalist and historicist' and saw themselves as 'contingent through and through'. So the reason why the average sixteenth-century Christian might not be bothered by the question 'Why are you a Christian?' is simply unavailable to the non-intellectual nominalist and historicist liberal. Whatever reason they have for not being bothered by sceptical questions, it will not be the same as for the sixteenth-century Christian.

Rorty does not altogether deny that there would be doubts about the public culture of liberalism. And he is surely right not to do so for, given his own emphasis on the centrality of freedom within a liberal culture, there is every reason to believe that not everyone in a liberal society will wholeheartedly accept its values. Rorty tends to write as if either there are no 'concrete alternatives or programmes' to those embodying the values of a liberal culture or, if there are, that they are obviously inferior. But there is unlikely to be a shortage of alternatives, some of which will have attractions, and the very fact of such alternatives is likely to generate doubts. Indeed one would expect the presence of ironists in a liberal society to be a fertile source of both doubts and alternatives.

Rorty is fully aware of the potential tensions between irony and his commitment to solidarity. Typically, he puts the objection very clearly when he writes:

Ironism, as I have defined it, results from awareness of the power of redescription. But most people do not want to be redescribed. They want to be taken on their own terms – taken seriously just as they are and just as they talk. The ironist tells them that the language they speak is up for grabs by her and her kind. There is something potentially very cruel about that claim. For the best way to cause people long-lasting pain is to humiliate them by making the things that seemed most important to them look futile, obsolete and powerless.[13]

We need look no further for an example of the harmful potential of redescription than the pain caused to many Muslims by Salman Rushdie's novel *The Satanic Verses*.[14] This is a good instance of the way in which redescription may humiliate. Muslims clearly felt their most sacred beliefs and images were being ridiculed and desecrated by Rushdie. And whether or not he would be prepared to put it in Rorty's terms, something like this was what Rushdie intended. He knew that the novel would cause immense resentment among Muslims and this was not an unwelcome prospect to him, although the form that resentment eventually took certainly was.[15]

The furore caused by *The Satanic Verses* also shows the inadequacy of Rorty's other strategy for dealing with the tension between irony and commitment. This is the proposal to rigorously separate the private sphere of irony from the public sphere of commitment. In order to deal with the potential of redescription to humiliate people he seeks to distinguish between redescription for private and for public purposes.[16] I do not want to suggest that such a distinction could never do some of the work Rorty wants it to but it is pretty clear that in many contexts it will not be up to the task. How are we to conceive of Rushdie's novel in relation to the private/public distinction? I would suggest that the distinction is unhelpful – if one had to decide that the novel fell in one or the other category, it would have to be the public. But accepting that would inevitably lead one to wonder whether there was going to be much space in the private sphere.[17] If private purposes are at most limited only to the thoughts one thinks (leaving aside whether even these would always qualify), the public will clearly overwhelm the private, providing almost no scope for untrammelled irony or the pursuit of private perfection which Rorty so obviously values. If the sphere is so narrowed, it is also likely to further undermine the ironist's commitment to liberalism.

As Rorty develops this line of defence, he places great emphasis on the importance for public and political purposes of acquiring a sensitivity to the suffering of others which requires a skill at imaginative identification rather than a justification for caring about it. There is, it seems to me, much that is right in Rorty's claims about developing our affective capacities rather than just our narrowly intellectual ones. However, it is hard to see how this contributes much to the problem which Rorty has been addressing. We can see why if we notice that there is a gap between cruelty – which for Rorty's liberal is the worst thing we can do – and causing others suffering. We should bear in mind the, admittedly much abused, Shakespearian maxim that there are occasions when we may need to be cruel to be kind. At a mundane level, if I want to help a friend improve the quality of her piano playing, there may be no way around telling her that her performance was very poor, even though I know she will be hurt by it. If I want to avoid unnecessary suffering, I should not do it gleefully and I should try to put it in as constructive a way as possible, but still it must be done in a way in which the judgement is clear. But more fundamentally, especially in political contexts, there are occasions when causing others suffering is not being cruel at all, and when the liberal is likely to be in favour of it. Should I refrain from redescribing the white supremacist's views in a way that makes them seem less persuasive because the white supremacist might feel humiliated? Is this being cruel to the white supremacist? It is perhaps a virtue of Rorty's position that he reminds us that however much we detest the white supremacist's views we should not forget that he too has feelings and can suffer. But this can hardly be an argument for refusing to challenge his views. And if I think that Islam is misogynistic and illiberal, why should I not try, imprudence aside, to do something akin to what Rushdie did, even though it will offend and cause pain to many Muslims?

The problem for Rorty's liberal is that we cannot get directly from the observation that 'my redescription makes that person suffer' to 'I am being cruel'. Standardly what people think makes the difference to whether or not I am being cruel (or if it is preferred whether the cruelty is okay) is whether or not I am justified. This, of course, is a response which is problematic for Rorty. Since I doubt that he would want to say that we should desist from any and all redescriptions which may make others suffer, he must say something else. I suspect what he would say is that this only reinforces his anti-foundationalism because it shows that there is nothing external to which liberals can appeal to justify their actions other than their liberalism. Unfortunately, as it stands, since liberalism just is the view that cruelty is the worst thing we can do, it is quite unclear how liberals, even in terms of their liberalism, can get a handle on when causing suffering to others is cruel, or when the cruelty is none the less not what the liberal most wants to avoid. The issue here to be clear is not, directly at least, why the liberal wants to avoid cruelty but what counts as cruelty, or the wrong sort of cruelty, for the liberal. Many Muslims certainly thought that the publication of *The Satanic Verses* was cruel. Do Rorty's liberals agree? How do they decide? These are not just philosophers' questions, they are questions which liberals themselves can hardly avoid asking.

This criticism is, I believe, quite telling against what Rorty says about the liberal but it is not one which need disturb him too much. For what it essentially points to is that Rorty's liberal is underdescribed; that the characterization of liberals as people who believe that cruelty is the worst thing we can do is too thin. One does not need to be a liberal to agree that cruelty, if not literally the worst thing we do, is none the less very bad. It is only that the behaviour nonliberals think is cruel would, in some instances at least, differ from what a liberal would regard as cruel. Former communist secret policemen and white South Africans can tell sentimental stories about their own suffering and humiliations but these are unlikely to commend themselves to liberals. The reason for this is not necessarily that such stories are unbelievable – in some cases they are all too believable – but because their suffering, arising as it does from the removal of injustice, does not count. So what Rorty needs to say more about is the content of cruelty – to characterize it in terms of redescriptions which humiliate others will not do, unless Rorty really does want to say that *any* such redescription is what the liberal most wants to avoid. But I see no reason why Rorty could not say more. We simply need a 'thicker' description of what it is to be a liberal.

However, even if Rorty were to provide us with a richer conception of what it is to be a liberal, there remains the more serious question of whether there is any reason to think that ironists are likely to be particularly committed to that conception of liberalism. It is not obvious why they will be, other than perhaps for narrowly instrumental reasons. So long as liberalism affords them the best chance of the space to pursue their own projects of self-creation, they may favour it. However, this kind of support is likely to be rather precarious. First, it is hard to see why the ironist should regard anything in liberalism as worth fighting for. The ironist is likely to be too detached from those values for them to be strongly motivating. It is quite unclear how the ironist can keep her detachment for private values and really commit herself to liberal values in public. Secondly, as we have seen, the ironist is simply unlikely to feel a sense of solidarity with the unironical majority. The ironist will be rather like the woman without faith among religious believers – she may go through the motions, mouth the same slogans, observe the same ritual, but these cannot really unite her with the true believers. Indeed, there is every reason to think that the reverse will be the case. The solidarity ironist is likely to be uncomfortable in the public world of commitment, at best feigning a solidarity which cannot genuinely be felt. Indeed cynicism must be an abiding temptation for the ironist.

Rorty is understandably rather equivocal about the impact of adopting his anti-foundationalist picture of the world, of understanding ourselves as contingent all the way down, on our ordinary ways of carrying on. Sometimes he seems to think the impact will be negligible and we can pretty much carry on as before. With respect to some of our beliefs and practices this is highly plausible. For instance, it seems unlikely that our confidence in science will be much shaken by whatever philosophical view we take of the status of its results. This is not to suggest that nothing ever could shake that confidence but only that it does not seem to depend upon whether we accept the claim, say, that science describes the world as it really is. However, the view that we can carry on much as before whatever our conception of the status of those beliefs and practices is much less plausible when we consider moral and political beliefs. Here it seems that being told that we should view those commitments simply as the result of some mixture of causes (such as socialization) and choices seems to undermine the claim they have on us. Here the grounding really does seem to matter. To his credit Rorty is clearly worried by this issue. His boldest attempt to overcome the problem is the portrayal of the liberal ironist as someone in whom his anti-foundationalism and commitment to a liberal political culture are combined. But neither dividing the self between private ironist and public liberal nor dividing society between ironists and commonsense historicists provides a persuasive picture of how the two can coherently coexist.

By contrast I want to suggest that there is a deep tension between moral commitment and the conditions which promote it on the one hand, and the detachment of the ironist on the other. The case for anti-foundationalism is a strong one and the picture Rorty paints of us as contingent through and through coheres well with many features of modern culture. Many but not all – for we retain also a sense of moral and political commitment which rests on a very different picture of our relation to the world. This view requires those commitments to be something other than the contingent products of a combination of choice or circumstance. In short we have two perspectives which are not merely distinct but basically contradictory, both of which none the less seem persuasive. One of Rorty's many merits is that, partly unintentionally, he shows us how difficult it is to combine these different perspectives and yet how difficult it is honestly to jettison either one of them.

Notes

1 This hostility is perhaps only exceeded by that provoked by the work of Jacques Derrida.
2 Richard Wolin, *The Terms of Cultural Criticism* (Columbia University Press, New York, 1992), ch. 7.
3 See, for example, Bernard Williams, 'Auto-da-Fé: Consequences of Pragmatism', in A. Malachowski (ed.), *Reading Rorty* (Blackwell Publishers, Oxford, 1990).
4 See, for instance, Richard J. Bernstein, 'Rorty's Liberal Utopia', in his *The New Constellation* (Polity, Cambridge, 1991).
5 Rorty's critique is to be found most fully set out in his *Philosophy and the Mirror of Nature* (Princeton University Press, Princeton, 1979). For critical assessments of Rorty's treatment of the view he attacks see the essays in parts II and III of Malachowski, *Reading Rorty*.
6 Richard Rorty, *Contingency, Irony, and Solidarity* (Cambridge University Press, Cambridge, 1989), p. 73.
7 Ibid., p. 74.
8 Ibid., p. 75.
9 Ibid., p. 76.
10 Rorty sometimes gives the impression that we can just decide, as we like, whether or not something is right or wrong. But the whole point of the language of right and wrong is that it is not for us to decide *as and when we like*. If this is the best picture of what we are doing when we think we are making judgements about right and wrong, it is, I argue, effectively to abolish the distinction.
11 Rorty, *Contingency, Irony, and Solidarity*, p. 87.
12 Ibid.
13 Ibid., p. 89.
14 Salman Rushdie, *The Satanic Verses* (Viking/Penguin, London, 1988).
15 For a discussion of these and other issues raised by Rushdie's book see the essays in the second half of John Horton (ed.), *Liberalism, Multiculturalism and Toleration* (Macmillan, London, 1995).
16 Richard Rorty, *Contingency, Irony, and Solidarity*, p. 93.
17 Rorty himself distinguishes between novels for the public purpose of enlarging our sympathies and ironist novels directed towards self-perfection. However, the questions of how these are to be distinguished and of how the latter are to be kept in the private sphere are not considered by Rorty. See in particular *Contingency, Irony, and Solidarity*, ch. 7.

Response to John Horton

Richard Rorty

John Horton is right to point out that since final vocabularies are 'final' in the sense of providing the terms in which one's criteria are phrased, and since there is therefore no categorical distinction between wondering if you are using the wrong criteria and wondering if you are using the wrong vocabulary, it is hard to answer the question 'what exactly is the ironist worrying about?' But I have problems with his ensuing suggestion that the ironist's worries may be 'the manifestation of a psychological state' rather than 'a matter for cognitive inquiry'. Of course they are such a manifestation, but to say that they are not a matter for cognitive inquiry seems to presuppose that where criteria end, so does the need to think about a problem.

Again, when Horton says, 'We need an account which will bring out the point of such worry. For in the absence of such a point the ironist's worry is likely to seem merely neurotic', he seems to be saying that where criteria end, neurosis begins. The implication would seem to be that if you can't state the criteria you will be using in the process of solving your problem, your problem is a merely neurotic one which you should try to stop having.

Looming in the background here is an ancient conundrum of how to stop the regress of criteria. On the one hand, philosophy is supposed to supply you with the ultimate, wholesale criteria you ought to use for picking retail, regional criteria. On the other hand, it is supposed to leave nothing unquestioned, to put every presupposition in doubt, etc. – including proposals for ultimate criteria. As soon as you get a disagreement between philosophers (between Plato and Nietzsche, say) about what ultimate criteria to use, you seem to be stuck with the ancient dilemma: either find some still higher-level criteria to invoke in figuring out which philosopher is right (and expect that the problem will repeat itself at this higher level), or else become 'arbitrary' and 'non-cognitive'.

This dilemma seems to me highly artificial. We know how people come to terms with the disagreement between Plato and Nietzsche – most of us philosophy professors have done it at some point in our lives, or are still in the process of doing it. We do not do it by applying criteria, nor by asking ourselves the question 'What exactly am I worried about?' Nor do we become arbitrary and decisionistic. What we do is pretty much the same sort of thing we do when we realize that we do not love our long-term spouse, and that he or she quite possibly despises us – or when we realize that we loathe our job or our profession, and wish to God we had never taken it on. In the latter cases, we may wind up changing spouses or jobs, but it is not clear that we have criteria for choosing the new ones, nor that we choose them arbitrarily.

Sometimes dissatisfaction with marriage or employment or ultimate criteria is merely a neurotic symptom. These are the cases when our friends are right to say that we would be much better off just getting on with our marriage/job/way of life, rather than contemplating alternatives to it. Analogously, sometimes bishops are quite right to tell curates troubled by Intellectual Doubt to 'just get over it'. Sometimes, however, this is very bad advice indeed. It would be nice if we had criteria for figuring out when such advice is good or bad, but life is not that easy.

Horton says that what people who worry about final vocabularies 'actually' often worry about is the possibility of being mistaken, of being in error. He also says that I deny that this is what the ironist worries about. The latter claim would be correct only if the absence of an Archimedean point for deciding whether one is mistaken entails that the term 'mistake' is out of place. I can see nothing wrong with saying that the reader of Nietzsche who begins to wonder if she is a long-time victim of Socratism, or the person whose long-term and previously beloved spouse suddenly seems repulsive, wonders whether she has made a big mistake. But I would think this compatible with saying, as Horton paraphrases me as saying, that 'there is nothing to which being right [not having made a mistake] corresponds.'

It seems to me that the central issue between Horton and myself is whether, as he says, 'dropping the foundationalist picture does create problems for our understanding of our deepest moral commitments'. I see Horton as committed to the doctrine that the vocabulary of 'criteria', 'mistake', 'getting it right', 'cognitive inquiry' and so on is so interwoven with foundationalism that anti-foundationalists cannot consistently use it.

Suppose that, for the sake of argument, I grant him this point, and agree to strike all references to criteria, mistakes, etc. from my description of the ironist's predicament. Then the issue between us can be narrowed down to: can an anti-foundationalist have deep moral commitments? If so, can she understand them? Since deep moral commitments are the sort of social glue necessary to having any sort of culture, this question is equivalent to: is a nominalist and historicist culture possible?

I think our answer to this latter question should be: let's experiment and find out. What we should not do is to try to deduce its impossibility from the state of mind of inhabitants of our present culture, from what Horton calls '*our* [emphasis added] sense of what it is to have deep moral and political commitments'. Certainly anti-founationalism 'does not fit' with this sense. That is because it is a proposal to change our sense of what it is to have such commitments.

Horton would have been quite right to identify the ironist with 'the alienated intellectual who stands outside the society observing the assumptions and aspirations of its denizens' had he not continued with 'with at best benign amusement and at worst malign contempt.' He would have done better to have concluded his sentence with 'at best enthusiastic hope to change those assumptions and aspirations for the better and at worst benign amusement or malign contempt'. Such a conclusion would have done justice to alienated intellectuals like Socrates, Voltaire and Rushdie who hoped to help the denizens of the societies in which they were brought up change their assumptions and aspirations. One of the things they wanted to change was those denizens' sense of what counts as a sensible proposal for change.

We could only argue from the way we think now to the limits of what we should experiment with if all suggestions for social change could be tested by presently accepted criteria. But the idea that this is how moral and social progress occurs is, once again, a philosopher's fiction. It is a fiction which is natural to a foundationalist culture. In the first section of his essay, Horton seems to me to have successfully shown that anti-foundationalism is presently counter-intuitive. But what anti-foundationalist would deny this?

In the second part of his essay, Horton asks my liberal to do something nobody has ever been able to do: offer some general principles to tell whether one is being cruel only to be kind or whether one is instead being unconsciously sadistic. Certainly 'it is quite unclear how liberals, even in terms of their liberalism, can get a handle on when causing suffering to others is cruel'. That is not because of some special problem which liberals have. Lots of people, liberals and non-liberals, have wondered whether Rushdie, by publishing *The Satanic Verses*, was trying to be helpful to the Muslim world (in the way in which Socrates was trying to be helpful to the Athenian world) or was just being sadistic. I should not be surprised if Rushdie himself had not, during his worst nights, wondered about this.

Horton writes as if I were deficient in failing to provide a way of resolving this puzzlement. We need, he says, a 'thicker' description of what it is to be a liberal. Yet no matter how thick I made this description, I still would not be able to equip the liberal with a criterion for detecting her own unconscious sadism, or for resolving the sorts of moral dilemma which Socrates, Voltaire and Rushdie faced. The unfortunate effects of the aspiration to have such criteria are among the reasons I should cite in favour of experimenting with a non-foundationalist culture.

3
Richard Rorty on Truth, Justification and Justice

Simon Thompson

Introduction

Many critics of Richard Rorty's liberal ironism argue that one important reason for rejecting his account of politics is that it would deprive us of the ability to make a sufficiently strong case for our political values. Some of these critics argue that Rorty is an out-and-out nihilist who denies that we can claim that our political values are rationally justifiable or that statements endorsing these values are true. It follows, say these critics, that liberal ironism reduces political discourse to a matter of rhetorical persuasion and reduces politics itself to no more than a struggle for power. Others, putting a slightly different twist on things, argue that Rorty is a relativist who indexes the validity of political values to local standards of justification. In this case, they believe, his political theory discounts the possibility of radical social criticism and so offers nothing more than an apologia for the status quo. Either way, the critics conclude, liberal ironism represents a serious threat to the possibility of a rational and humane politics in which we engage in critical inquiry together in order to come to a reasonable agreement on well-founded values and principles that can shape the framework of our shared political life. Following their assessment, these critics demand a more robust account of political values. While they deny that such an account need claim that such values are in some way ahistorical, universal or transcendental, they nevertheless argue that it must make stronger claims for them than Rorty himself is prepared to provide.

My aim in this essay is to show that this critique rests on a serious misunderstanding of the character of Rorty's political theory, and, in particular, of his account of the relations between truth, justification and justice. Such a critique assumes that there is an exclusive and exhaustive choice between foundationalist and relativist accounts of truth: either a proposition is true since it corresponds to reality, or it is true only in the sense that it coheres with other propositions characteristically made by a particular community of inquirers. Since Rorty does not endorse the former account, the critics argue, he must endorse the latter. And this unacceptably weak account of truth also undermines our ability to justify our political values. I intend to challenge this critique by showing that there are alternative conceptions of truth that are neither foundationalist nor relativist. I argue that, while Rorty does not suggest that true propositions are somehow grounded in an unchanging reality, he offers an account of truth that makes it significantly more than a matter of coherence with other strongly held beliefs.

In order to make good this claim, I focus on what, if these critics' readings were accepted, would be a fairly blatant discrepancy in Rorty's account. If the critics are right to argue that he refuses to offer a rational justification for his values, or that, at best, he relativizes truth claims to local standards and conventions, then how can they explain his remark that it has 'always been true' that slavery is 'absolutely wrong' (1998: 125n42)? If, as he says, nothing is 'intrinsically decent' or 'intrinsically abominable' (1998: 207), then on what grounds could he declare the absolute wrongness of slavery to be a timeless truth? I argue that the best way to solve this puzzle is to establish a clear distinction between truth and justification. On most everyday occasions no distinction is made between these two since, if asked whether my assertion is true, I can only respond by showing it to be well justified. In certain circumstances, however, truth and justification can come apart: sometimes I may not have good reasons for asserting what is actually a true proposition; at other times I may be justified in asserting a proposition that turns out not to be true. By distinguishing between truth and justification in this way, it becomes possible to acknowledge that, while justification is a practice that always employs a particular set of standards, truth cannot be reduced to such standards. Hence we can declare that it is true that slavery is always wrong – even in circumstances in which no one had good reasons for thinking so. The crucial move, then, is to develop an account of truth according to which what we hold to be true is grounded in and yets exceeds our notions of what is currently justifiable. I believe that, on such an account, liberal ironism could make claims about normative truth, about justice, that would satisfy at least some of its critics' demands; and, in this case, they have one fewer reason for rejecting liberal ironism than they thought they had.

Although this has certainly not been the most prominent theme in the debate between Rorty and his critics, there have already been a number of important discussions and exchanges on this issue (e.g. McCarthy 1990a; McCarthy 1990b; Rorty 1990). But I believe that this debate is worthy of further consideration for two reasons. First, a number of critics continue to attribute various indefensible positions to Rorty, some of which cannot fairly be read into what he says – indeed some he explicitly denies. A first task, then, is to make the best possible sense of what Rorty actually says. Second, certain criticisms of Rorty's account are based on things that he *does* say in less cautious moments – and commentators are not slow to remark that such moments are not so few and far between. This means that a second task is to modify Rorty's account where necessary. In this case my argument is also worth making because I end up with a position that is more defensible than his own. For example, I suggest that if more weight is placed on what Rorty calls the 'cautionary' use of truth, this will take much of the sting out of criticisms of his ethnocentrism. To put my interpretive approach in terms of Ronald Dworkin's criteria of 'fit' and 'value' (1986), I begin by applying the first of these, and try to fit as many as possible of Rorty's remarks into a coherent whole. Whenever there is ambiguity, I turn to the second criterion, and choose the alternative that gives his account the most value. More strongly, I am also prepared to abandon fit for value: I ditch some parts of Rorty's account in the interests of a more defensible whole. I would argue that the result remains recognizably 'Rortian', although it differs from Rorty's own account in several ways.

What the critics say

Some criticisms of Rorty's account of truth and justice focus on his rejection of any form of metaphysical justification for beliefs and values. In the first place, he argues, the principles and institutions of liberal democracy simply do not need philosophical 'backup', 'presuppositions' or 'foundations' (1991: 178, 179, 189). Sometimes he claims that the liberal ironist should not even engage with the metaphysicians' arguments since it is fruitless to meet enemies on their own ground. On other occasions, however, Rorty cannot resist such engagement: in a number of places he makes direct claims about the impossibility of certain forms of metaphysical justification. For example, he says that we should deny that 'true moral judgments are *made* true by something out there in the world' (1998: 205). Similarly, he declares that 'the moral world does not divide into the intrinsically decent and the intrinsically abominable' (1998: 207). In short, his position is that, even were it possible, metaphysical justification would not be necessary in the defence of liberalism.

In light of these remarks, the critics contend that Rorty is guilty of irrationalism in the sense that, as Richard Bernstein puts it, he gives us 'no *reason* for believing that one vocabulary is better than any other' (1991: 275; and see Anderson 1991: 364; Freeman 1991: 8; Geras 1995: 123). It is a short step from here to the claim that, on Rorty's account, any particular moral stance is 'as good as' any other. Critics contend that it is fair to draw this implication – despite Rorty's explicit denial – since he cannot or will not give sufficient support to the contrary position that one particular political viewpoint is *better* than another. The critics conclude that, by denying the existence of a moral reality composed of moral facts, and by rejecting the possibility that our moral propositions represent or correspond to such facts, Rorty leaves us adrift in a nihilist universe.

Other critics focus on the account of truth and justice that Rorty does offer, arguing that this amounts to a form of relativism according to which these notions are indexed to local standards of justification. For example, he offers an approbative gloss of William James's notion of truth, according to which it is 'something inherently relative, inherently temporary' (1985: 109, quoted in Stout 1988: 248). He seems to endorse a similar relativism with regard to justice, claiming that 'the rightness and wrongness of what we say *is* just for a time and a place' (1998: 60, quoted in Okrent 1993: 382). Bringing both cases together, he declares that 'what counts as rational or as fanatical is relative to the group to which we think it necessary to justify ourselves' (1991: 177). Thus it seems that Rorty analyses both truth and justice in terms of a practice of justification that takes place within a particular community of inquiry, and in accordance with local norms.

On the basis of these and other comments, Rorty's critics have concluded that despite his protestations to the contrary, he is a relativist since (1) he reduces truth and justice to a matter of justified belief or value; and then (2) he relativizes such justification to particular communities of inquiry. As Norman Geras puts it, for Rorty, 'knowledge is to be treated as justified belief or warranted assertability, one's community, whether social or scholarly, being the source of epistemic authority' (1995: 112–13). Thus he makes 'all truth and coherence relative to competing language games' (1995: 128). One important criticism that is then made of this sort of relativism is that, since it constrains political theory to existing standards of justification, it forces it into a conservative acceptance of the status quo. Thomas McCarthy, for example, argues that Rorty abandons an idea of truth that has regulative, transcendental and critical force (1990a: 367–70). The implication is that, without the ability to go beyond current social norms, such a relativist political theory would not be able to reach a standpoint from which it could criticize those norms.

Other specific criticisms follow from these general charges of irrationalism and relativism. One of these suggests that Rorty's position gives us no help in securing the claims of justice; thus Michael Freeman claims that 'relativism or nihilism... are either useless or dangerous in the face of evils such as genocide' (1991: 3). In a similar vein, Geras believes that '[i]f there is no truth, there is no injustice' (1995: 107). In particular, he suggests, liberal ironism deprives the oppressed of what could be their most powerful weapon: their ability to tell others what really happened or how things really stand – to tell the truth about the injustices they have suffered or are suffering (1995: 132–3). To take a specific example, Sabina Lovibond believes that liberal ironism prevents feminists saying that sexual harassment 'is a feature of *social reality*' (1992: 66). The idea here is that the language of truth and reason is a potentially powerful weapon that can be used in the fight for justice; without it, the victims of injustice are left with what is no more than their own particular description of the situation they find themselves in – a description which is in some sense 'just as good as' that of their oppressors.

A final criticism focuses on the damaging effect that Rorty's account of truth and justice would have on politics. It is argued that liberal ironism would reduce political discourse to a matter merely of rhetorical persuasion. Rather than a medium of reason and truth-determination, the language of politics would become no more than rhetoric in the service of power (Bernstein 1991: 281; Lovibond 1992: 60–2). Extending this line of argument, Rorty's critics contend that, rather than regarding politics itself as a practice of collective deliberation and decision, he reduces it to nothing more than struggles for power. For example, it is suggested that, on Rorty's account, a given convention or standard that defines truth or justice in a particular society only prevails because its exponents have had the power to impose it in that situation (e.g. Honneth 1995: 292, 297). At the heart of this sort of criticism is the belief that reason should govern the conduct of our political life, and the consequent claim that, by eliminating reason, Rorty eliminates the possibility of principled politics. In short, his critics argue that he abandons the idea of a rational politics as an activity in which we engage in collective deliberation in order to come to reasoned and voluntary agreement together on the values that are to govern our common life. By offering no reasons stronger than those read off local standards and conventions, Rorty leaves us without reliable moral guidance in the conduct of our political affairs.

Rorty's tour de force

Some of these criticisms of Rorty's account of truth and justice can be set aside fairly swiftly. On the charge that Rorty is a nihilist, I would argue that this makes little sense of his own political writings: he clearly prefers some political practices and institutions to others, and provides reasons for his preferences. Thus he favours liberal regimes over illiberal regimes since, for one thing, the former seek to eliminate avoidable cruelty. If the critics then shift to the claim that Rorty cannot provide strong enough reasons to back up his preferences, I would respond by saying that, in some very basic cases, it is difficult to know what could be said in support of some preferences that would be more certain than those preferences themselves. If you didn't think that cruelty was wrong, it would be difficult to see how any sort of theoretical back up could make you change your mind. Of course, this argument will not work when it comes to other more complex cases, such as choosing a relative weighting of liberty and equality. Perhaps it is here that Rorty's critics could score a victory against him by showing how some sort of foundationalism would allow them to specify such a weighting. In practice, however, most of the critics fail to make good their potential advantage here since they shy away from defending anything stronger than what Bernstein calls a 'reasonable sense of justification' based on 'historically contingent fallible reasons' (1991: 276–7). Rorty would be able to endorse reasons of this kind even if the relativist reading of his position were true. On the charge that his account eliminates the possibility of radical social criticism, I would again look at Rorty's writings. His support for a form of Rawlsian

liberalism puts him in opposition to the current practices and institutions of the rich North Atlantic democracies in all sorts of ways.
Social criticism is always possible, whether it is a matter of pointing
out gaps between principles and practices, showing up inconsistencies
between principles, or introducing new principles from subaltern
groups, forgotten traditions or other places. If the critics then substitute the charge that, according to Rorty's relativism, and despite
aspects of his own practice, we *should* not criticize a community in
terms of values alien to it, then I would suggest that we need to look
more closely at what he says we can and cannot say in support of our
political values.

According to his critics, Rorty is either unable or unwilling to claim
that political values are rationally justifiable or true, or, at best, he
says that they are true only relative to local conventions. However,
while the critics' account may seem to be a plausible reading of a
number of Rorty's remarks, it does make one particular comment
stick out like a sore thumb. In the course of a discussion about the
possible relationship between feminism and pragmatism, he says that
'[i]t was of course *true* in earlier times that women should not have
been oppressed, just as it was *true* before Newton said so that gravi-
tational attraction accounted for the movements of the planets.' In a
footnote he expands on this remark: 'pragmatists should agree with
everybody else that "Slavery is absolutely wrong" has always been
true – even in periods when this sentence would have sounded crazy
to everybody concerned' (1998: 225–42). Lovibond takes note of this
passage and argues that it sits very ill at ease with many other things
that Rorty says. With reference to his denial that slavery is 'an
intrinsic evil', she argues that it is 'something of a *tour de force*' to
argue both for this and for the timeless truth of the absolute wrongness of slavery (1992: 61).

Let us be clear about the size and nature of the interpretive problem
presented here. On the one hand, there are plenty of occasions where
Rorty explicitly repudiates various forms of moral objectivism and
realism. To give just one more example, he advises feminists to
employ an account of their values and objectives that 'gives up the
claim to have right or reality on its side' (1998: 218). On the other
hand, in the passage to which Lovibond refers, Rorty claims that
'[p]ragmatists need not deny that true sentences are always true'
(1998: 225–42). So here it appears that Rorty does not reduce truth
to a practice of justification that takes place in particular communities
of inquiry. Thus the problem is this: at some points Rorty denies that
anything is intrinsically right or wrong – in which case it is difficult to
see how he could declare that it is true that sexual harassment is

always wrong. But, at other points, he declares that true sentences are always true – in which case he would be able to make such a declaration. What sense can be made of Rorty's position?

At least three solutions to this conundrum present themselves. First, it could be argued that Rorty's claim about the wrongness of slavery is an isolated aberration which cannot be rendered consistent with the rest of his account of truth and justice. In this case, if we are to make the best possible sense of Rorty's account, we should ignore this remark, seeing it as an uncharacteristic lapse from the line that he otherwise follows. Put in terms of Dworkin's interpretive criteria, the critics would argue that this reading has a fairly high degree of fit with Rorty's account, but it gives this account low value since it would leave it with all the problems that they have identified.

A second solution to the conundrum suggests that the problem goes rather deeper than the first implies, since it reveals a deep split in Rorty's account. Rather than an uncharacteristic lapse, it could be argued, the remark about slavery is just one example of a more general tendency that Rorty has to waver between his official position and the sort of objectivism that he claims to repudiate. That is, while he publicly rejects various forms of metaphysics, it is possible to identify a number of lingering metaphysical claims in Rorty's work. Thus Freeman argues that he has recourse to a 'minimal realism' about human nature when he describes the nature of cruelty and humiliation (1991: 8). And Bernstein suggests that Rorty's position depends on all sorts of universalist claims (1991: 278). One way of accounting for this fundamental inconsistency would be to say that in practice it is impossible to do without the sort of philosophical claims that Rorty tries to renounce (Geras 1995: 136–8). This reading would give Rorty's account a very low degree of fit (since no interpretation could render it consistent), and consequently low value.

A third solution – and this is the option that I want to pursue here – is that we should apply a principle of charity to Rorty's work and assume that his remarks about the wrongness of slavery are consistent with the rest of his position. If this argument can be made good, it would have at least one significant implication: it would be possible to be an anti-foundationalist ironist and still make claims about the truth of certain normative statements, where truth would not simply mean 'valid relative to local standards of justification'. In some cases, I believe, this implication may be sufficient to persuade sceptics that liberal ironism is an attractive theory since it would make possible a politics based on strong normative principles. To put this again in Dworkin's terms, this reading would have a high degree of fit with Rorty's account, and would give it a high degree of value. So how could it be argued that, although nothing is intrinsically good or evil, it is true that slavery has always been wrong?

Truth versus justification

I now argue that the best way to render Rorty's remarks on truth and justice consistent is to maintain a clear distinction between truth and justification. Consider, first of all, what would follow from such a distinction. If truth is not reducible to practices of justification, so that what is true is not necessarily what is justifiable by our current standards, then any proposition we choose to consider will fall into one of four categories. Propositions must fall into one of the first two categories if we restrict our attention to the current time and place.

(1) *Justified and true*: If I said, here and now, that 'the world is round' and that 'slavery is evil', these propositions would be both justified and true. In these circumstances, in practice, no distinction between justification and truth will be noticeable. As Rorty says, '[i]f I have concrete, specific doubts about whether one of my beliefs is true, I can resolve those doubts only by asking whether it is adequately justified' (1998: 19).[1] That is, such a resolution can take place only by measuring this belief against the standards of justification that currently prevail in whatever area of inquiry – whether it be literary criticism or genetics – that my belief falls into. If asked why I believe that the world is round, I cite the best available scientific evidence; if asked why I believe that slavery is wrong, I invoke arguments about the equal dignity of all human beings.

(2) *Not justified or true*: If, on the other hand, I said that 'the world is flat' or that 'slavery is defensible', then, following from the previous case, my propositions are not justified or true since they do not meet our standards of justification. In these first two cases, then, no gap between truth and justification is visible in practice.

Propositions can fall into the third and fourth categories when we judge assertions made in other times and places from our current standpoint.

(3) *Justified not true*: If someone in fourteenth-century Europe said that 'the world is flat', or someone in fourth-century B C Athens said that 'slavery is defensible', then the assertion of these propositions

would have been warranted by reference to the standards of justification prevailing at that time, but we can now say that these propositions were false since we know that the standards by which they were judged were inadequate.

(4) *Not justified but true*: The final case is the reverse of the third. If someone in fourteenth-century Europe said that 'the world is round' or someone in fourth-century B C Athens said that 'slavery is evil', their assertion of these propositions would not be justified but they would nevertheless be true. That is, the local standards of justification would not permit them to make such assertions; nevertheless, if they did assert such things, we now know that they would be true. In short, things we now know to be true could not have been justifiably asserted in other circumstances. In both these cases, then, truth and justification come apart.

If this analysis is accepted, then it becomes possible to render Rorty's account of truth and justice consistent. To be specific, on the reading I have offered, liberal ironists can endorse the truth of all of the following propositions: (a) slavery is wrong; (b) it has always been wrong; (c) it was wrong in fourth-century B C Athens; and (d) slave-owners at that time may have been justified in thinking that it was acceptable. Rorty's principal claim – that '"Slavery is absolutely wrong" has always been true' – corresponds to propositions (a) and (b), while his further claim – 'even in periods when this sentence would have sounded crazy to everybody concerned' – corresponds to (c) and (d). This account is possible so long as a distinction is maintained between truth and justification, so that the belief that is currently best justified isn't necessarily true, and, contrariwise, there may be no warrant at present for asserting what is in fact a true belief. If we restrict our attention to the present time and place, then there is no difference between truth and justification that makes a difference in practice. That is, I can only defend the truth of my proposition by showing that it is well justified, that I have a warrant for asserting it. But truth isn't *reducible* or *definable by reference* to particular procedures of justification. This becomes clear once we compare other standpoints to our own. If we look back to periods in the past, governed by standards of justification different to our own, then we can say that certain propositions made then were justified but were not true (and others were true but not justified). Similarly, if we look forward to a future governed by other and better standards of justification, then we can say that certain propositions that we now believe with good reason to be justified will turn out not to have been true.

It should be noted that this position rests on two important pre-conditions. First of all, it depends on the endorsement of a limited notion of *ethnocentrism*. We must be prepared to declare that our current standards of justification are the best available and, in particular, that they enable us to determine the truth of a state of affairs (compare Lovibond 1992: 65). In this case we are prepared to judge other standards inferior to our own: when there is a disagreement over values, we believe that we are in the right and those who disagree with us are in the wrong (since we believe that others' standards of justification are inferior to our own). Second, it is also necessary to endorse a certain form of what I will call *fallibilism*. We must accept that, since better standards of justification may come along in the future, our presently well-justified propositions may turn out not to be true.[2]

It may be thought that this is a strange and perhaps contradictory combination of commitments. While Rorty's ethnocentrism is often condemned for its arrogance, fallibilism, by contrast, suggests humility. In fact I would argue that this combination of ethnocentrism and fallibilism – at least in the sense that I intend them here – is much more plausible than it might initially seem. Indeed it is necessary to make sense even of our very everyday practice of argumentation. When we disagree over values, I must believe – at this moment – that I am right and you are wrong; for otherwise it is difficult to see in what sense the values I am defending are mine. At the same time, I do not think it impossible that I could change my mind. Whether in light of your arguments or on some other grounds, I could come to believe that I was mistaken. In short, I can believe that I am right, although I know I may be wrong. If this analysis of argumentation is plausible, it follows that it is quite possible to combine the conceptions of ethnocentrism and fallibilism that I have proposed here.

What is truth?

The reading of Rorty's account of truth and justification that I have developed up to this point will not convince all critics. The obvious question that it throws up is this: if only justification is relativized to local standards, then what is truth? If Rorty rejects a 'deflationary' view of truth as warranted assertability or justified belief, as well as rejecting what could be called an 'inflationary' view of truth as the representation of or correspondence to facts embedded in an unchanging reality, then what is left? At this point one particular escape route may seem attractive: if truth is not simply a matter of warranted assertability, then one alternative candidate that does not reintroduce the idea of foundations is some notion of 'assertability under idealized conditions' or 'idealized rational acceptability' (McCarthy 1990a: 369; compare Brunkhorst 1996: 9–11). That is, if we do not know for sure that our current standards of justification will lead us infallibly to the truth, then we may try to specify ideal conditions under which we are certain that the truth will be determined. Unfortunately this proposal faces just the same problem as the account of truth as warranted assertability. The latter account comes unstuck since it is always possible to ask: 'Even though we believe that we have good reasons for condemning slavery, is it *really* wrong?' In exactly the same way, the account of truth as idealized rational acceptability fails since it can always be asked: 'Even if under some set of ideal conditions, we would believe that we had good reasons for condemning slavery, would it *really* be wrong?' (see Rorty 1998: 22). This strategy also faces an awkward dilemma: on the one hand, if we are now able to specify these ideal standards of justification, then they should be our current standards and not ideal standards that have yet to be spelt out; on the other hand, if these ideal standards have not yet been spelt out, then the belief now that such standards will enable us to determine the truth in the future is no more than an act of faith.

So, having ruled out a number of possible ideas of truth, what conception could we fit into a broadly Rortian philosophy and politics? One principle that might help to guide us here states that an adequate conception of truth must be able to map the customary and familiar uses of 'truth' and its cognates. If such a conception did not fit the ordinary and everyday ways in which we use the word 'true', it would not be an account of truth. It is in this spirit that Jeffrey Stout declares that all that is interesting about the notion of truth can be found by 'empirical inquiry into the "nature" of reason-giving as a social practice' and 'detailed study of our use of the relevant expressions in ordinary language' (1988: 251).[3] Unfortunately, things are not quite as simple as this. It is well known that Rorty tries to josh us out of certain habits and rituals in which we routinely engage. At the most general level, he seeks to persuade us that we should not try to ground our liberal culture in metaphysics. But to this extent he is making a proposal for a change in our use of words like 'true', 'rational' and 'just' (1998: 29). To put the matter in Dworkin's terms once more, if we accept the need to make such proposals for reform, then our account of truth must begin by offering a conception that *fits* everyday usage; but if this everyday conception of truth lacks *value* – that is, if it is unhelpful or actively hinders our broader political purposes – then we must be prepared to suggest that this everyday conception should be changed.

If we begin, then, with everyday usage, we can follow Rorty in distinguishing three different ways in which we employ the word 'true'. First, every competent speaker must be able to understand the 'disquotational' use of truth, seen in propositions such as '"Snow is white" is true if and only if snow is white.' Our ability to talk about the nature of language requires us to be able to use 'true' in this way. Second, Rorty, following Donald Davidson, suggests that we also have an 'endorsing' use for the truth predicate. He contends that 'true' is just a term of endorsement, rather than a term of explanation (1991: 127–8). As he says, '"truth"... is just the reification of an approbative adjective' (1998: 53). Here Rorty follows William James's controversial analysis which claims that what is true is what is 'good in the way of belief'. And in this case Rorty must face the charge that, by appearing to try to reduce the true to the useful or the expedient, such an analysis flies in the face of the fact that the truth can often be uncomfortable to live with. In fact, it is possible to offer a reading of the Jamesian claim that protects it against simplistic utilitarian interpretations. Robert Brandom emphasizes what he calls the 'performative' element of this conception of truth: he argues that when pragmatists endorse a truth claim they adopt it 'as a guide to action' (1987: 77). On this account, to call something true is not to explain anything about its nature or to offer a description of it. Rather it is simply to recommend to other speakers that they should also adopt the belief or value that the speaker calls 'true'. The importance of this analysis here is that, if we focus on the act of calling-true rather than on the quality of the thing called true, we can avoid the usual assumption that to call something true is to describe it. And this can help us resist the temptation to adopt some kind of foundationalist or correspondence account of truth.

However, given the distinction between truth and justification presented in the previous section, it is clear that these disquotational and endorsing senses of truth do not exhaust the ways in which we use the word 'true'. Hence Rorty identifies a third and final use of the truth predicate which, again following Davidson, he calls the 'cautionary' use (1991: 128). This is the use of 'true' that we find in phrases such as 'fully justified, but perhaps not true' (1998: 22). It serves to indicate to us that although a particular proposition may meet all our current standards of justification, it is nevertheless possible that it will turn out not to be true. To endorse the cautionary use of 'true' is to be a fallibilist in the sense in which I defined this in the previous section. I would argue that, if we give this final use of 'true' its due importance, and so hold open the gap between truth and justification, then we can characterize truth simply in terms of its similarities to and differences from justification. I would suggest, then, that what we mean by 'true' is *something which is the case, whether or not it is currently believed, albeit with good reason, to be so.*[4] Or, to put it slightly differently, truth is *what there is anyway, no matter what we happen to think.*[5] More than this, I would argue, it is not possible or advisable to say. It should be clear that here I am recommending a change in everyday usage, a change that makes truth a much more mundane notion than that often invoked in a culture that still has lingering ambitions to provide metaphysical foundations for its values.

Ethnocentrism and toleration

Given that this essay began by considering the charges of relativism and nihilism brought against liberal ironism, it will seem ironic that the reading of Rorty that I have developed is likely to be criticized on the grounds that it proposes too strong an account of the truth of moral and political values. On my reading of Rorty, ironists can declare that it's true that slavery is everywhere and always wrong – no matter what values may prevail in particular places at particular times. This is closely related to accounts of Rorty's ethnocentrism, according to which ethnocentrists are committed to saying that, if we disagree, I'm right and you're wrong; similarly, where whole ways of life differ, our way is superior to that of others. Ethnocentrists believe that their standards of justification enable them to determine true beliefs and values, and they think that other standards of justification – whether in the past, future or other places today – are inferior to their own to the extent that they differ from them. Thus slavery is wrong in light of what we now know about (and value in) human beings.

The critics argue that, while this may be uncontroversial in the case of slavery, it is less clear-cut in many other cases – such as practices of monogamy or animal slaughter. Surely, the critics contend, there can be both reasonable disagreement between individuals and 'blameless variation' of ways of life.[6] For example, if one society values monogamy, and another doesn't, there is no need to declare that one is right and the other wrong. This line of criticism concludes that both my reading of Rorty on truth, and his broader account of ethnocentrism, are far too intolerant of difference: by judging all other views and ways of life inferior to our own, we leave no space for others who are simply different. Rorty's own reply to this charge cuts little ice with his critics. He claims that, since liberals are 'connoisseurs of diversity' (1991: 206), their ethnocentrism is in fact uniquely tolerant of others. But the critics retort that, since such connoisseurship is a matter of coming to see that some others are just like us, it is a process of empathy through identification. As such, they conclude, it is unable to appreciate the *distinctiveness* of those others, and hence it is unable to mark out a space *between* liberal citizens and illiberal fanatics.

I want to argue that in fact Rorty's theory contains resources with which he can make a necessary and desirable concession to the critics without giving way on any vital ground. He can do this by raising the profile of the cautionary use of truth, and by increasing emphasis on the fallibilism that I believe must accompany ethnocentrism. In the first case, then, when I believe that I am right, I still know that I could be wrong. And in the second case, when we believe that our standards of justification enable us to determine the truth, we are nevertheless aware that a better set of standards could come along in the future. This should encourage in us an attitude of humility when encountering different others: once we accept that our present standards of justification may well be bettered by others in the future, we will be less prone to make the bald assertion that our current standards of justice determine the only justifiable set of moral and political values. In this way an increased emphasis on the cautionary use of truth lets us concede that there can be reasonable disagreement across a wide range of issues, and acknowledgement of fallibilism enables us to accept that there can be blameless variation across a wide range of ways of life.

I would emphasize, finally, that making these concessions to the critics' case does not mean that, to use Rorty's cutting phrase, 'we have become so open-minded that our brains have fallen out' (1991: 203). Nothing in what I have said leads to the indefensible and indeed incoherent position that any set of standards is 'as good as' any other. It does not commit liberal ironists to endless patience with other points of view or infinite toleration of alternative ways of life. It simply requires us to accept that it is possible to make sense of and see merits in different sides of a range of arguments and in many different ways of life. This does not prevent us from judging – by our lights – that certain values and practices of others – while justified by their own lights – are in fact beyond the pale.

Conclusion

The line that I have taken in this essay is somewhat unusual if only because I have offered a qualified *defence* of Rorty's political theory. In particular I have argued that, subject to modification, his account of truth, justification and justice can be successfully defended. The principal modification that I would make has both negative and positive aspects. First, the negative: liberal ironism should avoid Rorty's temptation to offer what Stout calls 'pithy little formulae' (1988: 246) that summarize his position by collapsing the distinction between truth and justification. For example, liberal ironists should not say that truth is a matter of 'what one's peers, *ceteris paribus*, let one get away with saying' (Rorty 1979: 176),[7] or that '[f]or pragmatist social theory, the question of whether justification to the community with which we identify entails truth is simply irrelevant' (1991: 177). Given the cautionary use of truth, it always makes sense to ask: although it's justified by local community standards, is it really true? At one point Rorty accepts that he should not offer such pithy little formulae (1998: 225–42), but elsewhere he admits that he is tempted towards the sort of reductionist analysis of truth that they tend to embody (1998: 2). The problem is that these one-line summaries invite the all too common misunderstandings that motivate the all too common and misguided criticisms of liberal ironism.

The positive aspect of my proposed modification follows from this: liberal ironism should place greater emphasis on the cautionary use of truth and on the fallibilism that I believe must accompany ethnocentrism. By doing so, it will be able to avoid drawing too rigid a line between liberal citizens and fanatics. Rorty tends to contrast 'us' and 'them': the fellow citizens whom we regard as our equals and to whom we owe a justification of our actions, and those whom we regard as our inferiors and to whom we have no obligation to justify ourselves. But I would argue that there is space between these two groups for *different* others: those who are not the same as us, but whom we should not regard as our inferiors, and for whom we should make some attempt at justification. A greater emphasis on the cautionary use of truth would make it possible to mark out this space between citizens and fanatics, and in so doing it would take much of the sting out of the critique of ethnocentrism.

If liberal ironism adopted the version of Rorty's account of truth and justice that I have developed here, it would be able to repel many of the criticisms levelled against it, and so would be better able to achieve its broader political purposes. The most important implication of my reading is that a conception of truth based on a distinction between it and current practices of justification makes it possible to assert strong claims about the truth of moral (and non-moral) propositions without referring to any kind of unchanging moral reality. If we argue that truth, unlike justification, cannot be reduced to warranted assertability, then we can say that certain things are truly just or unjust – regardless of what other people at other times might think. Thus liberal ironism does not reduce political discourse to simple rhetoric, nor does it make politics merely a struggle for power. On the contrary, it can support a politics based on strong moral principles, in which we can roundly declare certain things always and absolutely good or evil, right or wrong. In this way, I have sought to render liberal ironism a defensible and indeed attractive political theory. More cautiously, I would say that I have removed certain reasons for *rejecting* this theory. Whether, without these obstacles, liberal ironism holds sufficient attractions to tempt waverers, is of course a matter on which only they can pronounce.

Notes

1 Note that, in order to make good my reading, I must deny that this observation provides a generally valid reason for collapsing the distinction between truth and justification.
2 Note that Bernstein contends that Rorty *rejects* fallibilism (1991: 280).
3 Compare Wittgenstein's declaration that '[w]hat *we* do is to bring words back from their metaphysical to their everyday use' (quoted in Lovibond 1992: 64n47).
4 Here I adapt a phrase from Lovibond (1992: 65).
5 Here I adapt a phrase from Sorell (1990: 13).
6 See Rawls (1993) on the idea of reasonable disagreement, and compare Nagel (1979) on the 'fragmentation of value'. The phrase 'blameless variation' is an adaptation of a remark by Crispin Wright, found in Rorty (1998: 31).
7 A modified formula, which does not cover all possible cases, could be defended: 'In the present time and place, truth is, to all practical intents and purposes, a matter of what our peers let us get away with saying.'

References

Anderson, Charles 1991: 'Pragmatism and Liberalism, Rationalism and Irrationalism: A Response to Richard Rorty', *Polity*, 23, 357–71.

Bernstein, Richard 1991: 'Rorty's Liberal Utopia', in his *The New Constellation* (Cambridge: Polity).
Brandom, Robert 1987: 'Pragmatism, Phenomenalism, and Truth Talk', *Midwest Studies in Philosophy*, 12, 75–93.
Brunkhorst, Hans 1996: 'Rorty, Putnam and the Frankfurt School', *Philosophy and Social Criticism*, 22, 1–16.
Dworkin, Ronald 1986: *Law's Empire* (London: Fontana).
Freeman, Michael 1991: 'Speaking about the Unspeakable: Genocide and Philosophy', *Journal of Applied Philosophy*, 8, 3–17.
Geras, Norman 1995: *Solidarity in the Conversation of Humanity: The Ungroundable Liberalism of Richard Rorty* (London: Verso Press).
Honneth, Axel 1995: 'The Other of Justice: Habermas and the Ethical Challenge of Postmodernism', in Stephen White (ed.), *The Cambridge Companion to Habermas* (Cambridge: Cambridge University Press).
Lovibond, Sabina 1992: 'Feminism and Pragmatism: A Reply to Richard Rorty', *New Left Review*, 193, 56–74.
McCarthy, Thomas 1990a: 'Private Irony and Public Decency: Richard Rorty's New Pragmatism', *Critical Inquiry*, 16, 355–70.
McCarthy, Thomas 1990b: 'Ironist Theory as a Vocation: A Response to Rorty's Reply', *Critical Inquiry*, 16, 644–55.
Nagel, Thomas 1979: 'The Fragmentation of Value', in his *Mortal Questions* (Cambridge: Cambridge University Press).
Okrent, Mark 1993: 'The Truth, the Whole Truth, and Nothing but the Truth', *Inquiry*, 36, 381–404.
Rawls, John 1993: *Political Liberalism* (New York: Columbia University Press).
Rorty, Richard 1979: *Philosophy and the Mirror of Nature* (Princeton: Princeton University Press).
Rorty, Richard 1985: 'Epistemological Behaviorism and the De-transcendentalization of Analytic Philosophy', in Robert Hollinger (ed.), *Hermeneutics and Praxis* (Notre Dame, Ind.: University of Notre Dame Press).
Rorty, Richard 1990: 'Truth and Freedom: A Reply to McCarthy', *Critical Inquiry*, 16, 633–43.
Rorty, Richard 1991: *Philosophical Papers*, vol. 1: *Objectivity, Relativism, and Truth* (Cambridge: Cambridge University Press).
Rorty, Richard 1998: *Philosophical Papers*, vol. 3: *Truth and Progress* (Cambridge: Cambridge University Press).
Sorell, Tom 1990: 'The World from its own Point of View', in Alan Malachowski (ed.), *Reading Rorty* (Oxford: Basil Blackwell).
Stout, Jeffrey 1988: *Ethics after Babel: The Languages of Morals and their Discontents* (Boston: Beacon Press).
Vision, Gerald 1990: 'Veritable Reflections', in Alan Malachowski (ed.), *Reading Rorty* (Oxford: Basil Blackwell).

Response to Simon Thompson

Richard Rorty

I quite agree with Simon Thompson that I should have been more careful to distinguish between truth and justification, and to remark that the one notion is absolute and the other relative. I have done this fairly consistently in the last decade or so, but there are some unfortunate passages in my earlier writings in which I run truth and justification together (something William James also did sometimes, though not in his better moments). The Davidsonian point Thompson emphasizes – the indefinability of the word 'true' – is one which I only came to appreciate late in life. But it now seems to me the beginning of wisdom in this area of philosophy.

Sometimes, even in recent years, I have spoken in incautious ways. When, for example, I said in 1993, in 'Putnam and the Relativist Menace', that 'the rightness or wrongness of what we say is just for a time and place', I was taking it for granted that my readers would interpret 'rightness' as a matter of conformity to current justificatory practice. But of course those who think of truth as correspondence to reality often construe 'the rightness of what we say' as 'fitting unchangeable reality', and so my remark was easy to misinterpret as saying something wildly paradoxical. I hope that I am gradually learning to be less aphoristic and less susceptible to accusations of paradox-mongering. My strategy is, or at least should be, to try to shift the burden of argument. I should stick to the claim that those who want to make 'truth' more than 'the reification of an approbative and indefinable adjective' should tell us more than they do about what meaning they assign to the term.

Thompson says that 'In certain circumstances...truth and justification can come apart.' I should say that they will always come apart when, but only when, we step back from the attempt to justify and take a sceptical stance towards the justifications we have been accustomed to accept. The circumstances in question are simply those that arise when we start speculating that some familiar pattern of justification should perhaps be superseded. Such speculation revolves around the thought that, although a given proposition coheres better with our present beliefs and desires than does its contradictory, those beliefs and desires might someday be so extensively revised that the contradictory would become clearly preferable. Such speculations about the partial replaceability of our networks of sentential attitudes are occasions for what I have called the 'cautionary' use of 'true'.

Thompson paraphrases Thomas McCarthy as saying that I abandon 'an idea of truth that has regulative, transcendental and critical force'. Indeed I do. Cautionary force is not the same as critical or regulative force. Nothing can have critical or regulative force – can serve to change our beliefs – except a concrete contribution to argument. The caution 'fully justified, but maybe not true' is not such a contribution. It is just a reminder of human finitude, a confession of fallibility. (I am not sure what to make of the notion of 'transcendental' force. But perhaps the suggestion that 'true' has such force is simply a reminder that, if a proposition is true, it is true in all possible contexts. But that too is just one more reminder of our finitude – of the fact that we shall never know all about all possible contexts, and therefore may always be wrong in our attribution of truth to propositions.)

Thompson rightly says that Norman Geras and others think that 'the language of truth and reason is a potentially powerful weapon which can be used in the fight for justice'. Can it? As far as I can see, this language can be used for self-congratulation, but not as a weapon. The only 'weapon' in the area is, once again, a concrete contribution to an argument. Many people, after going through the relevant arguments and adopting a view, pat themselves on the back by exclaiming: 'Now we have found the TRUTH!' 'REASON is on our side!' Such people enjoy saying, of the people unconvinced by the arguments that have convinced them, that these unfortunates 'have Truth and Reason against them'. But these bits of rhetorical exuberance are as available to the Nazi bad guys as to the democratic good guys. They can be used in the fight for injustice just as easily as in the fight for justice.

The temptation to think of this sort of language as weaponry which the bad guys cannot appropriate is, I think, to be explained by our unfortunate habit of using 'Truth' not as an hypostatized adjective but as the name of a causal power. I argued in my 'Pragmatism as Anti-authoritarianism' that the main reason why a lot of people hate pragmatism so much is that it takes away their sense that, by having become convinced by a certain argument of a certain proposition, they have gained a big, powerful ally – one which must finally prevail.

This personification and apotheosis of an hypostatized adjective seems to me a bad idea. After all, the only assurance I have that my view will finally prevail is the possibility that the argument that convinced me will convince everybody else. This is certainly a possibility, but hardly a certainty. It is no good saying that the fact that I was convinced by the argument gives good reason to think that all *rational* people will be so convinced. This would be an interesting claim only if we had an independent test for rationality – a test other than being convinced by the arguments that convince us. To have such an independent test, as I have urged in various articles, would require identifying a natural order of reasons – reasons which were *intrinsically* good reasons, rather than simply reasons found good by one or another human community. I do not see how this could be done.

This last point brings me to ethnocentrism. In introducing this topic, Thompson defines being ethnocentric as believing 'that our current standards of justification are the best available and, in particular, that they enable us to determine the truth of a state of affairs.' I am not happy with this definition. As I see it, 'our standards of justification' are simply our antecedent beliefs and desires, coherence with which is better achieved by the proposition we call 'justified' than by its contradictory. Philosophers, however, sometimes try to pull out, and privilege, certain specifically criteriological beliefs and desires, and to identify this subset of our beliefs and desires as our 'standards' or 'methods' of justification.

But I do not think that such plum-plucking exercises have met with much success. Consider, for example, the difficulty philosophers of science have in formulating 'criteria of theory choice'. I consider myself justified in believing that Smith is the better candidate, T the better theory, E the better explanation, and Jones the better choice as a business partner if, all things considered, that is the way they strike me. But it is a philosopher's fiction to insist that in the course of my reflections I must have been employing 'standards' and 'methods'. (We can always abstain from judgement, from fixation of belief, if we do not think that the coherence we have attained among our beliefs and desires is sufficient. That would be my description of the situation Thompson describes as believing that our 'standards of justification' do *not* enable us to determine the truth of a state of affairs.)

The fuzzy boundaries of the community of those who make up the relevant ethnos – the community of those whom we count as qualified inquirers – are set by the degree of overlap between their beliefs and desires and our own (and will of course vary as we shift from topic to topic). So when Thompson goes on to say that I should acknowledge that 'other standards of justification may simply be different from and not necessarily inferior to our own', I am inclined to rejoin that if the other guys have different beliefs from ours, and if we are trying to accomplish the same goals, then one of us just *has* to be inferior to the other. Pragmatists like me think that beliefs are habits of action. So insofar as projects are identical and habits of action differ, somebody is doing something wrong.

Of course we shall refrain from such invidious attitudes if projects differ, and if the differences between them strike us as not worth arguing about. (Their culinary tastes and projects are different, and so their beliefs about what spices to cultivate are different, but so what?) But this is not exactly *tolerance* of their differences in belief from our own, it is indifference to them. On any serious question – that is to say, any question about whether an important project should or should not be adopted – both indifference and tolerance are impossible. (But, of course, this inability to be indifferent may not lead to action – as when a nation of slave-owners abuts one in which slavery is illegal, yet neither country thinks it could win a war with its infuriating neighbour.)

Towards the end of his essay, Thompson suggests that I need to leave a space between fellow citizens and fanatics, to be filled by those who are simply, harmlessly, 'different'. I see his point, but would prefer to speak of a continuum of variation in belief and desire with us at one end, the fanatics at the other, and a lot of progressively less sane and reliable people stretching from us to them.

Different such spectra have to be envisaged for different topics, obviously. For you may be 'one of us' for political purposes but a kook when it comes to religion, or one of us for scientific purposes but a hopeless fanatic when it comes to politics. We do indeed live in what Thompson calls a '"post-metaphysical" age of radical plural-ism', but all this comes to for me is that we are somewhat more willing than our ancestors to stop asking 'Good, rational person or bad, irrational person?' and to say things like 'OK as a physicist but don't try to talk politics with her' or 'A good citizen and worker, but in private he lives in a screwball fantasy world'.

4

Irony, State and Utopia
Rorty's 'We' and the Problem of Transitional *Praxis*

Daniel Conway

Richard Rorty is often accused of staking out a position that effect-ively marks the end of politics as we know it.[1] Although it is true, as his critics regularly observe, that he proposes a relatively modest political agenda,[2] it is also true that he recommends this agenda as uniquely suited to the historical conditions that prevail over the transitional period in which he situates himself and his readers. The historical and global triumph of liberal democracy has dramatically altered the terms of political engagement, and Rorty wishes to pro-mote a vision of utopia that is consistent with these developments. His sketch of utopia thus reflects the influence of a historically specific political reality that is distinctly post-revolutionary in character. As he sees it, the most pressing political task at hand is for 'us' to complete the incipient transition to a post-metaphysical articulation of liberal democracy. His sketch of utopia is thus designed both to honour the historical conditions of our transitional epoch and to facilitate the transition to forms of liberal democracy that fit more perfectly with 'our' evolution beyond a reliance on metaphysical principles.

Rather than chide Rorty for celebrating the end of politics, it may be more accurate to treat him as attempting to transact liberal politics under the aegis of pragmatism. Although he boldly salutes liberalism as the optimal general structure for ordering political life in the wealthy North Atlantic democracies of late modernity,[3] he does not mean to suggest (and does not say) that the liberal democratic revolu-tion in political theory has delivered us to stasis or perfection. The details concerning the optimal articulation of liberal democracy must still be sorted out, and many of these details are likely to remain both contested and contestable for the foreseeable future. Critics and theorists should therefore engage in piecemeal melioration, tinkering with the prevailing forms of liberal democracy while leaving untouched its general institutional structure.[4] In undertaking this task of perfecting the practices of liberal democracy, the Rortian 'we' need not wield the heavy metal of metaphysical system-building, for no revisions of the basic structure of liberalism are needed. Instead, his 'we' must take up the sharper, subtler instruments of pragmatic melioration.[5] If Rorty has accurately described the historical context in which his 'we' labours, then this utopian vanguard should eventually be in a position to retire the blunt, heavy instruments favoured by orthodox metaphysicians.

In this essay I wish to focus on the transition that Rorty outlines for 'us' liberals in 'our' advance towards the utopia he envisions. In particular, I am concerned to investigate the nature of the political activity of the proto-utopian vanguard that he entrusts with the task of guiding this transition. It is my contention, *contra* Rorty, that this vanguard is obliged to make use of historically specific resources drawn from the (fading) tradition of Western metaphysics. I raise this contention, moreover, on what I take to be the historicist grounds that Rorty himself honours. If our late modern epoch is marked by the weaning of liberalism from the nourishment (ostensibly) provided by metaphysical ideals, then it seems likely that the governors of this transition are obliged to rely to some extent on the metaphysical resources they have involuntarily inherited. Rorty's 'we', that is, has no choice but to avail itself of metaphysical ideals in its campaign to deliver liberalism to its desired, post-metaphysical incarnation. His identification of late modernity as a transitional age thus places his 'we' in the same boat (or the same fleet) as those marginalized political agents who are obliged to seize the tools and strategies of their oppressors. On this interpretation Rorty is far closer than is generally acknowledged to those postmodern critics (e.g. feminists, advocates of critical legal studies, theorists of race, class and gender) who are obliged by their historical situation to make use of cultural resources that they hope eventually to retire from general circulation.

In what is intended as a friendly amendment to Rorty's blueprint for utopia, I thus apply to *him* the historicism that he productively applies elsewhere. By historicizing the historicist, or so I claim, we gain a clearer sense both of the unique political activity reserved for Rorty's 'we' and of the dependency of this 'we' on the very metaphysical tradition that it has been charged to conclude. In this light, I believe, the transitional political agenda of Rorty's 'we' appears much more ambitious and far more interesting than his own account generally allows. The complex aims of this 'we' should be of particular interest to Rorty's sympathetic readers, who must similarly make judicious use of the metaphysical resources that they have inherited. The discerning judgement required of this 'we' in turn suggests the outlines of a model of citizenship for a transitional epoch like our own.

I

Rorty is often criticized for the utopian impulse that animates his political thinking. These criticisms typically target the 'liberal ironism' that he proposes as the defining political orientation of the citizens who populate his utopia. According to Rorty, the ideal post-metaphysical liberal community is one in which the twin goals of individual self-creation and collective human solidarity are pursued simultaneously and separately: 'I want to save radicalism and pathos for private moments, and stay reformist and pragmatic when it comes to my dealings with other people.'[6] He consequently proposes a 'firm distinction' between private and public, which would prevent the ironism that catalyses self-creation and the liberalism that enables solidarity from contaminating one another.

The liberal ironists who populate Rorty's utopia observe this distinction by publicly pledging allegiance to the guiding ideals of liberal democracy, while privately engaging (or not) in whatever ironic projects their historical situation and pedigrees of acculturation have led them to pursue. Alluding to the double consciousness that ensures the political stability of his utopia, he explains that

> the citizens of my liberal utopia would be people who had a sense of the contingency of their language of moral deliberation, and thus of their consciences, and thus of their community. They would be liberal ironists – people who ... combined commitment with a sense of the contingency of their own commitment.[7]

As far as Rorty is concerned, these citizens may ridicule liberal ideals, or deconstruct the metaphysical foundations of liberal theory, or even reject liberalism altogether as a withered vestige of the Enlightenment – so long as they restrict these ironizing activities to the privacy of their own homes and consciences.

Rorty's defence of liberal ironism is often alleged to underestimate the importance of 'deep' political attachments for the ongoing life of a liberal democratic society. In ironizing the metaphysical foundations of liberal political theory, his critics maintain, he effectively divests the citizens of his utopia of the only political commitments that could lend genuine meaning to their lives. These attachments are identified as 'deep' inasmuch as they emanate from, and inhere in, something like an ethical substance, which imparts to a particular age or people its distinctive identity. The kind of ethical substance his critics have in mind has traditionally been understood as 'metaphysical' in nature, for it ostensibly connects individual human beings with a realm, world or dimension that is not exclusively (or merely) human.[8] In the absence of an ethical substance that would warrant the sacrifices required by a collaborative pursuit of community, this criticism continues, a 'liberal' society would amount to nothing more than a convenient arrangement for transacting the superficial commercial concerns of contemporary bourgeois life. It is the enduring presence of this ethical substance that both requires and enables those deep attachments that Rorty's critics value for their civilizing and spiritualizing functions. Examples of these deep attachments might include religious traditions, ethnic identifications, tribal and familial customs, ancestral pieties, spiritual observances, chthonic rituals, patriotic allegiances and civic virtues.[9]

Rorty typically responds to this line of criticism by challenging its continued relevance for contemporary liberals. In more specific terms, he disputes the common assumption that we can adequately anchor our sustaining attachments only by recourse to metaphysics. Although he is willing in principle to acknowledge the validity of past appeals to the stability and order furnished by metaphysical commitments, he nevertheless believes that such appeals are no longer viable. Contemporary liberals, who believe that 'cruelty is the worst thing we do',[10] can no longer afford the illiberal luxury of grounding their political commitments in a foundation of metaphysical bedrock. They can no longer tolerate the collateral cruelties that are invariably involved in any clash of competing metaphysical ideals and systems. The social and cultural costs of these 'deep' metaphysical commitments now outweigh any benefits they may provide by way of stability and universality. Rorty thus believes that liberalism has evolved to a point at which its continued progress will require liberals to distance themselves from the metaphysical ideals that (may have) nurtured its nascence and adolescence.

Moreover, Rorty maintains, even if we liberals *were* inclined to tolerate the cruelties perpetrated in the name of 'human nature', 'manifest destiny', 'universal reason', 'teleological progress' and kindred metaphysical confabulations, we are no longer in a position to do so. Our unique historical situation is marked, he claims, by an inability to invest resolute belief in the deep metaphysical attachments that (may have) sustained predecessor generations of liberals. Simply put, we now know too much about the history of Western metaphysics to continue to labour acquiescently within its traditions. Rorty's primary justification for refusing to appeal to deep metaphysical commitments thus rests on his account of the irresistible trends of historical contingency: the unique confluence of historical currents that defines our historical situation suggests to him that metaphysical depth is neither credible nor desirable nor sustainable. Rorty's historicism thus sanctions a decisive movement away from the metaphysical ideals that contemporary liberals currently cherish with increasing scepticism and ambivalence.

Rorty's stolid embrace of contingency is thus designed to render the unique political truth of our transitional historical epoch. Although we are generally agreed on the superlative value of liberalism as an articulation of our best political insights, we are also too clever to believe the metaphysical myths that originally served to secure for liberal democracy a solid theoretical foundation. We are also too clever to believe the philosopher's myth that only a faultless theoretical foundation can sustain a sturdy political justification. In order to evoke this particular inflection of our unique historical situation, Rorty proposes the designation *postmodernist bourgeois liberalism*. He intends this designation to convey the loose aggregate of political allegiances shared by those citizens who continue to enjoy the bourgeois freedoms and opportunities afforded them by liberal democracy, while refusing the familiar metaphysical narratives that traditionally have been marshalled to justify liberal democracy. He thus views the passing of classical liberalism as an opportunity for us to extend – rather than terminate – our experiment in liberal democracy:

> I have been urging in this book that we try *not* to want something which stands beyond history and institutions. The fundamental premise of the book is that a belief can still regulate action, can still be thought worth dying for, among people who are quite aware that this belief is caused by nothing deeper than contingent historical circumstance.[11]

Rather than apologize for the robust historicism that guides his political thinking, Rorty presents it as one of the signal attractions of the utopian future that he envisions. It is his appeal to historicism, in fact, that enables him to trace a plausible trajectory that connects us postmodernist bourgeois liberals to the inhabitants of his utopia. Liberal ironism thus constitutes a utopian ideal only for *us*, that is, only for the postmodernist bourgeois liberals who inhabit the wealthy North Atlantic democracies, and only under the unique historical conditions that collectively define our contingent identities. Indeed, Rorty characterizes his liberal ironism as *utopian* precisely because the citizens he describes have successfully negotiated the challenges and dilemmas that currently exercise *us*. They have resolved the crises that we presently face; they have survived the transitional period that we presently occupy; and they have successfully installed a post-metaphysical version of liberal democracy. In short, they have perfected the balancing act that we struggle each day to perform. They are as happy and secure *without* any deep metaphysical commitments as liberals formerly were (or may have been) with the deep metaphysical commitments that Rorty's critics claim to honour.

The citizens of Rorty's utopia thus rely on no deep metaphysical attachments to cement their public allegiance to the liberal ideals they cherish. The 'social glue' that binds them is nothing more than the historically contingent sense of solidarity that arises from their sympathetic identification with one another:

> The social glue holding together the ideal liberal society...consists in little more than a consensus that the point of social organization is to let everybody have a chance at self-creation to the best of his or her abilities, and that that goal requires, besides peace and wealth, the standard 'bourgeois freedoms'. This conviction would not be based on a view about universally shared human ends, human rights, the nature of rationality, the Good for Man, nor anything else. It would be a conviction based on nothing more profound than the historical facts which suggest that without the protection of something like the institutions of bourgeois liberal society, people will be less able to work out their private salvations, create their private self-images, reweave their webs of belief and desire in the light of whatever new people and books they happen to encounter.[12]

As a consequence of their post-metaphysical orientation, the inhabitants of Rorty's utopia need no longer endure the peculiar – and potentially ugly – conflicts that typically arise from the clash of competing metaphysical ideals or systems. Their concrete articulations of social justice are therefore determined not by means of a theoretical exercise conducted by aspiring philosopher-kings, but by means of a consensus achieved through democratic discourse and participation. As he succinctly puts it, the truth of political life in his utopia is not discovered but created: 'a liberal society is one which is content to call "true" (or "right" or "just") whatever the outcome of undistorted communication happens to be, whatever view wins in a free and open encounter.'[13] He thus describes his utopian vision as realized in 'a society in which the charge of "relativism" has lost its force, one in which the notion of "something that stands behind history" has become unintelligible, but in which a sense of human solidarity remains intact'.[14]

Rorty's historicism thus motivates his challenge to the metaphysical depth that his critics claim to cherish. A polity fully disabused of its vestigial metaphysical ideals, he believes, would be better positioned to negotiate the complexities of liberal democracy in the increasingly diverse multicultural context in which we live. The convictions of contemporary liberals are sufficiently deep to sustain the rich plurality that textures their lives and practices. He thus rejects the familiar tendency of his critics to equate 'depth' with 'metaphysical depth'. While he is sensitive to the reluctance of certain individuals to relinquish their metaphysically grounded attachments, he nevertheless maintains that these attachments do not furnish the social glue that their champions prize. He is therefore willing to sacrifice the (alleged) depth of metaphysics in exchange for the harmony, civility and solidarity that characterize the public sphere of his liberal utopia. He defends this trade-off as true not only to the spirit of the times, but also to the spirit of American pragmatism.

II

In an important sense many of the familiar criticisms of Rorty's liberal ironism are either misplaced or misdirected. After all, Rorty candidly advertises his liberal ironism as the product of an exercise in utopian political thinking. He thus acknowledges from the outset that the utopian marriage of liberalism and irony is consecrated only by dint of his authorial fiat. He therefore fully appreciates the gulf that separates us postmodern bourgeois liberals from the liberal ironists who populate his utopia. In fact, he regularly characterizes this gulf as both expansive *and* navigable.

Yet critics regularly take him to task for his utopian excesses. His 'liberal ironists' are ridiculed as unreal, shallow phantoms, or, even worse, as willing parties to the 'collective solipsism' against which

Orwell warned us.[15] Expressing a sentiment that has become common among Rorty's critics, Richard Bernstein observes: 'When we turn to Rorty's attempt to privatize irony, to encourage the playing out of private fantasies, it is difficult to understand why anyone who becomes as narcissistic as Rorty advocates would be motivated to assume public responsibilities.'[16] If I read correctly the psychological basis of Rorty's utopianism, however, then Bernstein's reaction is entirely appropriate: in light of who *we* are, it *should* be 'difficult to understand' why 'narcissistic' private ironists would also contribute to the public quest for greater solidarity. That is, it should not be obvious at all how a balance that is so difficult for us to strike should become second nature for the liberal ironists whom we might someday beget. Indeed, it is precisely this unsettling difficulty, some version of which informs all depictions of utopia, that will (or may) spur our continued progress along the trajectory Rorty describes for us. Only this difficulty (or something like it) will galvanize our campaign to identify and eliminate the cruelties in which we are unwittingly complicit. Rorty, I take it, is in no position to counter Bernstein's objection, because he could never know in advance that his vision of utopia will in fact be realized. By the same token, however, Bernstein cannot know in advance that Rorty's utopian experiment will fail. He knows only that the complex motivation of these liberal ironists is 'difficult' – *but not impossible* – for us 'to understand'.

I thus interpret Bernstein's sceptical reaction as evidence of the success of Rorty's exercise in utopian political thinking. Rorty has sketched a vision of the future of liberal democracy that is neither completely familiar to us nor impossible to imagine. His vision stretches, but does not break, our imaginative projection of ourselves into an unknown future. His sketch is therefore productively disquieting, for it presents a possible future that we cannot know in advance to be impossible for us to realize. This is, after all, how utopian theorizing is supposed to work: it challenges and positions us, but without also compelling us to refuse the challenge for which we are now positioned. On my interpretation, then, Rorty should be pleased by Bernstein's reaction; in fact, he should fully expect his best readers to react in some such way to his utopian experiment. What remains to be seen is how his liberal readers will respond to their initial reactions: will they reify (and thereby sanctify) their own shortcomings as liberals, or will they permit his utopian vision to enflame their own political imaginations?

To object that the marriage of liberalism and irony would require a shotgun wedding is therefore to miss the point of Rorty's experiment in utopian statecraft. He has invoked his utopian prerogative precisely to stipulate the consecration of this union. In fact, his recourse to utopian theorizing is intended to convey, among other things, his awareness of the gulf that currently separates us from the 'liberal ironists' who inhabit his envisioned utopia. A utopia exists 'nowhere' precisely because it holds together in thought various ideals that coexist happily nowhere in the real world. The citizens of Socrates' 'city in speech' in the *Republic* are all content with their 'natural' placement within the pyramidal hierarchy, even though the three social classes are accorded very different privileges and responsibilities. Christine de Pizan's 'city of ladies' is populated by women who have gained access to educational and social opportunities that are ordinarily reserved for men. More's *Utopia* furnishes the eponym for the tradition as a whole only because the author has stipulated that the ideal city described by Raphael is free of the corruption arising invariably from the institution of private property. Voltaire's contented Eldoradans aggressively pursue research in science and technology but never venture beyond the confines of their hermetic valley. The feral Houyhnhnms merit the lavish praise of Lemuel Gulliver because Swift has endowed them with 'a general disposition to all virtues' and an unequivocal respect for the rule of reason. Rousseau's social contract is ensured in large part through the ministrations of a 'legislator' who more closely resembles gods than men in the reach of his sagacity. Hegel's nebulous 'corporations' harmonize the procedural considerations of 'right' with the private, pre-rational commitments of the citizens who belong to them. The communists who survive the 'dictatorship of the proletariat' will be free from class divisions and ideologies because Marx has identified the uprising of the proletariat as the 'last' of the historical revolutions predicated on underlying class struggles. Nietzsche's downbound Zarathustra imparts his teaching of human sufficiency without implying the deficiency of his auditors. Rawls's 'veil of ignorance' not only blinds the occupants of the 'original position' to morally irrelevant facts and contingencies, but also imparts to them an enviable insight into the basic conclusions of cutting-edge social scientific research. Haraway's cyborgs affirm their 'impure' origins without yielding to the otherwise ubiquitous impulse towards innocence and purity. And so with Rorty's liberal ironists: they happily privatize their labours of self-creation while publicly honouring the guiding ideals of liberal democracy. Indeed, if the marriage of liberalism and irony seems suspiciously miraculous,[17] then this objection is properly directed not to Rorty himself, but to the tradition and project of utopian political thinking.

Having diverted the critical focus from Rorty to the larger utopian tradition in which he works, we are now in a position to re-formulate the standard objections raised by his critics: Why should political theorists indulge their utopian fantasies? What is the ultimate value for politics of utopian speculations? In particular, why do 'we liberals' continue to participate in utopian statecraft? The traditional answers to these questions rest on an appeal to the generative power of the imagination: utopian theorizing frees us to dream of a better world, of a more perfectly just arrangement of our basic political institutions.[18] Utopian theorizing allows us to imagine the best within ourselves enacted on the grand stage of politics, thereby allowing us to behold 'writ large' what is ordinarily difficult to isolate and examine within ourselves. Indeed, although a utopia is, by definition, 'nowhere' to be found, it must also hover always nearby. We must believe it to lie just beyond our extended reach. If we could not see our next selves reflected in a vision of utopia, then it would amount to nothing more than an alien fantasy. That Rorty's readers can see themselves as (inadequate) liberal ironists, that they worry about their capacity to perform this important, if divided, office (as Bernstein's objection nervously intimates), thus speaks to the success of Rorty's experiment in utopian theorizing.

But in order for utopian theorizing not to degenerate into idle daydreaming, its nourishment of the political imagination must succeed in enriching our private *and* public lives. The salutary political consequences of utopian thinking are (at least) twofold. Its benefits are preparatory, in the sense that utopian thinking frees, stretches and emboldens the political imagination. Commending the 'preposterous political romanticism' of Roberto Unger, Rorty remarks that Unger 'also lives in an imaginary, lightly sketched future. This is the sort of world romantics *should* live in; their living there is the reason why they and their confused, utopian, unscientific, petty bourgeois followers can, occasionally, make the actual future better for the rest of us.'[19] The benefits of utopian theorizing are also indirect, for in the process of founding a 'city in speech' we may accidentally stumble upon truths about real social relations that we would otherwise not have discovered.[20] In both these respects utopian thinking holds great political value, even if the utopia itself remains frozen in speech, unrealizable by the human resources presently at our disposal. Indeed, although we are destined to fall forever short of our utopian aspirations, the limited progress we achieve will provide a dynamic measure of melioration, such that we might continually progress through less imperfect forms of imperfect justice.

This traditional defence of the political value of utopian thinking dovetails neatly with Rorty's own theory of moral epistemology, which rests on a fairly traditional appeal to the cultivation of the moral sentiments. The primary goal of moral education, he believes, is to expand the individual's overlapping spheres of sympathetic identification and thereby foster an enhanced sense of human solidarity.[21] This is best accomplished, he elaborates, by reading (and assigning others to read) works of imaginative literature, wherein the reader is introduced to people, places, problems and times radically different from her own.[22] The moral/psychological basis of this expanded identification with others is the common susceptibility of all human beings to cruelty, especially the cruelty of humiliation. If we can learn to see ever more others as fellow sufferers, then we can more readily extend our sympathies to them and thereby accommodate an expanded feeling of solidarity.[23] Rorty consequently places great emphasis on the catalysing role of the imagination in expanding our imbricated spheres of sympathetic identification.[24] By meeting imaginary people, or by imaginatively making the acquaintance of real, historical individuals, we might come to comprehend ever more fully the dizzying range of cruelties that featherless bipeds visit upon one another.[25] To apprise citizens of their complicity in heretofore unacknowledged regimes of cruelty thus becomes the primary goal of moral education in a liberal society.[26]

III

In the course of advancing his own defence of utopian political theory, Allan Bloom suggests that any exercise in utopian theorizing necessarily trades on metaphysical ideals. In a passage that is perhaps overly dramatic for Rorty's tastes and purposes, Bloom remarks that

> To attempt to suppress this most natural of inclinations [idealism] because of possible abuses is, almost literally, to throw out the baby with the bath. Utopianism is, as Plato taught us at the outset, the fire with which we must play because it is the only way we can find out what we are. We need to criticize false understandings of Utopia, but the easy way out provided by realism is deadly.[27]

Although Rorty would presumably resist the political implications of this particular interpretation of utopianism, the urgency of Bloom's prose is nevertheless instructive. Simply put, he reminds us that utopian theorizing can have a galvanizing effect on liberal citizens and institutions only if it mantles a fructifying moment of idealism – only, that is, if the envisioned utopia departs enticingly from the established status quo. Following Plato, Rousseau, Hegel, Nietzsche and other non-liberal political thinkers whom he admires, Bloom associates metaphysics with idealism and identifies utopianism, by virtue of its enabling idealism, as an irreducibly metaphysical approach to the enterprise of statecraft. If we compare what *is* the case to what *might* or *should* be the case, then do we not participate thereby in a form of idealism that is recognizably metaphysical?[28] If we untether the imagination from the real and allow it to roam, will it not eventually carry us upward, away from the human condition as we presently know it? It would seem, then, that Bloom's dramatic flourish shelters an important philosophical insight: utopian theorizing would be unacceptably tame (unlike Plato's potentially enveloping 'fire') if we did not dare to imagine the one, ideally true description of how human beings ought to live. We ignite the Promethean flame only in the event that we measure the flawed, empirical world in which we live against some utopian, ideal world in which we might prefer to live.[29] From the standpoint of politics, in fact, the whole object of utopian theorizing is to free the imagination for flights of metaphysical fancy. The prescriptive suggestions that emerge from an experiment in utopian theorizing derive their normative purchase in large part from the metaphysical ideals propounded by the theorist in question.

For his own part, Rorty readily admits that his utopia exists nowhere in the real world, that the happy marriage of private irony and public liberalism constitutes *his* ideal political arrangement. If Bloom is correct, then Rorty's admission would seem to imply an acknowledgement of the metaphysical entanglements of his utopian statecraft. If Bloom is correct, moreover, then the persistence of these entanglements would redound entirely to Rorty's credit. The inextricable complicity of his project in metaphysical idealism would attest to the incendiary possibilities resident within his utopianism.

This excavation of the metaphysical roots of utopian thinking thus positions us to ask after Rorty's own political activity. Why would a philosopher who is committed to the historical disenfranchisement of metaphysics avail himself so readily of the metaphysically freighted practice of utopian theorizing? That is, why do 'we liberals' continue to traffic in utopian ideals? Do they not contribute to the cruelties 'we' wish to expose and curtail? Rorty would certainly refuse the melodrama of Bloom's account of utopia, especially his characterization of utopianism as the potentially destructive 'fire' with which we must 'play'. Some examples of utopian theorizing (e.g. Socrates' 'noble lie' in the *Republic*) may warrant this characterization, he might object, but not all do; we would do well, he might add, to reject Bloom's blanket claims about the metaphysical provenance of utopian theorizing. He might protest, for example, that his own opposition to metaphysics does not commit him to a wholesale proscription of speculative ideals and abstractions; that he wishes to reject only that pathological quest for transcendent verities and ahistorical essences that has come to dominate modern philosophy. *His* approach to utopian theorizing, he might insist, projects the future only in vague outline, the details of which are to be filled in by practising liberals. Following his lead, we might thereby refuse Bloom's melodrama and continue to place ourselves in the venerable tradition of utopian political thinking.

In recommending Roberto Unger's 'preposterous political romanticism', Rorty attaches great importance to the 'lightly sketched future' to which Unger directs our gaze. If it is fair to generalize from his discussion of this particular case, then it would appear that Rorty objects primarily to the heavy hand employed by some utopian theorists. Rather than content themselves with gesturing towards a 'lightly sketched future', these theorists more typically bear down with their drafting pencils. Unable to erase or revise their sketches in the spirit of self-directed irony, unwilling to allow their drawings to suffer fading or smudging, these theorists favour the bold, confident, permanent strokes of the master architect. Rather than muse poetically about what a better future might hold, these theorists hold out for a reasoned account of what the best future must hold. For these theorists the political goal of attaining less imperfect forms of justice merges seamlessly with the personal goal of divining the one, true, ideal way to organize human affairs. It is to these theorists that Bloom's paean to pyromania is properly directed, and it is to these theorists that the siren song of metaphysics will always prove irresistible. For his part, Rorty need not prove himself right for all persons, for all times. He is content with the 'lightly sketched future' that he finds in Unger's writings and attempts to provide in his own. In utopian statecraft, as elsewhere, the devil lurks in the details. Rorty happily provides no details.

Still, Bloom's point is not so easily swept aside. Here we might ask: does one best avoid metaphysics by sketching only lightly an imaginary future, or by categorically refusing to sketch an imaginary future at all? It may be clear that the broad, dark strokes of the revolutionary are indelibly metaphysical, but it is not so clear that the faint, thin strokes of the poet are not also metaphysical. A great deal rests here on what Rorty ultimately means by 'metaphysics', and by its avoidance and/or discontinuation. At one point he acknowledges that he uses the term 'metaphysics' in the sense of 'a search for theories which will get at real essence'.[30] As he then goes on to explain, however, it is not this search *per se* that draws his disapprobation, so much as the perversion of this search into a blinkered quest for redemptive, trans-historical certainty. (On Rorty's account, the orthodox metaphysician more closely resembles Captain Ahab than Don Quixote.) While he is certainly right to remind us that the chequered history of metaphysics is rife with perversions of the 'search for theories which will get at real essence', he would not be warranted in claiming that such perversions are a necessary, inevitable result of the search itself. Surely there is a relevant difference to be explored between philosophers who disclose the continuities that inform human experience and those who inflate such continuities into the 'overarching conditions of possibility... which provide the space within which discontinuity occurs.'[31] Rorty wishes to abjure all reliance on principles or ideals that lie beyond the temporal, the physical, the human, the immanent and the contingent. Yet he also wishes to engage in utopian theorizing, which leads him to posit an imaginary society populated by 'liberal ironists', of whom no known exemplars yet exist.

The metaphysical ghosts that haunt Rorty's utopia are most obviously displayed in his promotion of a distinctly *human* ideal of solidarity. As we have seen, he proposes solidarity as the 'glue' that binds the citizens of his post-metaphysical utopia. We can contribute to the enhancement of human solidarity, he believes, by expanding our spheres of sympathetic identification with others. If we can come to see others as fellow sufferers, then we are more likely to extend our sympathies to them and thus foster an expanded feeling of solidarity. Without the luxury of a metaphysically inflected theory or model of human nature, however, how likely is it that an expanded sphere of sympathetic identification would ever deliver a distinctly *human* solidarity? If sympathy with fellow sufferers is the sole (or primary) impetus towards solidarity, then Rorty's campaign to extend our range of sympathetic identification seems more likely to promote a selectively enhanced feeling of solidarity. Rather than extend their sympathies to all other human beings, individuals may be more likely to embrace only those who are most like themselves, or even those animals, plants, artifacts and machines with which they most strongly identify. Rorty can realistically promise an enhancement – in both breadth and depth – of our feelings of solidarity, but his official anti-metaphysical stance precludes his access to the sort of vocabulary – including, for example, appeals to human 'nature', the human 'condition' etc. – that would best ensure the enhancement of a distinctly human solidarity. Indeed, if the goal of human solidarity has traditionally eluded the best efforts of liberalism, then it might become only more elusive for a postmodernist bourgeois liberalism that has forfeited its metaphysical stake in a common human 'nature'.[32]

It is not my intention here to endorse Bloom's description of utopian thinking or to brand Rorty a closet metaphysician. Nor do I wish to insist upon a necessary linkage between metaphysics and either utopianism or idealism. Rather, I simply wish to suggest that whatever 'metaphysics' does and does not involve, it may not be as neatly distinguished from its alternative pursuits (e.g. historicism, ironism, pragmatism) as Rorty occasionally seems to believe. More precisely, I wish to suggest that utopian thinking may properly occupy an indeterminate liminal space between metaphysics and historicism, reducible to neither and sharing in both. That is, if Rorty's exercise in utopian theorizing does not implicate him in metaphysics, then it would seem to involve him in something that bears a strong family resemblance to metaphysics. I should hasten to add that I do not intend this suggestion to essay a criticism of his utopianism. The success of his experiment in utopian theorizing is attributable in part to its provenance in metaphysics or something like it.

In attempting to map the liminal space in which utopian theorizing is nourished by metaphysics, I take myself to be working within the spirit of Rorty's historicism. In particular, I am concerned to place him (and his understanding of the transitional epoch he represents) within the environs of his own historicism. If, as he maintains, contemporary liberalism is (partially) eclipsed by the lingering penumbra of metaphysics, then we should fully expect that he too must toil within these shadows.

As we have seen, Rorty views our historical epoch as a transitional period, in which we might make significant progress towards the end of weaning ourselves from metaphysical ideals. The liberal ironists who populate his utopia have no truck with the priestly types who preside over cultures inured to the metaphysical comforts dispensed by philosophy and religion. These citizens instead honour various incarnations of the 'strong poet', who provides compelling narrative redescriptions that do not appeal to the validity of a single, immutable truth about the real world.[33] Strong poets provide their fellow citizens with the 'final vocabularies' they need in order to negotiate the fractal complexities of post-metaphysical liberalism, and they recommend these vocabularies solely on the limited authority of the historical epoch that they contingently represent. According to Rorty, then, a liberal culture over which strong poets preside

> would be one in which no trace of divinity remained, either in the form of a divinized world or a divinized self. Such a culture would have no

room for the notion that there are nonhuman forces to which human beings should be responsible...The process of de-divinization... would, ideally, culminate in our no longer being able to see any use for the notion that finite, mortal, contingently existing human beings might derive the meanings of their lives from anything except other finite, mortal, contingently existing human beings.[34]

This 'process of de-divinization' stands at neither its beginning nor its end, and our progress towards its completion measures the progress of our transition to the post-metaphysical utopia Rorty describes.

Hence the (apparent) paradox that attends Rorty's exercise in utopian statecraft: since the transitional 'process of de-divinization' precipitates the installation of the strong poet as the cultural hero of Rorty's utopia, this process cannot derive its own momentum from the ministrations of the strong poet. The transition to a post-metaphysical utopia must therefore occur at least partially under the (diminished) aegis of the metaphysician. This means, I take it, that the transition is guided, and its enabling poetry produced, by metaphysicians who also contribute somehow to the historical extinction of metaphysics. So although Rorty envisions a utopia in which the strong poet has replaced the metaphysician as cultural hero, his activity of envisioning *itself* presupposes the continued role of the metaphysician. In building his utopian bridge to the post-metaphysical future, he is thus obliged to rely (albeit in untraditional ways) on traditional implements of metaphysical engagement. If we are sympathetic to his vision of utopia, moreover, then we should not want him to boycott all metaphysical ideals, at least not immediately, for some of these ideals will contribute to the sturdiness of the bridge he proposes to construct. He may not want to temper his utopianism in the metaphysical flame that Bloom describes, but he may have no choice in the matter – especially if our historical situation is marked by a continued (if diminished) reliance on metaphysical thinking. In any event, we will gain greater insight into his utopianism if we treat his flights of political imagination as at least residually metaphysical.

Rorty's entanglements in the metaphysical undergrowth of a transitional epoch are revealed in his appeals to the subversive power of irony. The combination of his utopian aspirations with his ironic stance yields something he calls 'ironist theory',[35] to which he assigns the complicated task of freeing us from the urge to engage in metaphysical speculation. Borrowing a famous image from Wittgenstein, Rorty presents ironist theory as a self-consuming means to the end of moving beyond the need for metaphysical explanations:

The goal of ironist theory is to understand the metaphysical urge, the urge to theorize, so well that one becomes entirely free of it. Ironist theory is thus a ladder which is to be thrown away as soon as one has figured out what it was that drove one's predecessors to theorize.[36]

In light of the unique, self-consuming function of ironist theory in the economy of Rorty's political thinking, it is important here to bear in mind that the responsibility for ironist theorizing falls *not* to the liberal ironists who patrol his utopia, but to Rorty and his fellow transitioneers.[37] Ironist theorizing is therefore a necessary evil, in which Rorty's proto-utopian vanguard must participate if they are to make possible the utopia in which liberal ironists blissfully reside.

Rorty is fully aware of the daunting complexities involved in relying on a particular strain of theory to free us from the generic need to theorize. Ironist theory will bring an end to metaphysical theorizing only in the event that it consumes itself (and its psychological/sociological bases) along the way. Just as the urge to theorize is ironized and turned against itself, so the metaphysical impulse of utopian theorizing is deployed in a self-consuming assault on the sources of metaphysical speculation. Like Wittgenstein's oft-borrowed ladder, utopian theorizing is pressed into service only under the condition of its own planned obsolescence. As I understand Rorty's historicism, moreover, this is precisely what we should expect of a transitional epoch as it looses itself from the metaphysical moorings of its past. As an ironist, then, Rorty fights fire with fire – which is precisely what the exigencies of his historical situation demand of him.

IV

Rorty's reliance on the self-consuming teleology of ironist theorizing shifts our critical focus to the transitional period in which the metaphysical ideals of his 'us' will subvert themselves in the process of delivering us to utopia. Let us turn now to examine the transitional period in which we presently find ourselves. Having attempted to historicize Rorty, let us now attempt to historicize his project of utopian statecraft.

The metaphysical idealism that fuels Rorty's exercise in utopian statecraft thus raises the problem of transitional *praxis*: what is his preferred plan for steering contemporary liberalism towards the utopian ideal that he envisions? By focusing on the issue of transitional *praxis*, we may now inquire directly into the political activity that

Rorty's sketch of utopia presupposes. How, then, do we move from the postmodernist bourgeois liberalism that Rorty defends to the liberal ironism that he proposes as a utopian ideal? How do we connect the prescriptive, utopian dimension of his project to its descriptive, historical dimension? That is, how do we get 'there' from 'here', especially if 'there' is altogether devoid of the metaphysical entanglements that continue to encumber our 'here'? Or, more precisely: what is the nature of the 'we' that will preside over the transition to utopia?

Although Rorty more regularly refers to an inclusive 'we' that comprises 'we twentieth-century liberals', or 'we heirs to the historical contingencies which have created more and more cosmopolitan, more and more democratic political institutions',[38] he also alludes occasionally to the more exclusive 'we' that will guide contemporary liberalism towards the utopian ideal that he envisions. This proto-utopian 'we' comprises neither the liberal ironists who inhabit his utopia, nor the retrograde metaphysicians who cling anachronistically to their deep attachments, but the transitional agents to whom he entrusts the task of aligning contemporary liberalism with the utopian ideal he advances. Although he does not characterize this more exclusive 'we' as comprising a reformative vanguard, this characterization would seem to convey accurately the nature and aims of its political activity. Insofar as this 'we' is charged with the self-consuming task of purveying ironist theory, moreover, it ostensibly comprises a vanguard that will wither away over time.

With respect to Rorty's 'we' and its role in realizing the liberal utopia he envisions, the concerns that were raised earlier about the marriage of liberalism and irony become uniquely urgent. His liberal ironists may be immune to criticism, but the transitional vanguard of proto-utopian liberals cannot be described in strictly utopian terms. If his vision of utopia is to compel our assent, then the members of this vanguard must closely resemble *us*. That is, they must respond to historical problems and crises that we recognize as impending on the horizon of our future, and they must draw for their reformative labours from the complement of powers, faculties and resources that are uniquely available to agents in late modernity. If we cannot identify strongly with this 'we', then Rorty has perhaps failed either to measure accurately the historical epoch in which we dwell or to describe convincingly the transitional *praxis* that will advance us towards his envisioned utopia.

Rorty apparently charges his reformative 'we' with an important and complex task. This 'we' must continue his anti-metaphysical campaign, ruthlessly historicizing the supposedly transcendent verities that would otherwise frustrate the progress of public discourse in a liberal democracy. As the designated practitioners of ironist theory, they would 'aim at curing us of our "deep metaphysical need"' in order that we might understand 'freedom as the recognition of contingency'.[39] They must do so, moreover, from within a transitional epoch that is defined by its continued (if diminished) reliance on metaphysical ideals. If I understand correctly the brand of historicism that Rorty espouses, then this means that his proto-utopian vanguard will invariably avail themselves – wittingly of not – of metaphysical ideals and resources.

In light of the complex task that devolves to the Rortian 'we' we might characterize the problem of transitional *praxis* as the problem of simultaneously containing and harnessing the metaphysical fire of utopian theorizing. Rorty's vanguard must somehow dampen the flame that ignites its utopian speculations – lest it engulf liberal democracy in a potentially devastating conflagration – while taking care not to extinguish the smouldering embers of idealism. These proto-utopian agents are keepers of a flame that is both unusually excitable and unusually vulnerable to permanent extinction. This delicate task is best entrusted, Rorty believes, to a transitional vanguard of practising pragmatists, who are uniquely situated to make optimal use of the historically specific fund of resources arrayed before them. In this sense, then, Rorty's proto-utopian vanguard comprises 'we pragmatists'.

A flaw common to all metaphysicians, Rorty claims, is their constitutive hyperopia, which issues in their collective failure to take the measure of any particular historical epoch. Unable (or unwilling) to treat each epoch in turn as sponsoring a unique *bricolage* of specific relations and resources, metaphysicians typically tuck diverse epochs into a Procrustean bed of trans-historical abstractions. In fact Rorty occasionally opposes pragmatism to metaphysics precisely because the former is better attuned to those historical particularities that the latter habitually overlooks.[40] As a pragmatist, then, he is obliged to undertake a thorough inventory of the historically specific fund of resources at our disposal. And if it is the case, as he regularly suggests, that we are historically situated in the receding shadow of metaphysics, then a principled opposition to metaphysical speculation would be insufficient to release us from its thrall. Indeed, it would be fatuous for Rorty's 'we' to believe that it might immediately renounce its reliance on the antiquated tools of metaphysical system-building. Rather than attempt to deny or trivialize our residual weakness for metaphysical ideals, his 'we' ought instead to transform this contingent fact of our historical destiny into a productive, pragmatic tool.

Konstantin Kolenda has captured this aspect of Rorty's political thinking with his emphasis on the importance for pragmatists of *coping* with the world as it presents itself to us.[41]

Hence there is no prima-facie reason to assume that a pragmatized form of metaphysical thinking would not find a place in the toolbox of the Rortian 'we'.[42] Indeed, if our historical situation manifests even vestiges of our metaphysical past, then we ought to be prepared to turn these vestiges to our advantage. If the nature of our historical situation does not permit us simply to be done with metaphysics, then it is incumbent upon the pragmatists amongst us to determine how we might proceed most productively within the historical shadow of metaphysics. In fact, we might view the strategic appropriation of our metaphysical inheritance as a test case for Rorty's claim to the legacy of American pragmatism. The true pragmatist, after all, strives to devise a productive use for *all* available historical resources – including resources as apparently inimical to pragmatic adaptation as is metaphysics for Rorty.[43]

If there is a sense in which Rorty is not equal to the pragmatist legacy he claims for himself,[44] it may lie in the severity of his allergic reaction to metaphysics. While generally appreciative of the light touch and faint strokes applied by Unger and other proponents of 'preposterous political romanticism', Rorty tends to leaden his touch and darken his strokes when approaching the topic of 'metaphysics'. As we have seen, in fact his use of the term 'metaphysics' is perhaps too broad (and too pejorative) to suit his pragmatic ends. Indeed, the pragmatist must always attempt to appraise objectively the resources arrayed before him, independent of his own prejudices and predilections. So if, as Rorty believes, our historical situation is still partially defined by a reliance on metaphysics, then it is incumbent upon him, *qua* pragmatist, to undertake a historically sensitive assessment of our metaphysical inheritance. (To be fair to Rorty, he would presumably respond that he *has* undertaken a careful inventory of the metaphysical resources at his disposal, and that he has judged them all to be of no further constructive value.)

One way to achieve this pragmatic end would be to soften the effects of metaphysical speculation, perhaps by confining our metaphysical forays to the arena of utopian theorizing. If properly contained, that is, metaphysical speculation could perhaps be harnessed for the pragmatic task of sculpting ever less imperfect forms of liberal democracy. Rorty's 'we' might very well discover that a complement of self-consuming metaphysical ideals is perfectly suited to the transitional task at hand.[45] In this sense the utopian ideals formulated by the Rortian 'we' could function much like Wittgenstein's famously obsolete ladder: having relied on these utopian ideals to guide liberal democracy towards ever more just incarnations, the Rortian 'we' might eventually retire these ideals – and itself – from active service.[46] This self-consuming task would perhaps foreshadow the end of utopian theorizing. Rorty, rather than (Heidegger's) Nietzsche, would thus be the 'last metaphysician of the West'.

Once historicized, Rorty's critique of metaphysics more closely resembles a miniaturism than an outright opposition or renunciation.[47] He rejects the grand, sweeping, trans-historical narratives that he associates with the pernicious objectivism of the Western metaphysical tradition, but *not* in favour of the stringently empirical, concrete analyses that his critique of metaphysics would seem to recommend.[48] His potent ironism may fragment the grand, metaphysical narratives that formerly sustained the development of liberal democracy, but it does not pursue this process of fragmentation to its elemental, atomistic conclusion. Although he gamely resists the metaphysical urge to traffic in eternal verities, to speak for all humans and for all times, he nevertheless presumes – rightly, in my opinion – to speak from a trans-individual perspective that conveys the common experiences of the North Atlantic liberal bourgeoisie with which he most strongly identifies.[49] Trading the grand narratives favoured by orthodox metaphysicians for the humbler, fractured narratives preferred by pragmatists, genealogists and other champions of localism, Rorty restricts his focus to that community, place and time for which he may legitimately speak. Indeed, he remains surprisingly unironic about his prerogative to stand and speak for a 'we' greater than himself.[50]

Although he occasionally advertises his own historicist narratives as different in kind from those dispensed by predecessor philosophers – different by virtue of their post-metaphysical aims and aspirations – it might be more helpful to view them as different only in degree, as miniature versions of the sweeping narratives they supplant. As I read Rorty's historicism, in fact, an embrace of miniaturism would furthermore cohere with the general trends of his political thinking. The particular historical conditions that uniquely define our transitional epoch both require and justify the move to miniaturism. We can no longer sustain (or believe) the epic stories of the metaphysical tradition, but we need not yet capitulate to vulgar particularism and nihilism. Rorty urges us instead to miniaturize our narratives, to downscale our goals and aspirations to a measure commensurate with the limited resources at our disposal. His resource to miniaturism thus corresponds to the faint, delible strokes that he admires in Unger's presentation of a 'lightly sketched future'.

V

Although Rorty does not address himself directly to this problem of transitional *praxis*, he does outline a containment strategy that his 'we' might adapt to the pragmatic task of realizing his vision of utopia. I have in mind here the prophylactic regimen that the citizens of his utopia derive from their guiding distinction between public and private. As Rorty explains, his sketch of utopia is expressly designed 'to show how things look if we drop the demand for a theory which unifies the public and private, and are content to treat the demands of self-creation and of human solidarity as equally valid, yet forever incommensurable'.[51] Towards this end he incorporates into his blueprint for utopia a 'firm distinction' between public and private, in order that liberal ironists might simultaneously pursue the twin goals of self-creation and the achievement of solidarity.

Because there is no need for yet another revolution in political theory,[52] there is also nothing to be gained by liberal ironists who would incur the risks involved in making public their doubts about the theoretical foundations of liberalism.[53] It is not their wish, after all, to disestablish liberalism in favour of another general structure of political organization. They consequently keep to themselves any suspicions, concerns, worries and criticism they might harbour of liberalism itself. A similar containment strategy might be developed by the Rortian 'we' to pragmatize the metaphysical ideals that inform their utopian theorizing. As we progress towards the realization of Rorty's utopia, his 'we' might do well to privatize its utopian musings, indulging them only to reap the indirect benefits they promise by way of a fortified political imagination.

Rorty could thus apply to his own transitional *praxis* the guiding hunch that motivates his sketch of utopia. That is, he could recommend that his proto-utopian 'we' limit their metaphysical thinking, including all exercises in utopian theorizing, to the private sphere. While he candidly wishes that metaphysical thinking would simply disappear, he also acknowledges that metaphysical speculation (or something like it) is potentially galvanizing when it is restricted to the private pursuit of autonomy. On this interpretation, his 'we' could happily read Plato, Hegel, Derrida et al. in private, provided that they do not allow their illiberal ideas to bleed directly into the public sphere. Presumably he could extend this restriction to encompass utopian thinking as well, especially if he were to agree that utopian thinking is irreducibly metaphysical in nature. He might therefore confine the utopianism of his 'we' to private projects of *self*-perfection, thereby preventing its enabling fire from engulfing anything precious to the public articulation of liberalism. If, as Bloom suggests, utopianism is the fire with which we must play if we wish to continue to improve our serial approximations of justice, then perhaps it is best played with privately, by individuals whose self-directed irony leads them to greater self-knowledge. Rorty's 'we' would still be keepers of the utopian flame, but they would restrict their flame-keeping to private experiments in self-transformation.

Critics will surely protest that the privatization of utopianism would render it apolitical, solipsistic or simply inconsequential. But this need not be the case. The privatization of utopian theorizing need not sever the linkage of utopianism to politics. J. S. Mill, for example (who also happens to be one of Rorty's heroes), argues persuasively for the indirect public benefits of private 'experiments in living'. As Mill sees it, the (indirect) social benefits of 'individuality' are so great that even those citizens who do not wish to make use of expanded civil liberties should want them to be extended to others.[54] Following Mill, we might conclude that the most desirable social consequences of utopianism are indirect (rather than direct), concrete (rather than abstract), and embodied (rather than theoretical). On this model utopianism would enter the public realm not as a theory or thought-experiment, but as an already perfected 'experiment in living', in which the agents of political change are passionately invested. Only the most promising products of utopian theorizing would enter the public sphere, and they would do so only in the form of fully embodied habits and practices. All false starts, second thoughts, miscalculations and whimsical errors would be confined to the self-directed ironizing of the private sphere, where they would present no unwanted danger to the public pursuit of liberal ideals.

The privatization of utopian theorizing need therefore result in limiting only the expression of the theorizing itself. The serious products of this theorizing, literally incorporated into the practices of the proto-utopian vanguard, would play a central role in the ongoing campaign to improve our liberal institutions. More importantly for Rorty's project, the privatization of utopian theorizing would provide an additional safeguard against the dissemination of utopian principles that are antithetical to the guiding ideals of liberalism. In the privacy of their own homes and consciences, his proto-utopian vanguard can experiment with various utopian principles and reject those that cannot be harmonized with the basic aims of a liberal polity.

The privatization of utopian theorizing would also seem to cohere with Rorty's historicism. If, as he insists, we have witnessed the last great revolution in political philosophy, then no benefit is to be gained from the public dissemination of utopian principles that are inimical to the advance of liberalism. We might be better served in our transitional epoch by utopians who actually embody their guiding ideals. We would then have a preliminary indication that these ideals are both consistent with liberalism and worthy of further elaboration. Having witnessed the political lapses of philosophers as monumental as Hegel, Marx, Nietzsche and Heidegger – all of whom were unable to account for themselves within their respective theories of modernity – we might now hold out for thinkers who are *also* responsible citizens, thinkers who refine their own habits and practices before urging others to refine theirs.

This means, I believe, that the voluntary privatization of utopian theorizing would also honour the spirit of American pragmatism. Rather than fan the flames of utopianism or douse them altogether, Rorty's 'we' might well determine that the privatization of utopianism would hold the greatest pragmatic value for the advance of liberalism. Although the Rortian 'we' would voluntarily restrict utopian theorizing to the private sphere, this theorizing would also be allowed (and encouraged) to enter the public sphere in some indirect, attenuated – we might say 'pragmatized' – form. So although it may be true that liberal democracy depends for its stability on the privatization of self-creation, it also depends for its dynamism and growth on the eventual publicity – in some pragmatized form – of the utopian idealism that galvanizes the private sphere.

The greatest obstacle to the containment strategy I have outlined is the public/private distinction itself. No element of Rorty's utopian theorizing has elicited stronger challenges than his insistence on separating the public allegiance to liberal ideals from the private pursuit of self-creation. Rorty's critics have insisted, for example, that his public/private distinction is not sufficiently liberal;[55] that it is not sufficiently ironic;[56] that it allows too much seepage from private into public;[57] that it allows too little seepage from private into public;[58] that it represents an atavism of an unowned attempt at 'first philosophy';[59] that it is contrary to the fallibilist spirit of American pragmatism;[60] and that it is neither possible, nor desirable, nor necessary to maintain it.[61]

In fairness to Rorty's critics, it is difficult to imagine that he sincerely means to observe this 'firm distinction' as strictly as he claims. If the public discourse of liberal democracy is to sustain its signature dynamism, then the quickening exercises of the private imagination *must* have public, political consequences – even if these consequences are only indirect, elliptical, or diffuse. In fact, we need to take seriously the possibility that Rorty is in fact ironic (in his sense) about his public/private split, that the economy of liberal ironism actually succeeds in obliterating (or softening) this distinction.[62] On this point a favourable analogy may be drawn to the political philosophy of J. S. Mill, whom, as we have seen, Rorty admires as a kindred thinker. Mill, too, begins his political theorizing with a fairly rigid distinction between public and private – in his parlance, between 'self-regarding' and 'other-regarding' actions – only to modify (or sublate) this distinction along the way.[63] As this analogy suggests, we might treat Rorty's public/private distinction as a heuristic device, designed both to honour and to convey a basic, pre-theoretical sentiment shared by 'us liberals'. Having established the coeval value of privacy and solidarity, Rorty might then undertake a more nuanced negotiation of their competing claims, gradually softening his guiding distinction to accommodate a pragmatic melioration of the institutions of liberal democracy.

In this light, I wish to propose a friendly amendment to the utopian charter of Rorty's liberal ironism. If I have accurately measured the reach of his pragmatism, then his public/private split does not operate (as he often suggests) as an impermeable barrier. It is neither so 'rigid' nor so 'firm' as he is wont to maintain. Rather, his public/private split operates as a pragmatic filter, allowing the ripest fruits of utopian thinking to transit from private to public, but only after they have been adequately harmonized with the guiding ideals of liberal democracy. Perhaps we can achieve even greater precision on this point: Rorty's public/private split *does* function as an impermeable barrier, but only in *one* direction. Since public ideals should never be allowed to encroach upon the private pursuit of self-creation, the public/private split effectively safeguards the individual's inviolable right to privacy in a liberal society. With respect to transit from private to public, however, this distinction should be understood to function as a selectively permeable barrier, in order that some private labours of self-creation might eventually inform the public quest for greater solidarity. Indeed, if Rorty wishes to ensure the continued growth and dynamism of the liberal society he sketches, then he must make some provision for the salutary influence of private self-creation on the public discourse of liberal democracy.[64] Under the terms of this friendly amendment, moreover, Rorty's liberal ironism would still allow for the citizens of his utopia to harmonize the goals of privacy and solidarity. Indeed, if the public/private split erects a barrier that is only unilaterally impermeable, then his citizens can readily accommodate their need for privacy to their campaign to minimize cruelty. Private labours of self-creation therefore need be neither solipsistic nor unpolitical. The personal can become (indirectly) political.

A further attraction of this friendly amendment is that it reveals the extent to which Rorty expects the citizens of his utopia to exercise judgement with respect to the publicity of their private epiphanies. If their private irony is to contribute to the public campaign for less imperfect forms of social justice, then they must determine for themselves when, and in what form, to introduce their ironic insights into the common, public vocabulary of liberal democracy. If they interpret the public/private split as functioning in both directions as an impermeable barrier, then they risk the stagnation of the public discourse that animates their society. If they ignore the public/private split and introduce unfiltered irony into the public sphere, then they risk the subversion of their most cherished public ideals. In short, *they* must determine the optimal porosity of this barrier, by voluntarily harmonizing their ironic insights with the reigning ideals of their liberal society. Although it is true that Rorty invokes his utopian prerogative to endow his liberal ironists with impeccable judgement, it is important to note that, even in utopia, there is ample space for the exercise of practical, deliberative reason.

Conclusion

The central (if understated) role of judgement in the maintenance of Rorty's utopia suggests a similarly important role for judgement in the political activities of his proto-utopian vanguard. In determining the optimal flame for their utopian fire, these transitional agents must deliberate carefully and exercise discerning judgement. Unlike the liberal ironists who inhabit his utopia, however, his 'we' are not blessed by authorial fiat with perfect judgement. These transitional liberals must consequently educate themselves about the epoch in which they labour, in order that they might accurately appraise the limited historical resources at their disposal.

As a by-product of his sketch of utopia, Rorty thus presents a thoroughly historicized model of citizenship, for he demonstrates how we might be good citizens throughout the halting transition from postmodernist bourgeois liberalism to the utopia of liberal ironism. In more concrete terms, his model of citizenship can be presented in terms of the following exhortations: read good books; dream of a better future; publicly honour liberal ideals; expand the quest for human solidarity; privately pursue projects of self-creation; pragmatize the metaphysical ideals of utopianism; cherish the unprecedented freedoms secured by liberal democracy; swallow (or sublimate) all resentment; and don't be cruel. What we do not receive from Rorty is a *theory* of citizenship. If the exhortations articulated above are not sufficient to refresh one's commitment to the liberal ideals he espouses, then he has nothing more to say.

Notes

1 See, for example, Bernstein (1991: 282–6). According to Bernstein, 'Rorty never faces up to the (contingent) slide from irony to ruthless cynicism – a cynicism which corrupts liberal democracy...For all Rorty's manifest concern with liberal democracy, public responsibilities, and utopian politics, it is curious how little politics one finds in this book [*Contingency, Irony, and Solidarity*]. Indeed, despite his battle against abstractions and general principles, he tends to leave us with empty abstractions' (1991: 283–4).

2 Both Hickman (1993: 237) and Stuhr (1997: 123) describe the political agenda of Rorty's liberal ironism as 'timid' in comparison to the rich legacy of Deweyan pragmatism that Rorty claims to honour.

3 Rorty (1989: 63) thus explains, 'Indeed, my hunch is that Western social and political thought may have had the last *conceptual* revolution it needs'.

4 Here Rorty (1996: 17) follows Dewey, who, he believes, struck an admirable balance between politics and philosophy: 'When Dewey talked politics, as opposed to doing philosophy, he offered advice about how to avoid getting hung up on traditional ways of doing things, how to redescribe the situation in terms which might facilitate compromise, and how to take fairly small, reformist steps'.

5 See Hall's (1994) claim that Rorty is a plucky *bricoleur*.

6 Rorty (1996: 17).

7 Rorty (1989: 61).

8 A representative statement of this criticism is captured in the following rhetorical question, which is posed by Hartshorne (1995: 20): 'Why should we give up all efforts to satisfy such natural curiosity as that about the eternal or necessary aspects of reality, in contrast and relation to which the contingent and emergent aspects alone have their full sense and definition?'

9 In an observation that Rorty's critics might find apposite to his apologia for liberal ironism, Ferdinand Tönnies distinguishes between a bloodless, bourgeois *Gesellschaft* and the traditional *Gemeinschaft* from which all meaningful human communities arise. According to Tönnies, 'inherent in the concept of the *Gesellschaft*...[is a] tendency [which] necessarily

implies a dissolution of all those ties which bind the individual through his natural will and are apart from his rational will. For these ties restrict his personal freedom of movement, the saleableness of his property, the change of his attitudes, and their adaptation to the findings of science. They are restrictions on the self-determined rational will and on the *Gesellschaft* insofar as trade and commerce tend to make property or property rights as mobile and divisible as possible and require unscrupulous, irreligious, easygoing people' (1957: 234). Tönnies's sobering reference to the 'unscrupulous, irreligious, easygoing people' who characterize the *Gesellschaft* is similar in its rhetoric and tone to the standard criticisms of Rorty's liberal utopia.

10 Rorty (1989: xv).

11 Ibid., p. 189.

12 Ibid., pp. 84–5.

13 Ibid., p. 67.

14 Ibid., p. 190.

15 I originally explored this criticism in Conway (1991a), especially pp. 205–8.

16 Bernstein (1991: 287).

17 Critchley (1996: 25) argues that the difficulties involved in negotiating the divided office of private ironist/public liberal would require that Rorty's liberal ironists cultivate an 'impossible psychological bi-cameralism, which would be a recipe for political cynicism'. Mounce (1997: 207) similarly observes that 'the liberal is the same man in both spheres and one of the things he will be ironic about in private is precisely his liberalism. However he acts in public, he cannot avoid whilst in private . . . being ironic about his public values. The difficulty is to see how he can leave his irony behind when he passes through his front door. How, in short, can he prevent his private thought from affecting his public actions?' In the course of a summary dismissal of Rorty's vision of utopia, Haack maintains that 'There could be no honest intellectual work in Rorty's post-epistemological utopia' (1995: 139).

18 Seery has drawn attention to the importance of *death* to utopian political theory. In a fascinating attempt both to extend and rejuvenate the tradition of utopian political theory, Seery outlines a theory of 'plutonic' justice (1996: 176–92), wherein living human beings engage in imaginary conversations with the dead. The perspective of the dead, who presumably have nothing further to gain from self-interest and strategic discourse, is invaluable in envisioning the model of justice that we might wish to install in our utopia. The living thus gather sustenance and encouragement from the dead, whose mistakes of embodiment the living might presumably avoid.

19 Rorty (1991b: 183).

20 Donna Haraway writes persuasively of the value of utopian thinking for unleashing the power of the imagination. Haraway maintains that the primary objective of utopian thinking is not to bring into existence the

utopia that is sketched, but to free the imagination for the real work of political change. In this sense utopian thinking comprises a regimen of preparatory calisthenics, which exercises the imagination for the difficult revisioning work that lies ahead.

21 Rorty (1989: 192) thus explains that 'My position is not incompatible with urging that we try to extend our sense of "we" to the people whom we have previously thought of as "they".'

22 Ibid., p. 107.

23 For a critical evaluation of the 'tribal moralism' that emerges from Rorty's post-metaphysical campaign to enhance human solidarity, see Nielsen (1991: 149–57); Mounce (1997: 207–2); and Haack (1995: 138–9).

24 For Rorty's account of the importance of political imagination, see Rorty (1991b: 184–5).

25 For a critique of Rorty's reliance for democratic progress on expanded spheres of solidarity, see Mouffe (1996: 1–12). According to Mouffe, 'The progress of democracy, *pace* Rorty, will never take the form of a smooth, progressive evolution in which the "we liberals" get bigger and more inclusive as more and more rights are being recognized. Rights will conflict and no vibrant democratic life can exist without a real democratic confrontation among conflicting rights and without a challenge to existing power relations' (1996: 8).

26 For a consideration of the residual metaphysics associated with Rorty's anthropocentric campaign to promote human solidarity, see Conway (1992: esp. 286–9).

27 Bloom (1987: 67).

28 As Rorty (1989: 3) himself volunteers, 'Utopian politics sets aside questions about both the will of God and the nature of man and dreams of creating a hitherto unknown form of society.'

29 Acknowledging, perhaps, the flammatory perils to which Bloom alludes, Rorty (1991b: 191) refers to exercises in utopian statecraft as 'risky social experiments'.

30 Rorty (1989: 8).

31 Ibid., p. 25 n. 2.

32 I pursue this line of objection in Conway (1992), from which the present essay borrows a few sentences (pp. 287–8).

33 Rorty (1989: 53, 60–1).

34 Ibid., p. 45.

35 Ibid., pp. 96–121.

36 Ibid., p. 97.

37 The failure to distinguish between the liberal ironists who populate Rorty's utopia and the progressive, pragmatic liberals who, he hopes, will work toward the realization of this utopia is the source of some confusion on the part of Rorty's critics. See, for example, Haack (1995: 138–9); and Bernstein (1991: 278–83). That Rorty fully understands the difficulties for *us* in achieving a stable balance between the competing

claims of private irony and public solidarity is confirmed by his self-acknowledged recourse to *utopian* theorizing.

38 Rorty (1989: 196).

39 Ibid., p. 46.

40 Rorty (1991b: 181) thus remarks that 'As a pragmatist, I think philosophy is at its best when it is content to be "its own time apprehended in thought" and lets transcendence go.'

41 According to Kolenda (1990: 25–6), 'The notion of coping is likely to enlarge the scope of exploratory activity and spread it more widely among all kinds of intellectuals, that is, people, whom Rorty defines as those who worry about their final vocabularies. If there is no common grid from which one must start, one can concentrate on the particular position, viewpoint, orientation, and field of expertise one happens to be in.'

42 In Conway (1999) I pursue at greater length the question of the pragmatist's optimal orientation to the metaphysical resources that are available to representatives of a transitional epoch.

43 On this point I mean to follow the lead of Shusterman, who insists that 'historical purism is false to the forward-looking spirit of pragmatism' (1996: 68).

44 Perhaps no aspect of Rorty's philosophy has riled practising pragmatists more than his claim to the legacy of Deweyan pragmatism. According to Gouinlock (1995: 75), for example, 'Pre-Rortian students of Dewey's thought will be astonished to learn that Dewey was "beyond method", and their astonishment is justified.' Gouinlock insists that, in fact, 'Unwittingly but inexorably, Rorty threatens to undo Dewey's work, rather than carry it forward' (1995: 87). For other critical responses to Rorty's invocation of the legacy of Dewey, see Stuhr (1997: 121–4); Macke (1995: 169–70); Levine (1995: 47–9); Bernstein (1991: 233); Alexander (1993: 211–12); Haack (1995: 126–7); and Hickman (1993: 237–8). For more positive responses to Rorty's claim to the legacy of Deweyan pragmatism, see Hall (1994: 84–6); and Mounce (1997: 173–4).

45 See Shusterman (1996: 79–81).

46 For my appreciation of the extent of the sacrifices expected by Rorty from practising pragmatists, I am indebted to the argument articulated by Anderson.

47 In an apparently related claim, Rorty (1991b: 6) suggests that his 'essays should be read as examples of what a group of Italian philosophers have called "weak thought" – philosophical reflection which does not attempt a radical criticism of contemporary culture, does not attempt to refound or remotivate it, but simply assembles reminders and suggests some interesting possibilities.'

48 I investigate the metaphysical residue of Rorty's position in Conway (1991b: esp. 107–10).

49 On Rorty's practice of continuing to offer 'narratives', see Hall (1994: 60–3).

50 Here I follow the lead of Bernstein (1991: 247), who maintains that Rorty not only is 'insensitive to the dark side of appealing to the "we" when it is used as an exclusionary tactic', but also purveys the 'historical myth of the given', insofar as he speaks 'as if there is at least a historical fact of the matter'. Bernstein submits that 'Rorty's constant references to "we", a common tradition, a shared consensus, appear to be hollow – little more than a label for a projected "me"'.

51 Rorty (1989: xv).

52 Ibid., p. 63.

53 As Rorty (1996: 45) explains in his response to Critchley, 'As I see contemporary politics, we do not need what Critchley calls "a critique of liberal society". We just need more liberal societies, and more liberal laws in force within each such society.'

54 Mill (1978: 67–9).

55 Hall (1994: 136) thus asks, 'But if Rorty is worried that public uses of irony may undermine the socialization process, shouldn't he be fearful that his own severely ironic treatment of the authors of books will seep into the public consciousness and undermine our political idols? There is, after all, no nonpermeable membrane protecting us from such osmosis.'

56 Conway (1991a: 202–5).

57 Elshtain thus remarks, and apparently not in a charitable vein, that 'There is a lot of seepage of private to public and public to private within Rorty's argument' (1992: 204).

58 Critchley observes that 'it seems strange that the fact that we become ironists in the private realm seems to have few implications for our relation to the public realm' (1996: 25). Essaying a Deweyan critique of Rorty's defence of liberal privatism, Alexander (1993: 211) insists that 'Rorty's view of the incommensurability of private self-creation with any public concern abandons seeing how public affairs are really implicated in our private worlds or how our private actions may have broad public consequences. He thus encourages the retreat into the private world of aesthetic description with the hope that it eventuates in a "sentimental education" which somehow bolsters the project of liberal democracy.' As I explain below in my friendly amendment, however, Rorty almost surely wishes for some indirect consequences of private irony to enter the public sphere of his utopian society.

59 Referring to what he calls Rorty's 'logic of apartheid', Bernstein (1991: 286) notes that 'It seems curious that Rorty, who shows us that most distinctions are fuzzy, vague, and subject to historical contingencies, should rely on such a fixed, rigid, ahistorical dichotomy.' Derrida makes a similar point about the distinction between public and private, although not with explicit reference to Rorty's project. According to Derrida the distinction between public and private haunts any political philosophy that attempts to adhere strictly to it: 'And if this important frontier [i.e. between the public and the private] is being displaced, it is because the medium in which it is instituted, namely, the medium of

the media themselves (news, the press, telecommunications, techno-tele-discursivity, techno-tele-iconicity, that which in general assures and determines the spacing of public space, the very possibility of the *res publica* and the phenomenality of the political), this element itself is neither living nor dead, present nor absent: it spectralizes. It does not belong to ontology, to the discourse on the Being of beings, or to the essence of life or death. It requires, then, what we call, to save time and space rather than just to make up a word, *hauntology*. We will take this category to be irreducible, and first of all to everything it makes possible: ontology, theology, positive or negative theology' (Derrida 1994: 51).

60 Haack (1995: 138–9).

61 Mounce (1997: 207–9).

62 Conway (1991a: 205–6).

63 In the first, 'Introductory' chapter of *On Liberty*, Mill asserts 'one very simple principle' of liberty: 'That the only purpose for which power can be rightfully exercised over any member of a civilized community, against his will, is to prevent harm to others' (1978: 9). Apparently aware that his broad-brushed distinction between self- and other-regarding actions bears further elaboration and sophistication, Mill argues in his fourth chapter that any violation of 'a distinct and assignable obligation to any other person or persons' qualifies an action as 'other-regarding' (1978: 79). Here I follow the interpretation outlined by Elizabeth Rapaport in her 'Editor's Introduction' to *On Liberty* (1978: xv–xvii).

64 On the *need* for private irony to enter indirectly the public sphere, see Conway (1991a: 201–2). See also Kolenda (1990: 51–3).

References

Alexander, Thomas M. 1993: 'The Human Eros', in *Philosophy and the Reconstruction of Culture: Pragmatic Essays After Dewey*, ed. John J. Stuhr (Albany, NY: SUNY Press), pp. 203–22.

Anderson, Douglas R. (unpublished): 'Pragmatic Intellectuals: Facing Loss in the Spirit of American Philosophy'.

Bernstein, Richard 1991: 'Rorty's Liberal Utopia', in *The New Constellation: The Ethical/Political Horizons of Modernity/Postmodernity* (Cambridge: Polity), pp. 238–49.

Bloom, Allan 1987: *The Closing of the American Mind* (New York: Simon and Schuster).

Conway, Daniel W. 1991a: 'Taking Irony Seriously: Rorty's Post-metaphysical Liberalism', *American Literary History*, V 3/1, pp. 198–208.

Conway, Daniel W. 1991b: 'Thus Spoke Rorty: The Perils of Narrative Self-Creation', *Philosophy and Literature*, 15 No.1, (Spring), pp. 103–10.

Conway Daniel W. 1992: 'Disembodied Perspectives: Nietzsche *contra* Rorty', *Nietzsche-Studien*, 21, pp. 281–9.

Conway, Daniel W. 1999: 'Of Depth and Loss: The Peritropaic Legacy of Dewey's Pragmatism', in Casey Haskins and David I. Seiple (eds), *Dewey Reconfigured: Essays on Deweyan Pragmatism* (Albany, NY: SUNY Press), pp. 221–48.

Critchley, Simon 1996: 'Deconstruction and Pragmatism: Is Derrida a Private Ironist or a Public Liberal?' in Chantal Mouffe (ed.), *Deconstruction and Pragmatism* (London: Routledge).

Derrida, Jacques 1994: *Specters of Marx*, trans. Peggy Kamuf (New York: Routledge).

Elshtain, Jean Bethke 1992: 'Don't Be Cruel: Reflections on Rortyian Liberalism', in Daniel W. Conway and John E. Seery (eds), *The Politics of Irony* (New York: St Martin's Press), pp. 199–217.

Gouinlock, James 1995: 'What is the Legacy of Instrumentalism? Rorty's Interpretation of Dewey', in Herman J. Saatkamp, Jr. (ed.), *Rorty and Pragmatism: The Philosopher Responds to his Critics*, (Nashville, Tenn.: Vanderbilt University Press), pp. 72–90.

Haack, Susan 1995: 'Vulgar Pragmatism: An Unedifying Prospect', in Herman J. Saatkamp, Jr. (ed.), *Rorty and Pragmatism: The Philosopher Responds to his Critics* (Nashville, Tenn.: Vanderbilt University Press), pp. 126–47.

Hall, David L. 1994: *Richard Rorty: Prophet and Poet of the New Pragmatism* (Albany, NY: SUNY).

Haraway, Donna J. 1991: *Simians, Cyborgs, and Women* (London: Free Association Books).

Hartshorne, Charles 1995: 'Rorty's Pragmatism and Farewell to the Age of Faith and Enlightenment', in Herman J. Saatkamp, Jr. (ed.), *Rorty and Pragmatism: The Philosopher Responds to his Critics* (Nashville, Tenn.: Vanderbilt University Press), pp. 16–28.

Hickman, Larry A. 1993: 'Liberal Irony and Social Reform', in John J. Stuhr (ed.), *Philosophy and the Reconstruction of Culture: Pragmatic Essays after Dewey* (Albany, NY: SUNY Press), pp. 223–39.

Kolenda, Konstantin 1990: *Rorty's Humanistic Pragmatism: Philosophy Democratized* (Tampa: University of South Florida Press, 1990).

Levine, Thelma Z. 1995: 'America and the Contestations of Modernity', in Herman J. Saatkamp, Jr. (ed.), *Rorty and Pragmatism: The Philosopher Responds to his Critics* (Nashville, Tenn.: Vanderbilt University Press), pp. 37–49.

Macke, Frank J. 1995: 'Pragmatism Reconsidered: John Dewey and Michel Foucault on the Consequences of Inquiry', in *Recovering Pragmatism's Voice: The Classical Tradition, Rorty, and the Philosophy of Communication* (Albany, NY: SUNY Press), pp. 155–76.

Mill, J. S. 1978: *On Liberty*, ed. Elizabeth Rapaport (Indianapolis: Hackett).

Mouffe, Chantal (ed.) 1996: *Deconstruction and Pragmatism* (London: Routledge).

Mounce, H. O. 1997: *The Two Pragmatisms: From Peirce to Rorty* (London: Routledge).

Nielsen, Kai 1991: *After the Demise of the Tradition: Rorty, Critical Theory, and the Fate of Philosophy* (Boulder, Colo.: Westview Press).

Rorty, Richard 1989: *Contingency, Irony, and Solidarity* (Cambridge: Cambridge University Press).

Rorty, Richard. 1991a: *Objectivity, Relativism, and Truth, Philosophical Papers*, vol. 1 (Cambridge: Cambridge University Press).

Rorty, Richard. 1991b: *Essays on Heidegger and Others, Philosophical Papers*, vol. 2 (New York: Cambridge University Press).

Rorty, Richard, 1996: 'Remarks on Deconstruction and Pragmatism', in Chantal Mouffe (ed.), *Deconstruction and Pragmatism* (London: Routledge).

Seery, John E. 1996: *Political Theory for Mortals: Shades of Justice, Images of Death* (Ithaca, NY: Cornell University Press).

Shusterman, Richard 1996: *Practicing Philosophy: Pragmatism and the Philosophical Life* (New York: Routledge).

Stuhr, John J. 1997: *Genealogical Pragmatism: Philosophy, Experience, and Community* (Albany, NY: SUNY Press).

Tönnies, Ferdinand 1957: *Community and Society*, trans. and ed. Charles P. Loomis (East Lansing: Michigan State University Press).

Response to Daniel Conway

Richard Rorty

Daniel Conway writes as if you could not be deeply attached to anything, and *a fortiori* could not be politically idealistic, without being somehow metaphysical. This suggests that he and I are using 'metaphysical' in different senses. I use 'metaphysics' as the name of the belief in something non-human which justifies our deep attachments. So I should never agree, as Conway suggests I might, that 'utopian thinking is irreducibly metaphysical in nature'.

Conway uses 'metaphysics' and 'metaphysical' in much broader senses, as when he says that I 'rely on various metaphysical ideals to further the realization of [my] post-metaphysical utopia', and again when he says that 'we will gain greater insight into his [my] flights of political imagination as at least residually metaphysical.' He uses 'metaphysical' as if it were coextensive with 'deep'. In contrast, I think of the depth of an attachment (to a person, a *polis*, an ideal, a god, or whatever) as a matter of the inextricability of the object of that attachment from one's most cherished self-descriptions. This sense of 'depth' has nothing to do with intellectual depth, considered as one of the features which distinguished Socrates from Cephalus. One's deepest attachments may or may not be associated with religious or secular metaphysical beliefs – beliefs which provide assurance that one *should* cherish certain self-descriptions. Whether one has any such convictions depends largely upon the culture in which one has been raised, but the ability to have deep attachments swings free of culture.

Conway seems to agree with Richard Bernstein that unreflective and intellectually shallow narcissists cannot be deeply attached to ideals of social justice. Consider, as counter-examples, Walt Whitman and Lyndon Baines Johnson. You cannot get much more narcissistic than they were, but who would question the depth of either man's attachment to a utopian version of the United States of America, that 'greatest poem'? Conway seems to think that only metaphysics can, by saving us from narcissism, make us generously public-spirited. Perhaps he agrees with Plato, as I do not, that unselfishness is possible only for those who have climbed some way up the divided line, and that moral and intellectual virtues are intertwined.

In short, I protest in exactly the terms Conway predicts that I will protest: I insist that my 'opposition to metaphysics does not commit him to a wholesale proscription of speculative ideals and abstractions'. I wish, just as Conway suggests, 'to reject only that pathological quest for transcendent verities and ahistorical essences' which Plato initiated and Nietzsche mocked. I do not see why the replacement of the metaphysician by the strong poet as cultural hero presupposes the (albeit diminished) role of the metaphysician. It does not take a metaphysician to beat a metaphysician. Nietzsche was (despite some unfortunate bluster in his *Nachlass*, and *pace* Heidegger) a strong poet who managed to scrape off almost all residues of metaphysics. Treating Nietzsche as a metaphysician seems as pointless as saying to Shelley or Tom Paine, 'atheism is your religion.'

Since I question the 'inextricable complicity of this [my] project in metaphysical idealism', I cannot make much of 'the problem of transitional *praxis*' that Conway poses in section IV of his contribution to this volume. Much of what Conway says suggests that we anti-metaphysicians should try to turn metaphysics against itself. That is certainly an option, but I cannot see its attractions. Liberal anti-fundamentalist and anti-clerical critics of religion made sneaky use of scripture and other theistic equipment to accomplish their ends, but Shelley's and Paine's ingenuous frankness strikes me as, in the end, more effective. It was more effective because it suggested the glowing possibilities of a brave new atheistic utopia.

As with atheism, so with anti-metaphysics. Conway suggests that it would be antithetical to the spirit of pragmatism to reject these resources 'provided by our metaphysical inheritance' before determining their historically contextualized value. But surely we have already had enough experience with attempts to use the weapons of metaphysics against metaphysics? I think of British empiricism, positivism, contemporary Australian philosophical physicalism, and the like, as such attempts. All they accomplished was to replace one non-human source of justification (the Will of God, the Idea of the Good) with another (the Intrinsic Nature of Physical Reality). The spirit of pragmatism, I should think, dictates that, given a history of failed experiments with half-measures, we try more radical remedies. So I think we should follow Nietzsche's and James's leads, and break with the onto-theological tradition more radically than did Comte or Bertrand Russell.

Conway speaks of 'the stringently empirical, concrete analyses that his [my] critique of metaphysics would seem to recommend'. I am not sure what he has in mind. Analyses of what? Increasing inequality of educational opportunity in the old democracies? The role of the IMF in pauperizing Third World peasants? I am all for providing stringently empirical, concrete analyses of such things. But Conway and I are not the right people to pick out which things of this sort need which sort of analysis.

He also speaks of 'that community, place and time for which he [I] may legitimately speak'. I don't think of myself as doing anything like speaking for a community, a place or a time, nor do I have any idea what would 'legitimate' me in doing so. To be sure, I agree with Hegel that philosophy should be 'its time held in thought'. But offering a description of your community, time and place is hardly the same thing as speaking 'for' it. I would never describe myself, as Conway does, as trying to 'render the unique historical truth of our transitional historical epoch'. It is one thing to say, 'Let's try this; it might help', and a much more dubious thing to say, 'This is what the age demands'.

What about Conway's claim that 'If the public discourse of liberal democracy is to sustain its signature dynamism, then the quickening exercises of the private imagination *must* have public, political consequences'? If Conway had written 'an occasional quickening exercise ... ' I could have agreed entirely. If there are *no* private quickening fantasies (such as those of Jefferson, Whitman, Debs or King), then indeed liberal democracy will suffer a loss of dynamism – just as tyranny would have suffered such a loss without the loony private fantasies of a Hitler or a Mao. Presumably Conway does not think that any and every quickening exercise of the private imagination should have such public spill-over. But only if he did think something like that, it seems to me, should he find my 'firm distinction' between the public and the private as objectionable as he does.

I must have been very misleading in what I wrote about this distinction in *Contingency, Irony, and Solidarity*. For Conway is right that those passages have rubbed a great many people the wrong way. But, as I say in my response to Richard Shusterman in this volume, all I wanted was a firm distinction between responsibilities to oneself and to responsibilities to others. I cannot see that anything in the final section of Conway's paper shows that the latter distinction is philosophically or politically mischievous.

When Conway gets around to his 'friendly amendment', however, he seems to think that my private–public distinction is basically OK, and just needs more careful handling. Certainly I am happy to accept his amendment. But in proposing it, Conway seems to think that its principal effect will be to make clear the need for us admirers of Nietzsche to hide our irony from the masses.

This idea, familiar from the work of Leo Strauss and his followers, is one for which I have no sympathy. It presupposes that the masses are still unable to kick their metaphysical habit, and that we ironical types must therefore be prudently sneaky in our dealings with them. My hunch is that if the masses could learn – as a lot of them already have – that the powers that be are not ordained of God, then they can learn to get along without metaphysical backup for their deep attachment to democratic institutions.

I envisage a global liberal utopia in which nobody – neither the philosophers nor the masses – thinks that democratic institutions need any more than pragmatic justification. Conway fears that that sort of attitude would provide insufficient social glue, insufficiently deep attachments. Maybe he is right. Time will tell. But I do not think there is any good argument from what he might call the continuities that inform human experience that backs up his pessimistic prediction. We have seen all sorts of surprising discontinuities since 1789, and we may see more.

5

The Avoidance of Cruelty
Joshing Rorty on Liberalism, Scepticism and Ironism

David Owen

The political writings of Richard Rorty eschew the rigorous tone of the academic philosopher for that of the light-minded critic who seeks to seduce the young and josh his fellow citizens out of their contentment. Consequently it might not surprise us that the price for communicating in broad, bold brushstokes is an occasionally careless disregard for detail. It is not, after all, as if we don't know whether Rorty is capable of playing the more studied role of professional analytic philosopher – he has done so on too many occasions for this to be in doubt. So if Rorty chooses to be a cartoonist rather than an architectural draughtsman, we might begin by asking why he adopts this tactic. Fortunately, Rorty tells us:

> The encouragement of light-mindedness about traditional philosophical topics serves the same purposes as does the encouragement of light-mindedness about traditional theological topics...such philosophical superficiality and light-mindedness helps along the disenchantment of the world. It helps make the world's inhabitants more pragmatic, more tolerant, more liberal, more receptive to the appeal of instrumental rationality.
>
> If one's moral identity consists in being a citizen of a liberal polity, then to encourage light-mindedness may serve one's moral purposes. Moral commitment, after all, does not require taking seriously all the matters that are, for moral reasons, taken seriously by one's fellow citizens. It may require just the opposite. It may require trying to josh them out of the habit of taking those commitments so seriously. There

may be serious reasons for so joshing them....I should argue that in the recent history of liberal societies, the willingness to view matters aesthetically...has been an important vehicle of moral progress. (1991: 193–4)

So, crudely speaking, Rorty is engaged in a rhetorical and pedagogic wager. This wager has two related elements: first, that light-mindedness acts as a corrosive on philosophical and theological metaphysics; second, that light-mindedness deployed for serious moral reasons is an aesthetic form of moral education. In Rorty's case the primary serious moral reason for engaging in this activity is an unconditional commitment to putting cruelty first, to cruelty as the *summum malum*.

But what is involved in putting cruelty first? In *Ordinary Vices* Judith Shklar provides the following characterization:

> To put cruelty first is to disregard the idea of sin as it is understood by revealed religion. Sins are transgressions of a divine rule and offenses against God; pride – the rejection of God – must always be the worst one, which gives rise to all others. However, cruelty – the willful inflicting of physical pain on a weaker being in order to cause anguish and fear – is a wrong done entirely to *another creature*. When it is marked as the supreme evil it is judged so in and of itself, and not because it signifies a denial of God or any other higher norm. It is a judgement made from within the world in which cruelty occurs as part of our normal private life and our daily public practices. By putting it unconditionally first, with nothing above us to excuse or to forgive acts of cruelty, one closes off any appeal to any order other than that of actuality. To hate cruelty with utmost intensity is perfectly compatible with Biblical religiosity, but to put it *first* does place one irrevocably outside the sphere of revealed religion. For it is a purely human verdict upon human conduct and so puts religion at a certain distance. The decision to put cruelty first is not, however, prompted merely by religious skepticism. It emerges rather from the recognition that the habits of the faithful do not differ from those of the faithless in their brutalities, and that Machiavelli had triumphed long before he had ever written a line. To put cruelty first therefore is to be at odds not only with religion but with normal politics as well. (1984: 8–9)

If we reflect on this passage, we can locate the impetus for Rorty's advocacy of both ironism and liberalism. On the one hand, ironism is proposed as a (necessary?) condition of putting cruelty first. Ironism rules out appeals to any metaphysically secured 'higher norm'; it limits us to the order of actuality. On the other hand, ironist liberalism simply is putting cruelty first. Such a liberalism is a form of politics committed to the avoidance of cruelty. So Rorty expresses his commitment to putting cruelty first through his advocacy of the figure of the liberal ironist as an exemplar of the type of human being that we should be. Consequently the initial task of this essay will be to try to clarify the constitutive characteristics of the liberal ironist (section I). However, Rorty also endorses – presumably as an exemplar of what an ironist liberalism would involve – Rawls's political conception of liberal justice. So the second task of this essay will be to ask if this is appropriate to a liberalism which puts cruelty first (section II). Finally, I will return to the theme of light-mindedness in order explore the use of this tone as a means of moral education, focusing on the relationship between joshing and cruelty (section III).

I

This section focuses on the figure of the liberal ironist. However, in order to clarify the constitutive features of this figure, I will begin by examining the figure of the ironist, before turning to the specific features of the liberal ironist.

Rorty describes the ironist as someone who stands in a particular sort of relationship to his or her 'final vocabulary', where a final vocabulary is characterized as follows:

> It is 'final' in the sense that if doubt is cast on the worth of these words, their user has no noncircular argumentative recourse. Those words are as far as he can go with language; beyond them is only hopeless passivity or a resort to force. A small part of the vocabulary is made up of thin, flexible and ubiquitous terms such as 'true,' 'good,' 'right,' and 'beautiful.' The larger part contains thicker, more rigid, and more parochial terms, for example, 'Christ,' 'England,' 'professional standards,' 'decency,' 'kindness,' 'the Revolution,' 'the Church,' 'progressive,' 'rigorous,' 'creative.' The more parochial terms do most of the work. (1989: 73)

The relationship in which the ironist stands to her 'final vocabulary' has three features:

> (1) She has radical and continuing doubts about the final vocabulary she currently uses, because she has been impressed by other vocabularies, vocabularies taken as final by people or books she has encountered; (2) she realizes that argument phrased in her current vocabulary can neither underwrite nor dissolve these doubts; (3) insofar as she philosophizes about her situation, she does not think that her vocabulary is closer to reality than others, that it is in touch with a power not herself. (1989: 73)

Crucially, on Rorty's account, being an ironist (i.e. recognizing the contingent historical causes of one's beliefs) is entirely compatible with having beliefs which are taken to be worth dying for (1989: 189). In other words, Rorty argues that recognizing the contingent historical causes of one's beliefs is consonant with having an unconditional commitment to a belief (such as cruelty as the *summum malum*). I will return to this point shortly, but first let's try to get clearer about what sort of figure 'the ironist' is.

In a recent essay on truth in ethics, Bernard Williams offers the following comment:

> We know that when people say that they want real truth in ethics, above all when they say they want objectivity in ethics, they want more than the local language of thick concepts and the associated minimal truth.... They want there to be one canonical, homogeneous ethical language. They want it to be conceptually homogeneous across cultures, and across disagreements within our culture (across pluralism). (1995: 240)

The predominant representatives of this impulse are Kantians and Utilitarians for whom this task of getting at objectivity entails the attempt to have recourse only to thin, univocal ethical concepts in order to show how we can both have a universal ethical language and that such a language does not require thick concepts to generate binding obligations. The main alternative to this construction of a 'morality system' is the attempt by neo-Aristotelians to build from thick ethical concepts and attempt to cope with the apparent lack of conceptual homogeneity by positing a distinction between the universal deep structure of thick ethical concepts and local surface variations, with or without a theory of error, which similarly attempts to meet the challenge of plurality but rejects the attempt to dispense with thick ethical concepts (Williams 1995: 240–2). Now, in the context of Rorty's account of final vocabularies, I take it that Rorty's ironist (like Williams) is sceptical of these endeavours, that is, the possibility of 'real truth' in ethics. This is just the sense of the third feature of the ironist, namely, that 'insofar as she philosophizes about her situation, she does not not think her vocabulary is closer to reality than others' (Rorty 1989: 73). Moreover if, as seems entirely reasonable, we take Rorty as an example of an ironist, then his view of sophisticated neo-Kantians like Jürgen Habermas and neo-Aristotelians like Charles Taylor support this conclusion. But how does this point connect to the first two features of the ironist?

Consider the following issue elaborated by Williams in his remarks on truth in ethics:

Statements of the kind 'X is chaste' and 'X is not chaste' are true, when they're true, in some language L, which is a certain ethical language but not the same as our ethical language Lo because the languages differ at least in the respect that one contains the concept of chastity and the other one doesn't. This doesn't mean that when some speaker of L gives approval to an utterance of another speaker of L, he or she is awarding that speaker only the qualified approval 'what you said was true in L'. As David Lewis has pointed out, if a person's utterance is true in L, and the person is speaking L, then the person's utterance is true. (1995: 238)

Williams goes on to point out that this does not entail that an ethnographer whose ethical language Lo lacked the concept of chastity could not understand L; all that follows is that

What he [the ethnographer] can't do is generate a Tarski-equivalent right hand side in his own language Lo for the claim that (e.g.) 'X is chaste' is true in L. The reason that he can't do this is that, given the way in which we set up the case, the expressive powers of his own language are different from those of the native language precisely in the respect that the native language contains an ethical concept which his doesn't. (1995: 239)

In such a situation, according to Williams, we recognize that our thick ethical concepts are not the only option and we may, under certain conditions (for example, the acknowledgement of ethnographic reports), recognize that L is a real, rather than simply notional, option for us. Williams does not attempt to specify these conditions in any general sense but he does assert that '[t]oday all confrontations between cultures must be real confrontations' (1985: 163).

Now, instead of the ethnographer, imagine a reasonably reflective person, A, committed to scepticism concerning 'real truth' in ethics, who has a particular final vocabulary F which lacks the concept of chastity, confronting another person, B, with a different final vocabulary Fo which includes the concept of chastity, and which A recognizes as a real option for her. Given Rorty's position concerning language and truth (at least insofar as I understand it), we can take this confrontation as identical in the relevant respects to that between the L-speaker and the Lo-speaker. In this context it is difficult to imagine how A can avoid reflecting on F *qua* sexual ethics and, insofar as she is impressed by Fo *qua* chastity, having doubts about F (the first feature of the ironist). Moreover, because F lacks the concept of chastity, arguments conducted in F can 'neither underwrite nor dissolve these doubts' (the second feature of the ironist). So, on

Rorty's strict definition of the ironist, all that is involved in being an ironist is (1) scepticism towards the idea of 'real truth' in ethics and (2) recognizing that there are other real options open to us. In other words, being an ironist is recognizing the force of the challenge of plurality.

In this respect, whatever one thinks of it, being an ironist is a readily intelligible position. But, with respect to the second feature of the ironist, Rorty seems to have something further in mind. For example, he remarks:

> There is no *neutral* noncircular way to defend the liberal's claim that cruelty is the worst thing that we do, any more than there is a neutral way to back up Nietzsche's assertion that this claim expresses a resentful, slavish attitude. (1989: 197)

This example points out that the second feature of the ironist is not simply a matter of engagements between ethical vocabularies which do not share the relevant concept (e.g. chastity) but also engagements where the relevant concept is held in common. How are we to understand this claim? If we try to grasp it in terms of the formal notion of a final vocabulary as a set of concepts, it is not clear that we can make much sense of this claim – unless we take the relations of values expressed in our world-guided and action-guiding thick ethical concepts as integral to what it is to have this final vocabulary. This would allow us to distinguish between final vocabularies which share the same concepts, yet where the ethical values expressed by these concepts are radically distinct; for example, 'brutality' as a term of condemnation in one vocabulary and as a term of praise in another, where the concept picks out the same actions. If we adopt this strategy to make sense of Rorty's position, then I take it that his point is this: 'It is not true that for each conflict of values, there is some value which can be appealed to (independent or not) in order rationally to resolve the conflict' (Williams 1981: 77).

Thus 'sane and honourable people can attach different importance to different values, so that they will not agree on the resolution of many different cases' (Williams 1981: 80). So, on this account, having a final vocabulary involves having a set of thick ethical concepts whose action-guiding character is structured by one's ethical beliefs and commitments. Support for this account of the sense of a final vocabulary is provided by Rorty's contention that 'nothing can serve as a criticism of a final vocabulary save another such vocabulary' (1989: 80).

With these observations to hand, let us return to Rorty's contention that 'a belief can still regulate action, can still be worth dying for, among people who are quite aware that this belief is caused by nothing deeper than contingent historical circumstance' (1989: 189). There are two ways of approaching the question of the degree to which Rorty is warranted in asserting this proposition. The first would be to cite examples of sane ironists who, as a matter of fact, have died for their beliefs (and, from a pragmatic point of view, if Rorty were to meet a suitably Socratic fate in a suitably Socratic manner, this would provide an exemplary response to his critics). The second route would be to note that being willing to die for a belief means simply that death is preferable to living a life which is a denial or negation of this belief. In other words, being willing to die for a belief involves two features: first, that the belief is integral to one's ethical understanding of what it is for a life to be liveable and, second, that one is 'confident' in this belief. Now I see no reason why the ironist should not have beliefs about what it is for a life to be ethically liveable and, given that the ironist is committed to the claim that this life is the only one that she has, one can reasonably suppose that they matter to her. It is the second feature which is crucial: can the ironist have sufficient confidence in a belief to be prepared to die for it? After all, the most commonplace philosophical route for generating reasoned confidence in a belief that is, holding it to be 'objective', is ruled out for the ironist. But is this the only way of generating confidence? At least one other option would seem to be open to the ironist, namely, reflective endorsement: that a belief has survived open and honest dialogic engagement with other incompatible or incommensurable beliefs, that is, with other types of final vocabulary. By 'open and honest dialogic engagement' I mean simply dialogue conducted in terms of recognition of, and respect for, the other. If she has engaged in this kind of imaginative or, preferably, actual dialogue with others, then that her belief, her final vocabulary, survives this plural fusing of horizons is all that is required for confidence in it, and she can reasonably say: 'Here I stand, I can do no other.' (Note that the ironist need not herself engage in this dialogue as long as she has sufficient confidence in some representative person(s) who do conduct this dialogue.) If this is plausible, modesty concerning the status of one's beliefs, one's final vocabulary, is compatible with unconditional commitments and Rorty is warranted in his assertion that ironism is compatible with being willing to die for one's beliefs.

This consideration of the ironist means that we are now in a position to specify the character of the liberal ironist as that ironist who is unconditionally committed to the belief that cruelty is the *summum malum*, that is, who is (ideally) willing to die for this belief.

So Rorty can state, first, that 'the citizens of my liberal utopia would be people who had a sense of the contingency of their language of moral deliberation, and thus of their consciences, and thus of their community' (1989: 61), that is, they would be ironists and, second, that such ironists as liberals just want 'our *chances of being kind*, of avoiding the humiliation of others to be expanded by redescription':

> She thinks that recognition of the common susceptibility of human beings to humiliation is the *only* social bond that is needed. Whereas the metaphysician takes the morally relevant feature of the other human beings to be their relation to a larger shared power – rationality, God, truth, or history, for example – the ironist takes the morally relevant definition of a person, a moral subject, to be 'something that can be humiliated.' Her sense of human solidarity is based on a sense of a common danger, not on a common possession or a shared power. (1989: 91)

In this context, solidarity

> is not thought of as recognition of a core self, the human essence in all human beings, but rather thought of as the ability to see more and more traditional differences (of tribe, religion, race, customs and the like) as unimportant when compared to our similarity in respect to pain and humiliation – the ability to think of people wildly different from oneself as included in the range of 'us'. (1989: 192)

Now it is fairly straightforward to see that an ironist who is unconditionally committed to cruelty as the *summum malum* is going to view solidarity in terms of our common human susceptibility to cruelty and, in particular, humiliation (a specifically human form of cruelty). Consequently, in just this respect, the liberal ironist *must* be committed to the development of human solidarity, not least insofar as the non-recognition of beings who are susceptible to cruelty and humiliation as human beings is necessarily itself a significant form of cruelty.

In this context criticisms such as the following misrecognize the issue:

> Rorty assures us that the only species universal is 'the ability to feel pain', to which he sometimes adds the 'susceptibility to humiliation' as a distinctive human form of pain. Why not the ability to speak, act, think, work, learn, interact, play roles, be guided by norms, have desires and feel feelings other than humiliation? Rorty's answer seems to be, Because there is no universally shared language, system of actions, and so forth. That may be, but the empirical evidence suggests that there are common features in all of these areas and that they are at

least as extensive as the shared features of humiliation. (McCarthy
1993: 36)

Contra McCarthy, it is not that the ability to feel pain is the only
species-universal but that, from the perspective of an unconditional
commitment to cruelty as the *summum malum*, it is our susceptibility
to cruelty (and thus our ability to feel pain as a necessary condition of
our susceptibility to cruelty) which is the ethically salient feature of
our common humanity. That we also share the abilities listed by
McCarthy is relevant only precisely insofar as these features are
integral to the multiplicity of ways in which we can act cruelly with
respect to one another.

However, we might reasonably pause to wonder about the fact that
Rorty appears on occasion to identify cruelty with humiliation *qua*
human beings. It is not, after all, immediately apparent that humiliation exhausts the forms of cruelty to which human beings are susceptible and, if this is the case, it is not clear why the liberal ironist should
regard 'the morally relevant definition of a person, a moral subject, to
be "something that can be humiliated"'. Consider that, to be susceptible to humiliation, one must have some minimal sense of self-worth;
where to have a sense of self-worth (however minimal) requires the
recognition of ethical bounds to the self. In other words, to be
susceptible to humiliation requires that one must have at least one
identity-conferring commitment which places limits on the actions
that one is prepared to perform. This is just to point out that a human
being who lacks any integrity cannot be humiliated – or, as
Lynne McFall elegantly puts it, that 'in order to sell one's soul, one
must have something to sell' (1987: 10). Does this mean that such
human beings cannot be susceptible to cruelty? It may entail that such
human beings are not susceptible to most (perhaps all?) forms of
moral cruelty, but it certainly does not entail that they are not susceptible to non-moral forms of cruelty such as physical cruelty. The
integrity-lacking individual can scream with pain under torture as
much as anyone else (although the lack of integrity may make it
more likely that he or she will avoid situations of being subject to
torture insofar as torture is often, but not exclusively, tied to the
attempt to break down identity-conferring commitments). Consequently, I take it that we should understand Rorty's commitment
to cruelty as the *summum malum* as not being, despite occasional
utterances, reducible to humiliation as the *summum malum*.

We might suppose that an even quicker argument against Rorty's
lapses on this point would be to claim that one cannot experience
humiliation unless this concept is part of one's final vocabulary but

that this does not make one any less susceptible to other forms of cruelty, such as physical cruelty. However, although lacking the concept of humiliation limits one's capacity to discriminate between – and one's expressive range for recounting – experiences of powerlessness, it does not entail that one does not experience powerlessness nor that, if one acquired this concept, one could not retrospectively pick out some of one's range of such experiences as experiences of humiliation.

Similarly, we should also not identify this commitment to cruelty as the *summum malum* with susceptibility to pain and humiliation as Rorty may occasionally appear to suggest (1989: 182). There are, after all, numerous sources of pain which are not products of cruelty but simply of being a human being, a fragile and vulnerable creature who lives in awareness of her own finitude. In other words, a commitment to cruelty as the *summum malum* directs us to injustice, not to misfortune (although failing to exhibit sympathy for the plight of those subject to misfortune may itself be a significant form of cruelty); it directs us to the products of human agency, not of blind nature – although discriminating between the two is likely to be an activity fraught with difficulties, even when the parties concerned hold common conceptions of human agency.

With these clarifications in place, let us turn to the issue of the liberal ironists' maintenance of reasoned confidence in their unconditional commitment to cruelty as the *summum malum*. As the discussion of the ironist makes clear, under conditions of plurality the maintenance of confidence in this overriding obligation to avoid cruelty entails another unconditional commitment on the part of the liberal ironist – a commitment to engage, directly or via representatives, in free and equal dialogue with those who do not hold that cruelty is the *summum malum*, that is, those who hold other types (or genres) of final vocabulary. We should note that this second commitment is entirely compatible with the first in that it simply requires that one engage with non-liberals and/or non-ironists in a manner consistent with recognition and respect; indeed, insofar as failing to recognize and respect the other is a form of cruelty, this second commitment is already required by the commitment to cruelty as the *summum malum*. This latter point becomes clear if we consider what recognition and respect involves on the part of the liberal ironist – namely, to recognize the other as a human being who is susceptible to cruelty and who may have a final vocabulary (i.e. various identity-conferring commitments), and, if so, to engage with them by attempting to see the world from the perspective of their final vocabulary and acknowledging the significance of this final vocabulary for them. The negation of this commitment to recognition and respect is to deny either the humanity of the other (non-recognition) or the significance of their relationship to their beliefs and commitments (non-respect). Thus the former is that cruelty which consists in denying the susceptibility to cruelty of a being who is susceptible to cruelty and the latter is that cruelty which consists in humiliating a being who is susceptible to humiliation. Thus, given her unconditional commitment to cruelty as the *summum malum*, the liberal ironist *must* be committed to dialogic engagement characterized by recognition of, and respect for, the other. Indeed, it may be regarded as one of the strengths of this liberal position that the condition of an ironist holding *any* unconditional commitment with reasoned confidence is internally embraced by the unconditional commitment characteristic of liberal ironists.

We can conclude this section, then, by summarizing the constitutive features of the liberal ironist. First, the liberal ironist as an ironist is sceptical of 'real truth' in ethics and recognizes that other final vocabularies than her own are real options for her. Second, the liberal ironist as a liberal is committed to the claim that cruelty is the *summum malum* – this commitment defines the type or genre of her final vocabulary. Third, the liberal ironist as both ironist and liberal is unconditionally committed to dialogue, directly or via trusted representatives, with non-liberals and non-ironists conducted in terms of recognition of, and respect for, the other.

II

Given this characterization of the figure of the liberal ironist, the question taken up in this section concerns the sort of politics to which the liberal ironist should be committed given her recognition of the challenge of plurality *qua* final vocabularies. Rorty's general answer to this question is that: 'It is not evident that [our political institutions] are to be measured by anything more specific than the moral intuitions of the particular historical community that has created those institutions' (1991: 190). So where a society is characterized by shared moral intuitions, however illiberal they may be, then that its political institutions express its intuitions is the only justification required. This may appear to be an odd position for a liberal to advance but it expresses Rorty's ironism by eschewing the idea that there is anything deeper than our moral intuitions and it is consonant with his liberalism insofar as it would be cruel and humiliating to members of this society to override their moral intuitions if the political institutions of this society do *in fact* express their shared moral intuitions. However, to know that this is the case requires some mechanism or other for the members of such a society to express their moral intuitions freely, that is, it requires some appropriate mechanism (such as, for example, rights) for ensuring the freedom to express one's moral intuitions without fear or hinderance. In other words, Rorty's point is that political institutions are just insofar as they can be justified in reasons acceptable to the members of this society. It is, I think, for this reason that Rorty endorses Rawls's turn to political liberalism in which Rawls presents his argument in terms of the value of public justifiability. But before we turn to the question of whether or not Rorty ought to endorse Rawls's position, it may be worth raising one further point with respect to moral intuitions.

The point is this: does it matter if our moral intuitions are reflectively endorsed by us or not? By 'reflectively endorsed' I mean that our moral intuitions are endorsed under conditions where we are aware that there are other real options available to us. For example, if one is brought up with the belief that the monarchy is the best form of government and this belief is ongoingly endorsed by the other members of one's society, then political institutions which express this belief are extremely likely to be publicly justifiable – but is this adequate if we do not recognize any other possible way of thinking about this topic? If there simply are no other real options available, then this may not matter; but if there are other real options and we are blocked in one way or another from becoming aware of them, then it does because awareness of other real options might result in no longer endorsing a given set of moral intuitions and, if this were the case, it might also result in ceasing to endorse the political institutions which express those moral intuitions. In this respect it is not enough that there be freedom to express one's moral intuitions; public justifiability also requires, at the very least, that one is not prevented from envisaging or encountering other real options. In other words, public justifiability also requires the freedom to develop practices of critical reflection within a given society and the freedom to encounter societies characterized by different moral intuitions.

At this juncture, let's turn to Rorty's (reflective) endorsement of Rawls's political liberalism as an extension of the principle of toleration to philosophy which affirms the value of public justifiability. The issue that I want to focus on here concerns the nature of public justifiability. Rawls's position is this: public reason, understood as the reason of the public directed to the good of the public and matters of fundamental justice, should be restricted to reasons which are, in principle, acceptable to all as free and equal members of the polity

(Rawls 1993: 217). In other words, given the fact of pluralism, in exercising reason as citizens concerned with fundamental political issues (such as constitutional questions) which involve the use of the coercive power of the state, citizens 'should be ready to explain the basis of their actions to one another in terms each could reasonably endorse as consistent with their freedom and equality' (Rawls 1993: 218). In this respect reasons which are compelling for an individual or group in terms of her or their comprehensive conception of the good are ruled out of the public domain unless they are reasons which those holding other reasonable comprehensive conceptions of the good could also endorse, where reasonable comprehensive conceptions of the good refer to those which recognize both the idea of society as a system of fair cooperation between free and equal citizens (1993: 49–50) and the possibility of reasonable disagreement (1993: 61). The question which I want to pose is this: should Rorty, as a liberal ironist, accept Rawls's conception of public reason, that is, the rules of preclusion which Rawls proposes on the sorts of reason which may be appropriately expressed in public political debates on fundamental matters?

Consider first the case of the citizen who holds, on Rawls's criteria, a reasonable comprehensive doctrine in that while she is fundamentally opposed to abortion, she recognizes that others may reasonably disagree and that the coercive power of the state should not be used unless this policy can be accepted by citizens as reasonable and rational persons. There are two points to note here. First, in proposing a policy of either banning or restricting abortion, this reasonable citizen is barred from advancing the reasons that actually most matter to her, that is, the reasons why she holds that abortion is wrong. To be sure, she may be able to advance reasons which matter to her as a political liberal but these are unlikely to express the meaning of her commitment. The importance of this point is that while we may not recognize reasons expressed in terms of her comprehensive commitment as reasons for us and, in this respect, we may not accept her proposals with respect to abortion, it is hard to see how we can exhibit recognition of, and respect for, her as a person characterized by a particular final vocabulary – or express this in terms of accommodation and tolerance – unless we are aware of her comprehensive, and not just her political, reasons for advocating this policy. This point is sharpened further by the fact that exactly the same points apply to a person who advocates the right to abortion. So both main parties to the dispute can only advance their arguments in terms of shared political values. Apart from the fact that there seems to be something intuitively cruel about denying the expression in (and

relevance to) public political debate of a citizen's most deeply cherished commitments, there are further problems with this position
which can be drawn out by considering Rawls's own remarks on
this issue:

> Suppose first that the society in question is well-ordered and that we
> are dealing with the normal case of mature adult women. . . . Suppose
> further that we consider the question in terms of these three important
> political values: the due respect for human life, the ordered reproduc-
> tion of political society over time, including the family in some form,
> and finally the equality of women as equal citizens. . . . Now I believe
> that any reasonable balance of these three values will give a woman a
> duly qualified right to decide whether or not to end her pregnancy
> during the first trimester. The reason for this is that at this early stage of
> pregnancy the political value of the equality of women is overriding,
> and this right is required to give it substance and force. . . . A reasonable
> balance may allow her such a right beyond this, at least in certain
> circumstances. . . . [A]ny comprehensive doctrine that leads to a balance
> of political values excluding that duly qualified right in the first
> trimester is to that extent unreasonable; and depending on details of
> its formulation, it may also be cruel and oppressive; for example, if it
> denied the right altogether except in the case of rape and incest. Thus,
> assuming that this question is either a constitutional essential or a
> matter of basic justice, we would go against the ideal of public reason
> if we voted from a comprehensive doctrine that denied this right.
> (Rawls 1993: 243–4 n. 32)

The problem with these comments is that in the course of his 'burdens
of judgement' argument for reasonable disagreement, Rawls has
argued that: 'Even when we agree fully about the kinds of considerations that are relevant, we may disagree about their weight, and so
arrive at different judgements' (1993: 56). This argument applies to
the weighing of the three political values involved in this case and,
therefore, Rawls's judgement concerning what would be a reasonable
balance can be subject to reasonable disagreement, so he is utterly
unwarranted in asserting that any comprehensive doctrine which
departs from his judgement of reasonable balance is necessarily
unreasonable. In this respect Rawls's remarks serve simply as an
example of the sort of humiliation to which those opposed to abortion may be subject. Now, given that appealing to shared political
values does not remove the possibility of reasonable disagreement, we
might reasonably wonder whether there is any *reasonable* justification for precluding citizens from articulating their positions in terms
of their comprehensive commitments. This thought may strike us with

particular force if we recognize that any policy which we introduce is going to be one with which citizens may reasonably disagree and which may be a source of pain to them in terms of their comprehensive commitments – and that not allowing citizens to articulate their non-political comprehensive values removes the possibility of *either* seeking to accommodate these values as far as practicable within the framing and administration of the policy *or* being able to compensate such citizens through trade-offs in other policy areas where there is reasonable disagreement. Consequently, I would claim that in this type of case Rorty as a liberal ironist should reject Rawls's position.

As our second case, consider the citizen who is unreasonable on Rawls's account in that he or she is not committed to the idea of society as a system of fair cooperation between free and equal citizens (1993: 49–50). That is to say, the case of someone who is not committed to a liberal conception of the good society. Exactly how reasonable is it to describe such a person as unreasonable? Is not the idea of the good society one about which there may be reasonable disagreement? The liberal ironist, precisely because he or she admits the challenge of plurality in its full force, is constrained to recognize that there can be such reasonable disagreement – and that simply to presuppose a liberal conception of reasonableness such that any other conception of society is necessarily unreasonable is to abrogate the unconditional commitment to recognition and respect which is required both by the need to maintain confidence in one's own final vocabulary and by the unconditional commitment to cruelty as the worst thing that we do. Thus, again, Rorty as a liberal ironist should reject Rawls's political liberalism.

Finally, consider the case of someone (the non-ironist) who is unreasonable, on Rawls's account, because he or she rejects the idea of reasonable disagreement, that is, holds as a conjecture that the reasonable is reducible to the rational. Rawls notes that his own claim, that is, the claim that the reasonable is not reducible to the rational 'is simply a conjecture' (1993: 53). In fact, this situation resembles that of the liberal and the Nietzschean considered in the previous section insofar as there is no neutral way of deciding between these incompatible conjectures; that is, it is a matter about which there can be reasonable disagreement. Now it may be reasonable to claim that non-ironists are unreasonable if they do not acknowledge the conjectural status of their claim but it is not necessarily unreasonable for them to advance this claim. Consequently, to regard this claim as necessarily unreasonable (as Rawls does, cf. 1993: 152–3) is, again, to abrogate the commitment to recognition and respect which characterizes the liberal ironist.

So, if these arguments are sound, it follows that, as a liberal ironist, Rorty is mistaken in endorsing Rawls's political liberalism. This being the case, what kind of stance should the liberal ironist be committed to? The suggestion which I want to advance flows from our discussion thus far. It is simply this: the liberal ironist should be committed to a polity in which members bring their full, substantive, final vocabularies into processes of political deliberation conducted in terms of mutual recognition and mutual respect with the hope of reaching agreement with respect to which thick and substantive ethical principles are appropriate for them as citizens. The advantages for the liberal ironists of this proposal are that it expresses their commitment to cruelty as the *summum malum* and, concomitantly, to the value of public justifiability, while avoiding those forms of cruelty and humiliation which are structurally embedded in Rawls's political liberalism. Moreover, from the perspective of the liberal ironist as an ironist, this proposal also specifies the conditions under which we can be confident in our political commitments as citizens. I do not have space here to argue this case more fully (or to respond to possible objections to it) so I will simply refer to James Tully's *Strange Multiplicity: Constitutionalism in an Age of Diversity* (1996) as a brilliant elaboration – and example – of the case for this approach.

III

In this section I return briefly to the issue with which we began, namely, Rorty's advocacy of light-mindedness or joshing as a pedagogic strategy. The question I want to address is whether or not joshing is an appropriate strategy for liberal ironists, for persons committed to cruelty as the worst thing that we do.

We should note initially that Rorty is aware that light-mindedness involves redescription and that redescription 'often humiliates' (1989: 90). In this respect the ironist, 'by threatening one's final vocabulary, and thus one's ability to make sense of oneself in one's own terms rather than hers, suggests that one's self and one's world are futile, obsolete, *powerless*' (1989: 90). Now Rorty points out that the same is true of the metaphysician who redescribes in a tone of seriousness, but the point remains that light-mindedness can be cruel and humiliating. However, that it can be so does not entail that it need be so. To reflect on this point, consider light-mindedness between friends, noting that such light-mindedness often involves redescriptions which would, in other contexts, be cruel; for example, 'you lazy nigger', 'you utter bastard', etc. Yet in this context such redescriptions are not typically experienced as humiliating, rather they are experienced as expressions of care because we trust the speaker to be speaking as a friend. Now the relevant point about the example of friendship for our concerns is that relations of friendship involve mutual recognition and mutual respect, and it is this feature which provides the basis for our trust in the other, our trust that the other is not seeking to humiliate us (we may, of course, be mistaken in this). It is, I think, for this reason that Rorty adopts the term 'joshing', which is typically associated with, and evokes, an ethos of friendship. If these specula-tive observations are plausible, then we can grasp 'joshing' as an appropriate rhetorical strategy for Rorty in that, unlike ridicule, the concept of joshing (as used by Rorty) presents as a commitment to a form of persuasion which involves recognition and respect for the other. In other words, the person or group subject to joshing as a suasive strategy knows that they can reject our proposals without sacrificing this recognition and respect.

But do we have any reasons to suppose, on this account of joshing as an exemplary performance of the commitments of the liberal ironist, that it will be effective in gradually undermining that appeal of metaphysics/fundamentalism or encouraging a commitment to cruelty as the worst thing that we do? I think that Rorty has some grounds for this hope precisely because joshing exemplifies both the general fact that one can have unconditional commitments without metaphysics (pro-ironism) and that one can recognize and respect others' without agreeing with them (pro-liberalism). Of course, our world is widely characterized by forms of non-recognition and non-respect, and joshing is certainly not a sufficient strategy. Rorty recog-nizes this point when he advocates the use of sentimental education with respect to encouraging the spread of human rights culture (Rorty 1998: 167–85) and when he considers issues of economic triage (Rorty 1996) – but joshing, as a form of teaching by example, offers a plausible path for Rorty to adopt.

Conclusion

In its somewhat meandering way, the purpose of this essay has been to try to make sense of what is involved in being a liberal ironist – in terms of moral, political and rhetorical commitments – and to show that Rorty's adoption of the persona of the moral cartoonist is a performance of the liberal ironist position which he advocates. On the way, I hope to have given at least a prima-facie case for joshing Rorty out of his commitment to Rawls's political liberalism by stressing the political implications of the unconditional commitment to recognition of, and respect for, the other which is a constitutive feature of the liberal ironist.

References

McCarthy, T. 1993: *Ideals and Illusions* (Cambridge, Mass.: MIT Press).
McFall, L. 1987: 'Integrity', *Ethics*, 98, pp. 5–20.
Rawls, J. 1993: *Political Liberalism* (New York: Columbia University Press).
Rorty, R. 1989: *Contingency, Irony, and Solidarity* (Cambridge: Cambridge University Press).
Rorty, R. 1991: *Objectivity, Relativism, and Truth, Philosophical Papers*, vol. 1 (Cambridge: Cambridge University Press).
Rorty, R. 1996: 'Moral Universalism and Economic Triage', paper presented to the 1996 UNESCO Philosophy Forum.
Rorty, R. 1998: *Truth and Progress, Philosophical Papers*, vol. 3 (Cambridge: Cambridge University Press).
Shklar, J. 1984: *Ordinary Vices* (Cambridge, Mass.: Harvard University Press).
Tully, J. 1996: *Strange Multiplicity: Constitutionalism in an Age of Diversity* (Cambridge: Cambridge University Press).
Williams, B. 1981: *Problems of the Self* (Oxford: Oxford University Press).
Williams, B. 1985: *Ethics and the Limits of Philosophy* (London: Fontana).
Williams, B. 1995: 'Truth in Ethics', *Ratio*, 8/3, pp. 227–42.

Response to David Owen

Richard Rorty

I shall confine my discussion of David Owen's essay to the only criticism he makes of me – that I should be more chary of Rawls's views than I am. Most of his essay is a very sympathetic and accurate account of my motives and strategies. I particularly appreciate his extensive quotation from Judith Shklar, which helps bring out the connection I see between liberalism and the renunciation of religious and metaphysical sources for moral convictions. I wish that I had quoted at similar length from those pages of Shklar's in *Contingency, Irony, and Solidarity.*

Owen asks whether 'Rorty, as a liberal ironist, [should] accept Rawls's conception of public reason, that is, the rules of preclusion which Rawls proposes on the sorts of reason which may be appropriately expressed in public political debates on fundamental matters'. He reads Rawls as 'precluding', for example, a Catholic's attempt to drag her religion into the discussion of legislation concerning abortion. On this reading such a Catholic 'is barred from advancing the reasons that actually most matter to her, that is, the reasons why she holds that abortion is wrong'.

I am not sure what this preclusion would come to in practice. Here are some candidates:

(1) When mention is made in a public meeting (e.g. the local caucus of a political party, called to elect or advise candidates for legislative office) of the view of the Catholic Church, and of the speaker's ardent adherence to that Church, the speaker is gavelled down.

(2)   Such mention in such a meeting is not gavelled down, but practically everybody in the meeting finds it in very bad taste (though nobody says so).
(3)   Such mention in such a meeting is respectfully and sympathetically heard, but practically everybody in the meeting silently dismisses it as completely irrelevant to the discussion.

I doubt that Rawls would recommend gavelling down, but presumably he would sympathize with the reaction of the audience described in (3), and perhaps even that described in (2). I myself would sympathize with both of the latter reactions, while also seeing no need to gavel anybody down – assuming the speaker does not take up too much time. I expand on the appropriateness of such reactions in my 'Religion as Conversation-Stopper', included in my collection *Philosophy and Social Hope* (Harmondsworth, Penguin, 1999). For if speakers were gavelled down too frequently, or too soon, on such occasions, there would be an obviously undesirable chilling effect on political discussion.

If the speaker recognizes that (2) or (3) is the case, she will, quite possibly, feel humiliated. But nobody said that the practice of democratic politics could eliminate humiliation. You cannot teach schoolchildren to read and write, or workers to meet a production quota, or soldiers to complete an obstacle course, without inflicting a good deal of humiliation on the under-achievers. You cannot let movers of unpopular motions introduce them without exposing them to the humiliation of failing to have their motions seconded. You cannot forbid people to utter what they may well know in advance to be an impotent *cri de coeur* in order to protect them from the humiliation they will suffer as a result of the hard-to-conceal contempt and scorn of their audience.

Owen makes a different point when, after quoting Rawls's own reasons for legalizing first-trimester abortions, he says that Rawls 'is utterly unwarranted in asserting that any comprehensive doctrine which departs from his judgement of reasonable balance is necessarily unreasonable.' But Rawls would not and cannot say 'necessarily'. Nor would he deny that his own 'judgement concerning what would be a reasonable balance can be subject to reasonable disagreement'. If there could not be reasonable disagreement about what is reasonable, we should be able to substitute rational demonstration for reasonableness. The reasonable–rational distinction would lose its utility if we made room for the expression 'necessarily unreasonable'.

I suspect that Rawls and I could agree that the question 'whether there is any reasonable justification for precluding citizens from articulating their positions in terms of their comprehensive commitments' boils down to something like 'how far can political meetings go in cutting off speakers after it has become clear that most of what they say is regarded by most of the audience as simply irrelevant to the issue at hand.' I doubt that there is any general, principled, answer to be given here. We want a reasonable abortion policy, even though it is one which will deeply offend some people, and we also want a reasonable right-to-speak policy, even though it too will deeply offend some people.

So I am not inclined to agree that 'as a liberal ironist' I should 'reject Rawls's political liberalism'. Most of Rawls's views on appropriate compromises (e.g. first trimester OK, third trimester not OK) seem about right to me, though I should hate to have to explain what criterion I was using in accepting them. I suspect that Rawls and I might, as chairs at meetings, both adopt some rule such as 'five-minute *cri de coeur* OK, lengthy recitation of the Baltimore Catechism or of papal encyclicals not OK'), and that we would both be equally at a loss to explain why five, rather than fifteen, minutes seemed about right.

Perhaps Owen would not regard questions about gavelling down as the sort of 'preclusion' and 'barring' about which he is concerned. But outside of such concrete practical decisions, I am not sure what preclusion is in question, save perhaps the use of public funds to secularize, or de-metaphysicize, the world-views and vocabularies of the citizenry. But here again I see no reason not to agree with Rawls about the desirability of such use (as exemplified by, for example, the teaching of evolution, and of condom-use, in public schools). It is unquestionable that in most of the advanced democracies there have been, in the course of the last two hundred years, systematic uses of state power to diminish the status of the clergy. One can imagine, in the future, a similar use of state power to inculcate consequentialism at the expense of the idea that some acts are intrinsically abhorrent. (Considering how much Kant would have loathed the idea of legal protections for same-sex partners, and how heartily Bentham would have endorsed it, one can see the adoption of gay-rights legislation as showing that this latter possibility is already in the course of being actualized.)

The humiliations inflicted on the French clergy by the laicization of primary education were a lesser evil than permitting the citizenry of a constitutional democracy to be forced to imbibe Catholic doctrine. Analogously, the humiliation of people who were raised as Catholics, when their views are laughed off by what they regard as a tyrannical majority, seems to me a lesser evil than trying to enforce a public policy which guarantees that expressions of religious conviction are greeted with respectful attention. There are limits to the extent to which a liberal society can, in Owen's words, 'engage with non-liberals...in a manner consistent with recognition and respect'. Even in the best liberal society I can imagine, it is very unlikely that the non-liberal will think she gets enough recognition and respect. But I cannot see how to give her what she wants.

I should not speak, as Owen does, of my liberal ironist having an 'unconditional' commitment to cruelty as the *summum malum*. A commitment worth dying for is not the same as an unconditional commitment. For it is sometimes best to do the worst thing one can imagine: for example, to torture, in her presence, the children of the terrorist who has hidden a ticking thermonuclear device somewhere in a city. People who, like Owen and myself, resonate to the words he quotes from Shklar should agree with Dewey that 'every evil is a rejected good' and that most controversial actions are the choice of a lesser evil. I do not think that they can avoid invoking notions like Rawls's 'reasonableness' – messy, vague and subject to abuse as all such notions admittedly are.

6

Richard Rorty
Humanist and/or Anti-humanist?

Kate Soper

It seems to me that the most obvious – and perhaps the only possible – answer to the question posed in my title is the round-the-houses one: the one that approaches the issue by way of that classic philosophical opening gambit of saying 'well it all depends what you mean by humanism' and ruminates on from there. At any rate, it is this approach I am going to adopt here.

Let me begin, then, by briefly listing some of the themes and arguments associated with the humanist idea in Western culture and European philosophy. My list is by no means exhaustive, nor do I claim any particular rigour for it. For example, I am not claiming that there is any hard and fast delineation between its various strands or thematics. The point is simply to isolate those humanist themes which I deem to be most relevant to a discussion of Rorty's particular commitments, and to see where his pragmatism stands in regard to them.

1 Firstly, then, there is the anti-deistic or anti-theological thematic: humanism as atheism, the rejection of the idea of there being a divinity or supreme being in accordance with whose will the world has been brought into being, and who continues omnisciently to oversee its course. Clearly not all self-styled humanists are atheists (thus we encounter a variety of religious 'humanisms'). But this is perhaps the most common or lay sense of humanism, at least in Anglo-American culture, and the central strand of the philosophy of British and American humanist associations.[1]

2 Secondly, and closely allied with the anti-deist thematic, is what might be termed the 'anthropocentric' or 'Promethean' thematic. To be humanist in this sense is to celebrate freedom from superstitious fear of nature; to express confidence in human powers to control and master the course of history; to assert the superiority and self-sufficiency of the *Homo sapiens* species, or, at least, of its 'civilized' Western representatives.

3 This in turn has affinities with the 'progressive' thematic: to be of a humanist disposition, in this sense, is to have faith in human amelioration and progress; to be convinced of the essential benevolence and improvability of humankind, and to reject all forms of anti-progressivism and nihilism.

I have referred to these first three as 'thematics' of humanism, but one might also think of them as ideological conceptions associated with the humanist idea in Western culture. As such, I think they can be said to differ from humanism in the meanings the idea has acquired in much recent theoretical argument, particularly that associated with the so-called Continental school of philosophy. Here too I want to distinguish three related modes of thinking.

4 One of these is what may be termed 'essentialist' humanism: humanists are here defined as those who are prepared to defend the idea of 'human nature' even if only in the minimal sense that there are certain 'basic' needs held in common across the human community.[2]

5 This position is closely allied (though to be distinguished from essentialism on human nature) with what might be termed 'teleological' humanism: humanism conceived as a discourse about the telos or ends of man: as philosophical anthropology which refers us to the essential *humanitas* of the species, and speculates on our destiny in terms of that. There is, as it were, a way of being which is 'natural' or 'proper' to being human, which may be distorted or alienated under specific conditions of existence, and brought to its full realization under others. It is this which Heidegger understands by humanism when he argues that 'every humanism is either grounded in a metaphysics or is itself the ground of one'[3] (where what he means is that all forms of humanism seek to realize the essential *humanitas* of *Homo humanus*, and are metaphysical to the extent that they presuppose a knowledge of this essential nature). There may be differing conceptions of this 'nature' or 'essence' (Aristotle's, Marx's, Goethe's, etc.) but, says Heidegger, what is common to them all – and, in his eyes, damns them as 'metaphysical' – is that they 'presuppose an interpretation of being without asking about the truth of Being'.[4]

6 Finally, let me note what I shall term the 'existentialist' or 'self-creative' thematic, whose emphasis is on the irreducibility of the

element of human self-making or self-creativity (on our capacity, as Sartre put it, to make more of ourselves than we are made of). To be humanist in this sense is to defend the notion of free human agency against structuralist and constructivist approaches to the understanding of the subject, and to insist that there can be no adequate understanding, either of the individual or of historical process, that denies this active element. Sartrean existentialism, Marxist philosophy of *praxis*, E. P. Thompson's historiography, have all been described as 'humanist' in this conception.

Now Rorty is plainly a humanist in the sense that he is an anti-deistic thinker. Not only does he make clear his personal atheism, he also follows Nietzsche and much contemporary French 'postmodernist' theory in defending his anti-foundationalist stance as an escape from what Heidegger termed 'onto-theology'. Like them, and paradoxically in some ways, one may argue, he seeks to win acceptance to his position by invoking the quintessentially humanist idea of de-deification.[5] In fact Rorty not only frequently describes his pragmatism as a form of anti-theological therapy, he also presents it, if not as the 'true' philosophy or 'final vocabulary' for the irreligious (which would be self-subverting), as nonetheless the philosophy most appropriate or useful for beings who have accepted their own contingency in a godless universe.

Inveighing against the idea that the world splits itself up, on its own, into sentence-shaped chunks called 'facts', he argues that, 'if one clings to the notion of self-subsistent facts, it is easy to start capitalizing the word "truth" and treating it as something identical with God or with the world as God's project. Then one will say, for example, that Truth is great and will prevail.'[6] Or again,

> The very idea that the world or the self has an intrinsic nature – one which the physicist or the poet may have glimpsed – is a remnant of the idea that the world is a divine creation, the work of someone who had something in mind, who Himself spoke some language in which He described His own project. To drop the idea of languages as representations, and to be thoroughly Wittgensteinian in our approach to language, would be to de-divinize the world.[7]

Let me note in passing, here, that if such remarks are intended to figure as 'argument' against contemporary realists, they are pretty prejudicial. After all, one could readily accept that 'God is dead' and that humanity is not answerable to any transcendent deity without agreeing to this picture of the relations between language and world. In other words, there would seem no reason at all to accept Rorty's rhetorical presentation of representationalist theories of language or realist positions in social theory as in some sense 'theological', even less to agree to his implication that an argument such as, for example, John Searle's about 'facts', or Terry Eagleton's views on 'ideology' is a residue of religious dogmas about the divine creation of the world. The debate between Rorty and the anti-pragmatists is not, as he here implies, a debate between progressive Nietzschean atheists and old-fashioned theologians who have not quite rid themselves of the belief in divine creation, and Rorty can only suggest that it is by caricaturing his opponents. Realists do not maintain that truths are properties of the world rather than of sentences. All they maintain is that certain sentences are true in virtue of the way the world is. Nor are they after ahistoric verities in the manner that Rorty implies both in these remarks and elsewhere. It seems, to take but one instance here, quite mistaken to present Marx, along with other 'radical critics', as seeking to 'penetrate to the true, natural, ahistorical matrix of all possible language and knowledge'. On the contrary, in seeking to reveal the 'reality' beneath the 'appearances' of capitalist society, Marx saw himself as exposing its essentially historical form; and it is in general a distortion to present realists as denying the historicity of knowledge or as adopting an absolutist position on truth.[8] Rorty often seems to labour under the misapprehension that anyone looking for realities behind appearances is looking for something timeless or natural, which is not necessarily the case at all.

But I do not here want to get into a debate about realism, which has been extensively pursued elsewhere, and will doubtless run and run. My intent rather is to point out how keen he is to rescue us from any form of reverence for the idea of the world as it is 'in itself'. It is as if Rorty is saying that when realist thinkers acknowledge (in all humility!) that human practices and languages are conditioned by determinate features of the world, they are still living in an enchanted world, still subscribing to an essentially religious conception of it, still, in alienated fashion, imputing to nature powers that by rights belong to them as the 'makers' of their world or the 'poets' of their languages.

This, I suggest, is to invoke a very humanist rhetoric both in the anti-deist sense and in the sense that it appears to offer a rather straightforward endorsement of what I have referred to as the 'Promethean' strand of humanism. Advising us that we go wrong in metaphysically 'deifying' the world (though why it should worry Rorty, I'm not sure, given his urge to collapse the science/mythology divide), he at the same time recommends us to appreciate our capacity to construct the world according to our own lights, to credit as 'truthful' only those descriptions which advance our own interests, in short, to view ourselves as the all-powerful manipulators of truth and meaning.

Of course, Rorty is himself sensitive to the charges of those who have deplored pragmatism precisely because of the arrogance or complacency of the type of humanism to which it lends itself. As he recognizes, it is these implications of the pragmatist 'disenchantment' that accounted for Heidegger's disdain for it and so alarmed Horkheimer and Adorno.[9] If by freeing us from deism, the Enlightenment had ended by granting legitimacy to utilitarian calculus and instrumental rationality, then it had itself issued in a new form of dominance and human oppression (what Heidegger termed the 'forgetfulness' of Being under modern technology; what Horkheimer and Adorno deplored as the totalitarianism or 'one-dimensionality' of modern industrial society). So even as he emphasizes our endless capacity for reweaving our beliefs about the world in accordance with our changing interests and designs, Rorty is anxious to distinguish his (Romantic and Deweyan) brand of pragmatist humanism from the 'power-mad' pragmatism condemned by Heidegger and Critical Theory, and we can see this project reflected in his reading of Heidegger as an inconsistent compound of good, healthy pragmatist advice about the contingency of the human condition, and misguided nostalgia for the truth of being.

Thus, he argues, if we construe Heidegger as claiming that 'there is no hidden power called Being... There is just us, in the grip of no power save those of the words we happen to speak, the dead metaphors which we have internalized,'[10] then Heidegger had no good reason for associating pragmatism with the form of humanism he despised (a Promethean or power-mad humanism). Or again, when Heidegger says things to the effect that no understanding of Being is more or less true – in the sense of truth-as-disclosedness, *aletheia* – then, suggests Rorty, his outlook is appreciative of the contingency of the human condition; and from this perspective, he had no grounds for either nostalgia for an age prior to the 'forgetting of Being' or for the hope that this amnesia will be overcome, and no reason to dislike pragmatism as much as he does.[11] To the extent, however, that Heidegger *does* engage in this nostalgia, and associate the forgetfulness of Being with a Promethean and power-hungry humanism of which he regards pragmatism as a prime instance, then Rorty himself parts company with Heidegger, or presents himself as – like Derrida – wanting to 'stand him on his head': to cherish what he loathed.[12]

Rorty, then, certainly wants to distance his brand of pragmatism from that which has been associated with an overly complacent and anthropocentric perspective.[13] Yet the emphasis, common to every pragmatist argument, Dewey's and Rorty's included, on getting what we want (imposing our will on the world/reading the world in the light of our interests, changing our languages about it in the light of our needs, viewing language as a tool to serve our purposes rather than as representing the way the world independently is, and so on): all this can fairly be charged with subscribing to what I have termed a Promethean strand of humanist discourse, whether or not Rorty himself would want to acknowledge this.[14]

He is also, arguably, a humanist in my third ideological sense, since (in contrast to the anti-progressivist or nihilist perspective of many of his French fellow-anti-foundationalists whom he berates for their political quietism or Stoicism) he sustains an essentially optimistic outlook on human progress. Here, too, the argument is not quite clear-cut, and there is a vein of Rortian writing of a rather more despairing kind, where he dwells on the futility of theory, the failure to make advances, or even to know what to do to achieve them. In this mood he credits Orwell with helping us to 'formulate a pessimistic description of the political situation which forty years of further experience have only confirmed. This bad news remains the great intransigent fact of contemporary political speculation, the one that blocks all the liberal scenarios.'[15] Or again, of the horrors of our times, he writes that no one has yet come up with any proposal for ending them which draws on new conceptual resources: 'Our political imagination has not been enlarged by the philosophy of our century. This is not because of the irrelevance or cowardice or irresponsibility of philosophy professors, but because of the sheer recalcitrance of the situation into which the human race has stumbled.'[16]

But against this line of argument must be set all those passages where Rorty speaks more confidently of the progress that has been made, rebukes Heidegger (in an update of Heidegger himself on Heraclitus?[17]) for not seeing the goods that are under his nose, and offers his more congratulatory discourses on the achievements to date and future potential of North American liberalism. There is also a sense in which Rorty can be said to endorse a 'progessivist' or ameliorative humanism in the emphasis he places on the value and importance of continuously changing our beliefs and desires. Rorty is a conservative insofar as he accepts the standard pragmatist analysis of truth in terms of existing conventions and social agreements. But in his rhetoric he is a zealot for innovation. Indeed, at times he writes as if linguistic innovation was desirable simply in virtue of its novelty, and the preservation of old ideas and traditions of its nature a sign of stagnation or reaction.[18] This is particularly manifest in his essay on selfhood, where, drawing on Nietzsche's philosophy and Harold Bloom's account of the 'strong poet' as suffering a 'horror of finding himself only to be a copy or a replica' (i.e. of ending one's days in a world which one had no role in creating), he argues that the production of originality is of the essence of the good life, both communally and individually, and the only achievement that can provide us with genuine satisfaction.[19]

This surely endorses a humanist perspective in my progressivist sense of the term although its conception of human amelioration is open to the charge that it is both partial and patriarchal: partial in the sense that it operates with narrow and elitist assumptions about human gratification; and patriarchal because, despite Rorty's feminization of his 'poet', he offers us a picture of human self-realization which entirely abstracts from the labours, anxieties – and possible fulfilments – of reproduction. The 'strong poets' he so admires and recommends as models of human creativity seem also to have benefited (if only in the time available to them for their pursuit of originality) from a very traditional gender division of labour.

I'll come back to this question of partiality in a moment, but to sum up so far, Rorty's stance may be said to be 'humanist' in a number of generally accepted, though not necessarily entirely unproblematic, ideological senses of the term. But he is at the same time, of course, a radical anti-humanist in the sense that he agrees with Heidegger in rejecting what I have termed 'teleological' humanism as so much onto-theology or metaphysics. For Rorty there is no such thing as 'an intrinsic human nature' – no set of qualities defining of our *humanitas* as a species – towards whose fulfilment or redemption human society is tending or ought to be striving. History is to be viewed neither as an endless nightmare in which we are perpetually thwarted of the 'truth' of humanity nor as a vehicle in which it is finally brought to its realization.[20] And this is for the simple reason that there is no such 'truth' in the first place to be lost or redeemed.

But let us recall here that when Rorty endorses the Heideggerian argument against humanism, he does so – like Heidegger himself – in the name of avoiding metaphysical closure. (We might note here Heidegger's claim in the 'Letter on Humanism' that to think against humanism is not to advocate the inhuman but to open us to the metaphysical status of our 'humanisms' – an opening which Heidegger implies is more truly 'human' or 'humane',[21] and Rorty will certainly agree to that suggestion.) But those throwing stones at someone else's metaphysical presumptions about the *humanitas* of the species will need to be a little circumspect about their own presuppositions, and both Heidegger and Rorty, I submit, could be said to be living in something of a glasshouse in this respect: Heidegger, for example, in being so unthinkingly androcentric and intellectualist in his perspective; Rorty, as I've already suggested, in failing to see the more elitist and gender-blind dimensions of his own story about human creativity and self-fulfilment; and also, one might add, in abstracting as much as he does from the horrors perpetrated in the name of his favoured North American liberalism.

But the inconsistencies of Rorty's liberalism have been widely criticized elsewhere, and I shall here do no more than simply note that for all his strictures against onto-theology and metaphysical closure it is not clear to me that Rorty is as much out of the wood on this as he likes to think himself.

I am also unclear about his views on human nature, and thus about where he stands on what I have termed 'essentialist' humanism. It is true that Rorty professedly has no time at all for the idea of human nature. On numerous occasions he inveighs against the idea that there is any universally shared set of needs or aspirations, and on that ground claims that there is nothing to prompt any extensive solidarity with those who do not belong to our own community in time and space. Hence the impossibility, he argues, of finding any shared desires or beliefs to bridge the gap between the private and the public. We simply cannot, so he claims, hope to synthesize the desire for individual autonomy and self-creation with the project of a more just and equal society, and we must therefore cease to aspire to a philo-sophical outlook that would 'let us hold self-creation and justice, private perfection and human solidarity, in a single vision'.[22] To cite a fairly typical expression of his position on the issue:

> The traditional philosophical way of spelling out what we mean by 'human solidarity' is to say that there is something within each of us – our essential humanity – which resonates to the presence of this same thing in other human beings. This way of explicating the notion of solidarity coheres with our habit of saying that the audiences in the Coliseum, Humbert, Kinbote, P. O'Brien, the guards at Auschwitz, and the Belgians who watched the Gestapo drag their Jewish neighbours away were 'inhuman'. The idea is that they all lacked some component which is essential to a fully-fledged human being.
>
> Philosophers who deny... that there is such a component, that there is anything like a 'core self', are unable to invoke this latter idea. Our insistence on contingency, and our consequent opposition to ideas like 'essence', 'nature', and 'foundation', makes it impossible for us to retain the notion that some actions and attitudes are naturally 'inhu-man'.[23]

But even as he argues against any 'core self' or biological determinants, Rorty at the same time premises his whole philosophy on the claim that cruelty is to be avoided (several times citing Judith Shklar's definition of liberals as those who think cruelty is the worst thing we do[24]) and in explication of this he, not unreasonably, cites our shared capacity to experience pain and humiliation. He also recognizes that there is a tension in his doing so, and that the idea of our having an overriding obligation to diminish cruelty seems to take for granted that there is something within human beings which deserves respect and protection quite independently of the language they speak. As he puts it: 'It suggests that a nonlinguistic ability, the ability to feel pain, is what is important, and that differences in vocabulary are much less important.'[25] All the same, he proceeds to argue, the ironist will take a very different line on this from the 'metaphysical' liberal. For whereas the latter

> wants our *wish to be kind* to be bolstered by an argument, one which entails a self-redescription which will highlight a common human essence, an essence which is something more than our shared ability to suffer humiliation. The liberal ironist just wants our *chances of being kind*, of avoiding the humiliation of others, to be expanded by redescription. She thinks that recognition of a common susceptibility to humiliation is the *only* social bond that is needed. Whereas the metaphysician takes the morally relevant feature of the other human beings to be their relation to a larger shared power – rationality, God, truth or history, for example – the ironist takes the morally relevant definition of a person, a moral subject, to be 'something that can be humiliated'. Her sense of human solidarity is based on a sense of a common danger, not on a common possession or a shared power.[26]

For ironists, then, there is no common goal or truth, but simply a common susceptibility to pain and humiliation, nothing but the 'common selfish hope' that one's world will not be destroyed.[27]

But I think we may fairly ask what the argument is in these passages, and whether Rorty is not here offering a rather grotesque picture of the 'essentialist' theorist in order to sustain the difference between the ironist line on human nature and that of its putative opponents. After all, on my understanding an essentialist position on human nature need claim no more than Rorty does himself, namely a universal susceptibility to pain and humiliation. Rorty seems to think that it is after something in addition to this – 'an essence which is something more than our shared ability to suffer humiliation'. But why so? Why not just an admission that this is indeed an 'essence', that it is common to us in virtue of universal features of human biology and psychology, and that these minimal universal determinants are what we are referring to when we speak of human nature?

Put another way, it seems to me that Rorty here trades on a conflation between the types of humanism I have distinguished as teleological and essentialist rather than admitting to a clearer distinction between them. One can surely deny that people are simply 'incarnated vocabularies',[28] having no 'patterns' of biology in common, without insisting that human beings are linked by some common loyalty to God or truth or history. In short, one can be a realist on human nature (deny a wholly relativist position on human needs, insist that individuals are not exhaustively analysable as webs of belief or discursive constructions) without feeling the commitments which Rorty ascribes to his metaphysicians. So it seems to me that there is a certain equivocation in Rorty's 'humanism' in this respect – since he both denies that there is anything we share in common as human beings while in effect recognizing that his strictures against cruelty make no sense unless we accept that there is. Equally questionable is the distinction he then goes on to erect between those who are supposed to experience solidarity with others on the basis of 'inquiry' or 'reflection' and those who achieve it through 'imagination':

> In my utopia, human solidarity would be seen not as a fact to be recognized by clearing away 'prejudice' or burrowing down to previously hidden depths but, rather, as a goal to be achieved. It is to be achieved not by inquiry but by imagination, the imaginative ability to see strange people as fellow sufferers. Solidarity is not discovered by reflection but created.[29]

But again we can ask what the distinction is exactly, and how 'imagining' or 'creating' such identification differs from its 'discovery'. The only way in which I can here see it differing significantly would be if Rorty is suggesting that ironists come to the world with no presuppositions about who is or is not human (a position much closer to that of Derrida in some of his recommendations on 'messianic' hailing – where he has suggested that we should treat all our intuitive demarcations between human and non-human 'others' as a form of unwarranted conceptual policing).[30] But Rorty doesn't seem to be suggesting that we suspend all judgements of the kind that Derrida recommends we should (i.e. between the human and the animal, the living and the dead etc.), and personally I think he is right not to, since such a position becomes a *reductio ad absurdum* of the recommendation for solidarity. If we cannot impose any ideas about the 'nature' of the other for fear of failing properly to respect their strangeness or cultural difference, then strictly speaking we cannot empathize with their suffering either: we would be doing an injury in the very presumption of the other's agony or humiliation at the hands of torturer or oppressor, and might therefore do better not to intervene.[31]

I submit, then, that there is an equivocation in Rorty's position masked by a rather caricatured version of the realist position he is opposing. There is, moreover, something of a paradox about this since Rorty presents himself as a thoroughgoing conventionalist whilst in fact not taking the conventionalist position to anything like its logical conclusion. Rorty's universalism on the issue of pain and humiliation is not nearly as historicist as that of some of the French 'postmodernists', with Derrida, as I've suggested, but also Foucault offering the most obvious contrast here. At any rate, I interpret the postmodernist position in general as pointing to the partial and relative quality of Western conceptions of the divisions between humiliation and self-esteem, pain and pleasure, even life and death, and Foucault in particular as drawing attention to the always contextualized, ever fluid and inherently revisable character of these distinctions. Foucault's perspective, from which he has readily conceded that he has little interest in the furtherance of human 'happiness' (and at times espoused a sort of ethic of cruelty himself)[32] – is, it seems to me, much more consistent with Rorty's professed rejection of any essentialism on human nature than is the position on cruelty which Rorty actually espouses. This is in no sense to give preference to Foucault's argument. It is rather to suggest that Rorty is less radically anti-humanist than he likes to pretend. Or, if preferred, more confused than he is prepared to admit.

But where Rorty and Foucault are more directly comparable (though I shall simply have to throw this out as a last word and cannot develop it in more detail) is in their presentation of individuals as both creatures of discourse and existentially autonomous. Just as Foucault would have us view the subject as simultaneously both the worked-up effect of discourse and the site of autonomous resistance to its manipulative power, so Rorty would have us believe that individuals are both social all the way down – hence to be theorized as cultural constructs or, as he puts it, 'incarnations of vocabulary' – and at the same time self-creating poets whose genius for weaving entirely novel patterns of belief is apparently unrelated to the social context in which they find themselves and unaffected by the vastly differing conditions of education and acquisition of subjectivity it makes available to differing individuals. Rather like Foucault, he wants to invoke an existentialist humanist rhetoric about ethical self-making and poetic creativity while theoretically denying the grounds of such autonomy. Conversely, he wants us to accept that people are social products all the way down, while turning away from the critical implications of this for a society which, despite being the wealthiest in the world, denies so many in its urban ghettos the barest conditions of subjectivity let alone of poetic creativity. But this is just one aspect of the more general tension to which Rorty's philosophy is subject in virtue of its attempt to combine an anti-essentialist theory of the subject with the politics and rhetoric of liberal humanism.

Notes

1 See further my account in *Humanism and Antihumanism* (London, Hutchinson, 1986), pp. 9–23.
2 See e.g. Len Doyal and Ian Gough, *A Theory of Human Need* (London, Macmillan, 1991).
3 Martin Heidegger, 'Letter on Humanism', in *Basic Writings*, ed. David Farrell Krell (London, Routledge and Kegan Paul, 1978), p. 202.
4 Ibid. To quote Heidegger's argument more fully: 'But if one understands humanism in general as a concern that man become free for his humanity and find his worth in it, then humanism differs according to one's conception of the "freedom" and "nature" of man. So too are there various paths towards the realisation of such conceptions. The humanism of Marx does not need to return to antiquity any more than the humanism which Sartre conceives existentialism to be. In this broad sense Christianity too is a humanism, in that according to its teaching everything depends on man's salvation (*salus aeterna*); the history of man appears in the context of the history of redemption. However different these forms of humanism may be in purpose and in principle, in the mode and means of their respective realisations, and in the form of their teaching, they nonetheless all agree in this, that the *humanitas* of *homo humanus* is determined with regard to an already established interpretation of nature, history, world, and the ground of the world, that is of beings as a whole': ibid., pp. 201–2.
5 One of the paradoxes, we might note, in this connection is that anti-foundationalism employs a certain form of humanist rhetoric to defend a theoretical anti-humanism. What I mean by this is that it recommends that we give up certain kinds of so-called 'metaphysical' or 'humanist' modes of philosophizing on the grounds that these represent a certain kind of 'theology'. It is in the name of realizing the 'death of God' that Nietzsche seeks to undermine the philosophical tradition; it is with a view to exposing the 'metaphysical' or 'onto-theological' commitments of all forms of humanism hitherto that Heidegger writes his 'Letter on

Humanism': it is similarly by reference to the necessity of avoiding 'onto-theology' that Derrida seeks to deconstruct the metaphysics of presence and its associated 'humanist' or 'logocentric' commitments. What are dismissed by the so-called 'postmodernist' thinkers pejoratively as 'humanist' modes of thinking are damned by association with a certain kind of religiosity or deification, and this is, of course, rather at odds with the ordinary or lay sense of humanism as more or less synonymous with atheism; as signalling disbelief in any transcendent deity.

6 R. Rorty, *Contingency, Irony, and Solidarity* (Cambridge, Cambridge University Press, 1989), p. 5.

7 Ibid., p. 21.

8 See e.g. Roy Bhaskar's critique in *Reclaiming Reality* (London, Verso, 1994); Norman Geras, *Solidarity in the Conversation of Humankind* (London, Verso, 1995).

9 On Horkheimer/Adorno objections, see Max Horkheimer, Theodor Adorno et al., *Dialectics of Enlightenment* (London, Verso, 1979).

10 Cf. R. Rorty, *Essays on Heidegger and Others, Philosophical Papers*, vol. 2 (Cambridge, Cambridge University Press, 1991), p. 36.

11 Ibid., p. 36.

12 Cf. Rorty, *Contingency, Irony, and Solidarity*, p. 113 n.13: 'If, as I do, one forgets about Being and thinks that beings are all there are, then this "humanist" outlook – one which Heidegger himself despised – will be what one understands by Heidegger's claim that "language speaks man" and by his exaltation of "the poetic" as what "opens up worlds". The first three chapters of this book, and especially the exaltation of "the poet" in chapter 3, are an attempt to enlarge upon the idea of "the world as picture" which Heidegger offers in this essay [i.e. in 'The Age of the World Picture' in Heidegger, *The Question Concerning Technology and Other Essays*. trans. William Lovitt (New York, Harper and Row, 1977).'].

13 He even goes so far as to claim (by a surely rather tortuous logic) that the quest for certain truths manifests a desire to be 'overwhelmed by something, to have beliefs forced on you', and that this desire may 'just be a sublimated form of the urge to share in the power of anything strong enough to overwhelm you': Rorty, *Essays on Heidegger and Others*, p. 31. But surely to present the world as subordinate to our Logos is to evince a more obvious and straightforward urge for power!

14 And the issue is not clear-cut. Sometimes Rorty seems ready to admit both his humanism and its interest in power (especially in the opening essay of *Essays on Heidegger*, on 'Heidegger, Contingency and Pragmatism', and see also *Contingency, Irony, and Solidarity*, p. 116, where he writes: 'Heidegger thinks that if we are to avoid just this identification of truth with power – to avoid the sort of humanism and pragmatism advocated in this book, forms of thought which he took to be the most degraded versions of the nihilism in which metaphysics culminates – we have to say

that final vocabularies are not just means to ends but, indeed, Houses of Being.' At other times, however, as I have tried to bring out, Rorty seems keen to repudiate this image: to have us see his and Dewey's pragmatism as love-oriented rather than power-driven, and Romantic rather than scientist-instrumental.

15 Rorty, *Contingency, Irony, and Solidarity*, p. 182.

16 Rorty, *Essays on Heidegger and Others*, p. 26.

17 Cf. Heidegger, 'Letter on Humanism', pp. 233–4.

18 Rorty, *Essays on Heidegger and Others*, p. 72.

19 The paradigm here is 'the life of the genius who can say of the relevant portion of the past, "Thus I willed it" because she has found a way to describe that past which the past never knew, and thereby found a self to be which her precursors never knew was possible... The fear in which Bloom's poets begin is the fear that one might end one's days in a world one never made, an inherited world. The hope of such a poet is that what the past tried to do to her she will succeed in doing to the past itself, including making those very causal processes which blindly impressed all her own behavings, bear *her* impress.' Rorty, *Contingency, Irony, and Solidarity*, p. 29.

20 Let me say here that despite the criticisms I go on to offer I have a good deal of sympathy with Rorty's resistance to speculative philosophical anthropology, and I certainly think he is right to object to 'big stories' about the 'Ends of Man', the fate of Europe, the destiny of the West, and so on, even if I find him too ready to follow Heidegger in viewing thinkers such as Sartre and the early Marx as offering clear-cut stories of this kind.

21 Heidegger, 'Letter on Humanism', p. 225–6.

22 Rorty, *Essays on Heidegger and Others*, p. xiv.

23 Ibid., p. 189.

24 Rorty, *Contingency, Irony, and Solidarity*, pp. xv, 74, 146.

25 Ibid., p. 88.

26 Ibid., p. 91.

27 Ibid., p. 92.

28 Ibid., p. 88.

29 Ibid., p. xvi.

30 In a recent interview, Derrida has recommended, for example, that the 'someone' addressed in a 'messianic opening' is a someone whom we cannot and must not define in advance – 'not as subject, self, consciousness, not even as animal, God, person, man or woman, living or dead' (*Radical Philosophy* (autumn 1994), 68, p. 32); cf. Derrida's discussion of messianic opening in his *Specters of Marx*, trans. Peggy Kamuf (New York, Routledge, 1994), pp. 65f.

31 See my critique of *Specters of Marx*, in *Radical Philosophy*, 75 (Jan–Feb 1996).

32 See Foucault's interview with *La Fiera Litteraria*, 39, 28 Sept 1967, where he dissociates himself from any 'humanist' politics which aims at

an increase in human happiness. On Foucault's 'ethic of cruelty', and his commitment to sado-masochism as a mode of questioning normative divisions around pleasure and pain, see James Miller, *The Passion of Michel Foucault* (London HarperCollins, 1993), and my review of this, *Radical Philosophy*, 66 (Spring 1994).

Response to Kate Soper

Richard Rorty

Kate Soper raises a lot of good questions, but I think that some of them can be disposed of by recourse to further terminological precision. If agreeing that human beings are, among other things, animals which can suffer pain is enough to make me a realist and an essentialist, then of course I qualify. I have never wished to deny that human beings share a lot of traits with the other animals. I only want to deny that they possess something distinctively 'human', an extra added ingredient, a description of which can be used to explain, for example, why they have dignity rather than mere value. My view is that the only extra added ingredient they have is the extra neurons which make them capable of becoming language-users, and thus of changing themselves by changing the way they talk.

Again, if all it takes to be a realist is to grant that 'human practices and languages are conditioned by determinate features of the world', then I certainly count as a realist. I recognize, for example, that if you cut some neurons out of somebody's brain, the person will probably not be able to engage in certain linguistic and other practices of which she was previously capable. To echo Yeats's Promethean slogan, 'Whatever flames upon the night / Man's own resinous heart has fed' is not to deny that certain determinate features of the world – a vulture pecking at your liver, for example – will alter your practices and languages.

But to be a realist in either of these senses is quite compatible with, in Soper's words, 'viewing language as a tool to serve our purposes rather than as representing the way the world independently is' and with being unable to agree with her that 'certain sentences are true in

virtue of the way the world is'. The Prometheanism to which I sub-
scribe says that there are lots of descriptions of the world, some more
useful and some less, but none that match the way the world independently is. The latter notion is one for which I can find no good use.

I find it very useful to talk about what humans share with other
animals, about the presence or lack of neurons, and so on – and to
explain, using this sort of talk, why we are not 'the all-powerful
manipulators of truth and meaning'. But one can be Promethean
without claiming any such omnipotence, and without presenting
'the world as subordinate to our Logos'. Prometheanism is not a
matter of claiming superior causal power. It is a claim about authority
rather than about power – namely, the claim that the non-human
things that have power over us (vultures, comets, and the like) have
no authority over us. My reason for presenting 'representationalist
theories of language' as 'theological' is that such theories are bound
up with the idea that descriptions which match the way the world
independently is have an authority not possessed by other descriptions. This idea leads to metaphysics (the inquiry into how the world
independently is, as opposed to how it might usefully be described). I
think Heidegger is right to think of this inquiry as theology by other
means.

To agree with the Prometheanism embodied in the lines I quoted
from Yeats is not to claim that 'the production of originality is of the
essence of the good life, both communally and individually, and the
only achievement that can provide us with genuine satisfaction.'
Obviously one can achieve such satisfaction by, for example, achieving perfect conformity to rules. (Think of the ascetic monks.) I would
only claim that one of the many ways in which human life has
improved in recent centuries is that it has left more room for the
people who get a kick out of the production of originality. I have no
wish to argue that these kicks are inferior to those that can be gained
by scrupulous conformity.

Soper is quite right that it would be an inconsistency for me to offer
such an argument – at least if I based such an argument on deep
theoretical principles. I am delighted to live in a world in which self-
creation is a more widely available option than it used to be, just as I
am delighted to live in one where picnickers can listen to Mozart on a
portable recorder, and in one in which there is a bit more socio-
economic equality than in the past. But to hold that human life has
gotten better lately, in various ways, is not to presuppose a view about
either the nature or the telos of our species.

I should also be inconsistent if I said that 'people are simply "incarnated vocabularies"' rather than that they are that, among other

things, or if I said that 'individuals are not *exhaustively* [emphasis added] analysable as webs of belief or discursive constructions.' It would do nothing for my Promethean purposes to say 'simply' or 'exhaustively'. I do not see that Soper has given any reason to doubt the feasibility of combining, as she puts it in her closing sentence, 'an anti-essentialism theory of the subject with the politics and rhetoric of liberal humanism'. I cannot see why she thinks that the weird, idio-syncratic refusal to hope for human happiness which Miller plausibly diagnoses in Foucault is more consistent with anti-essentialism than, for example, Dewey's liberal hopes. Dewey and Foucault seem to me equally anti-essentialist, and to have distrusted theories of human nature for exactly the same reasons.

Soper obviously believes that there is a tighter connection between one's political concerns and one's views on such philosophical topics as the representational character of language than I do. She thinks of me as blind to the fact that strong poets have profited from the victimization of women, and to the plight of the inhabitants of urban ghettos, and she associates such blindness with my doubts about realism and about essentialism. I should have thought that degree of blindness to suffering varied quite independently of atti-tudes towards God, representation, metaphysics, or any of the other issues raised by Heidegger's critique of Sartre, or by my critique of Heidegger. The biggest difference between Soper and myself, perhaps, is that she thinks it inconsistent on my part 'to invoke an existentialist humanist rhetoric about ethical self-making and poetic creativity while theoretically denying the grounds of such autonomy'. I do not understand the notion of 'grounds of autonomy', nor why it would not be even more inconsistent on my part to offer such grounds.

The best question Soper raises, and the one I have most trouble answering, is 'how "imaging" or "creating" such identification [with the suffering of others] differs from its "discovery".' I am not entitled to make anything out of the found–made distinction, which I have denounced in the past (see my 'Relativism: Making and Finding' in my collection *Philosophy and Social Hope*, Harmondsworth, Pen-guin, 1999). Yet in a passage Soper quotes, and in many others, I make a big point of saying that human solidarity is to be created rather than discovered. This now seems to me an unfortunate way of saying: you cannot offer any convincing reasons (either scientific or philosophical) why some exclusivist group which feels no fellowship with some other group (the attitude of many straight white males towards black lesbians, and conversely) should take an interest in the suffering of the members of that other group. But you can try to arouse such an interest by other means – sad stories, for example.

The point of saying that solidarity is not discovered was to say that when we look to either science or philosophy for an account of why such solidarity should be felt, we look in vain. Neither discipline is good at pointing out similarities between members of the two groups, attention to which persuades them to change their practices. Novels and other forms of narrative, on the other hand, sometimes do effect such persuasion.

Soper's question makes me realize that I have been in the habit of running together the discovery–invention distinction with the distinction between offering ineffective theological, philosophical or scientific arguments for human solidarity and using novels, songs and other appeals to fellow feeling for the same purpose. If one holds these distinctions apart, then I can say that the question of whether solidarity is found or made is idle, and that the only question I want to discuss is how it best be achieved. Soper has more confidence than I do that science and philosophy can be mobilized for this purpose.

Let me end by returning to the various senses of the word 'humanism' with which Soper begins. I am a humanist in the first two senses, but not in the third. I have no faith in human benevolence, though I have hopes for it. If I had to bet, I would bet that within a few centuries we shall have reverted to post-nuclear holocaust barbarism, and that all the good work done by the Enlightenment and by Romanticism will have to be done again. But I do not think such a reversion is inevitable, any more than I think that continuous progress is inevitable.

So Soper is right in saying that I want to distance my brand of pragmatism from power-madness. She is also right in saying that 'the emphasis common to every pragmatist argument, Dewey's and Rorty's included, on getting what we want...can fairly be charged with subscribing to what I have termed a Promethean strand of humanist discourse.' But I see no slippery slope leading from my version of Prometheanism (the Yeatsian refusal to stand in awe of anything save the human imagination, and the Habermasian commitment to take nothing as authoritative save free human consensus) to power-madness.

7

Reason and Aesthetics between Modernity and Postmodernity
Habermas and Rorty

Richard Shusterman

I

The past few centuries of secular Western thought present two main utopian strategies: the rule of reason with its measured, rationalizing improvement of life, and a libidinal aestheticism with its hedonistic *promesse du bonheur*. As the project of modernity (with its Enlightenment roots and rationalizing differentiation of cultural spheres) has been identified with reason, so the postmodern is contrastingly characterized as dominantly aesthetic. Though pragmatism may deploy these contrasting terms to make its points, it should not regard them as denoting dichotomous, inimical essences. The rational/aesthetic and modernity/postmodernity oppositions must not be taken too rashly. Modernity clearly has its aesthetic, while postmodernism has its reasons. As art typically displays a rationality of order, unity and purpose, so reason reveals its own deep aesthetic dimension. For many of its central notions (coherence, balance, proportion, completeness, simplicity, fairness) not only have aesthetic connotations but, even when mechanically defined, require a kind of cultivated aesthetic perception or taste for their proper understanding and application.

A project advocating philosophy as the reasoned pursuit of aesthetic living cannot harbour an essential dualism between reason and aesthetics, reflected in an unbridgeable divide between the modern and postmodern. To explore and temper these oppositional notions, this essay confronts the influential theories of Jürgen Habermas and Richard Rorty, around whom much of the debate has centred: the former championing the claims of reason and modernity, the latter representing the aesthetic and postmodern.

Despite their apparent disagreements, Habermas and Rorty agree in choosing philosophical narrative (rather than synchronic analysis) as the method for theorizing the postmodern. Both also ply the same central story line: the path from modernity to postmodernity is portrayed as the undermining of reason by the aesthetic. Rorty welcomes this aesthetic turn as liberating us from a stiflingly rigid, homogenizing, and ahistorical conception of reason; as instead encouraging the flexibility of creative imagination that seems better suited to our increasingly decentred contexts and rapidly changing times. Habermas, on the other hand, defends modernity by portraying postmodernism's aesthetic turn as an unnecessary, misguided, and subversive response to a false idea of reason – subject-centred reason. The *malheurs* of modernity can thus be remedied not by abandoning reason for the aesthetic but by replacing subject-centred reason with a communicative model of reason.

As Rorty and Habermas insist on the primacy of language, it is there that the reason/aesthetic debate is ultimately focused. Thus Habermas criticizes Rorty for 'aestheticizing' language by privileging metaphor and rhetoric as semantically more central than truth and argument. This leads to a disastrous 'leveling [of] the genre distinction between philosophy and literature' in which philosophy's long-standing commitment to truth and the rational consensus of problem-solving is replaced by the poetic quest for exciting new metaphors.[1] Rorty responds not only by questioning the foundationalist 'universalism' implicit in Habermas's theory of communicative reason, but by challenging the very distinction 'between rationality and irrationality' as an 'obsolete and clumsy' piece of rhetoric. Even in its historicized Habermasian form, the ideal of reason represents a restrictive remnant of religion's need to supply a redeeming, unifying human essence, while what we need instead is to give free play to aesthetic 'fantasy' and its enriching multiplicities. Opposing modernity's 'Enlightenment hope' for rationalized society, Rorty advocates that 'culture as a whole...be "poeticized"'.[2]

Through such polemics, Habermas and Rorty project a misleading dualism between reason and aesthetics that seems inconsistent with their own basic pragmatism. This troubling dualism can be undone by showing that its duelling theorists actually agree on more than they differ, though such agreement is concealed by the rhetoric of contrast so central to our habits of philosophical thinking and reinforced by the institutional frameworks in which theory takes place.[3] We should begin by seeing how the reason/aesthetic opposition arises in Habermas's and Rorty's narratives of postmodernism's aesthetic turn.

II

For Habermas the story starts with Schiller's and Hegel's dissatisfaction with the tradition of subject-centred reason and its philosophy of reflection, a tradition that stems from Descartes and reaches its apotheosis in Kant. This concept of reason could not escape the self-referential dilemma of having to reflect critically on the subject's knowledge while basing such criticism wholly on the subject's own reason. Moreover, in focusing on the individual subject and thus neglecting the communicative dimension of human understanding, it heightened social fragmentation and prevented philosophy from fulfilling the role of promoting cultural unity, a role it had inherited from religion (*PDM*, 19–22). Yet, for Habermas, reason – properly understood as communicative – constitutes the absolute power of unification (*PDM*, 32). Philosophy's failure to grasp the idea of reason not in terms of subjectivity but in terms of communicative intersubjectivity – an idea implicit in Schiller's and the young Hegel's view of *art* as the genuine embodiment of a communicative reason and a noncoercive unifier – constitutes for Habermas the philosophical catastrophe of our epoch (*PDM*, 48).

Blindness to this alternative model of reason has locked us in the relentless self-critique of subject-centred reason, so that we have become suspicious of reason altogether. To escape this divisive dialectic of Enlightenment – the self-critique of reason by its own immanent activity (complemented by its repressive self-control of the rational subject) – Nietzsche turned instead to the aesthetic as 'reason's absolute other' (*PDM*, 94). Since Habermas affirms 'the internal relationship between modernity and rationality', he sees Nietzsche's aestheticism as 'the entry into postmodernity', and characterizes this aesthetic as an anti-rational, Dionysian 'decentered subjectivity liberated from all constraints of cognition and purposive activity' (*PDM*, 4, 94–6).

Of course, already in modernity's cultural economy of aesthetic autonomy (through the tripartite division of science, ethics-politics and art), aesthetic experience was aimed at freeing subjectivity both from narrow self-centredness and the constraints of scientific and moral-practical judgement. But such aesthetic freedom was essentially confined to the sphere of art. Hence aesthetic experience was not only directed by the rational discourse of art criticism, but also controlled in being framed by the regulative boundaries constituted by the corresponding autonomy of the more clearly reason-governed domains of science and morality. With Nietzschean postmodernism, however, the aesthetic no longer remains content with such rational limits. Displaying an irrational, limit-defying 'anarchistic intention' of Dionysian will to power, it 'reduces everything that is and should be to the aesthetic dimension', presenting itself as not only reason's other but its sovereign (*PDM*, 95–6, 123).

Habermas's story thus contains two very different notions of the aesthetic, though often neglecting to distinguish between them. The first concerns the rational, compartmentalized, and disciplined domain of art. Embodying communicative reason, seeking artistic progress, and providing the pleasures of meaningful form, this classic aesthetic of modernity is, for Habermas, one of 'aesthetic harmony' and 'artistic truth' (*PDM*, 207).[4] In contrast, what Habermas typically identifies as the aesthetic is an anti-rational drive of unconstrained hedonism and radical transgression, an aesthetic of 'body-centred experiences of a decentered subjectivity', aimed at 'limit-experiences' of 'mystical' 'ecstasy', producing 'dizzying effects of... shock... [and] excitement without any proper object'. As the dominating aesthetic in Habermas's polemic, it is demonized as 'aesthetically inspired anarchism' and attacked as postmodernism's grave threat to modernity's project of progressive emancipation through reason (*PDM*, 5, 306–10).

This aesthetic challenge is traced from Nietzsche to Georges Bataille's 'aesthetically inspired' eroticism and then to Foucault's theory of bio-power. It can also be seen in their idea of limit-experiences, which decentre the rationally controlled subject experientially, just as their genealogical critique decentres it theoretically (*PDM*, 211–16, 221–93). Postmodern privileging of aesthetics over reason becomes, for Habermas, still clearer in Derrida's and Rorty's advocacy of 'the primacy of rhetoric over logic,' 'world-disclosing' literary artistry over 'problem-solving' argument, and metaphor over 'normal' speech: all of this captured in their vision of philosophy as just a kind of writing (*PDM*, 190–207). He also finds this dangerous aesthetic challenge in recent German philosophy. Most virulent in Heidegger's ecstatic appeal to an archaic disclosure of Being (an 'ontologized art') through a poetic 'thinking more rigorous than the conceptual', it can even be detected in a rational archmodernist like Adorno with his emphasis on the redemptive, nondiscursive truth of art's archaic 'mimetic content' (*PDM*, 104, 129, 136).

For Habermas, the anti-rational aesthetic derives its authority from the enormous power of aesthetic experience in modern times, particularly as it developed from Romanticism to the modernist avant-garde. By seeming to surpass rationality (and overwhelm our self-possession), such experience seems to offer an alternative to reason and an escape from the self-centred critical self. Yet such potent aesthetic experience, he argues, is only the product of modernity's progress towards avant-garde art, and therefore depends on its rational discursive structures even while purporting to oppose and transcend reason. The aesthetic experiences employed by these anti-rational theorists 'are due to the same process of differentiation [and rationalization] as science and morality' (*PDM*, 339). Therefore, to appropriate aesthetic experience theoretically in order to escape or outflank rationality involves a performative contradiction. Moreover, to the extent that it negates the rationality embodied in modernity's artistic tradition, radical aesthetic experience loses all its meaning; 'the contents get dispersed . . . [and] an emancipatory effect does not follow.'[5]

Though plausible as *ad hominem* arguments concerning the modernist taste of anti-rational champions of the aesthetic, these arguments fail to clinch the case for the primacy of reason. They wrongly presume that powerful aesthetic experience always needs modernity's rationalized, differentiated conception of art, that it never existed before nor is ever achievable outside the framework of modernity's aesthetics. This presumption not only unconvincingly excludes the passionate aesthetic experience of ancient Greece (so inspirational for Nietzsche), but that of African cultures where such experience is not prestructured by modernity's cultural divisions.[6]

Habermas, however, still has his master argument for the primacy of reason. There is no escaping reason, because there is no escaping language and because language is essentially and necessarily rational. Language is the medium through which we live; and it is unavoidably rational because there is 'an internal connection between meaning and validity', that is between meaning and the rational, communicative assessment of truth claims and truth-related judgements (*PDM*, 313–14).[7] Aligning himself with Peircean pragmatism, Habermas insists that this defence of communicative reason makes no appeal to a transcendent 'pure reason that might don linguistic clothing only in the second place. Reason is by its very nature incarnated in contexts of communicative action and in structures of the lifeworld' (*PDM*, 322).

But in viewing language as the essence of rationality and the ground of its primacy, Habermas must resist Derrida's and Rorty's deconstructive efforts to portray language as more fundamentally aesthetic, as more a matter of disseminating creativity, persuasive rhetoric and world-making tropes than of logical validity. Their attempt to blur the distinctions between literature, literary criticism and philosophy is likewise condemned as a strategy to undermine the primacy of reason by denying its rationalizing process of differentiation of disciplines, a differentiation Habermas sees as essential to the achievement and progress of those disciplines. 'This aestheticizing of language', he claims, 'is purchased with the twofold denial of the proper senses of normal and poetic discourse.' Moreover, to deny all distinction 'between the poetic world-disclosive function of language and its prosaic, innerworldly functions' obscures the crucial fact that it is ultimately on such normal 'everyday communicative practice' that all 'learning processes' (including those of poetic production) are based, and 'in relation to which the world-disclosive force of . . . language has in turn to prove its worth' (*PDM*, 205).[8]

Habermas further argues that privileging the aesthetic language of innovative world-disclosure (paradigmatically expressed in 'the esoteric work of art') fosters not only an 'elitist contempt for discursive thought' but similar disrespect for the more ordinary and essential lifeworld practices of problem-solving and for the ordinary people engaged in them (*PDM*, 186). By endorsing the primacy of communicative reason through the ordinary linguistic practices of the lifeworld, by enlisting pragmatism's stress on consensual practice and Anglo-American philosophy's linguistic turn, Habermas seeks to overcome the Nietzschean-postmodern aesthetic turn that pervades so much contemporary continental theory – not only in France but closer to home in Heidegger and Adorno.

III

Rorty also advocates the primacy of language, but no longer sees it as the incarnation of reason or the expression of a deep human essence. Instead language is taken primarily as an aesthetic tool for new creation and self-fashioning; we revise science, self and society by redescription, by retelling their respective histories through different vocabularies. Philosophy should therefore also 'turn against theory and toward narrative' (*CIS*, xvi). Rorty's narrative of the path to postmodernity's 'ironist culture' is one of progressive liberation from the rule of reason through the advocacy and appeal of the aesthetic. This tale is structured on a series of parallel binary oppositions that elaborate the central contrast of reason versus the aesthetic. The oppositions can be lined up as follows: truth/metaphor, necessity/contingency, universal/particular, public/private, philosophy/poetry, inference/narrative, logic/rhetoric, discovery/creation, foundations/apologetics, deep reality/surface appearances, metaphysicians/ironists, theorists/novelists. Freedom and progress are functions of reversing the repressive privilege of the former terms.

Hegel began the aesthetic revolt against philosophy by historicizing it as narrative in his *Phenomenology of Mind*. However, he lapsed by taking his narrative as the definitive story with his own philosophy as the ultimate conclusion. Nietzsche advanced the cause of freedom by highlighting the aesthetic, by advocating an uncompromising perspectivism, and by rejecting truth and metaphysics for creative interpretation and genealogical redescription. But despite Nietzsche's professed anti-metaphysical perspectivism, there lurks a vestigial metaphysics and privileged perspective in his theory of the will to power.[9] Similarly, his anti-authoritarianism masks an autocratic injunction that the only worthy life is the sublime heroic one of the creative, striving *Übermensch*.

Heidegger, despite his attempt to overcome all metaphysics (including Nietzsche's), still falls victim to the same metaphysical impulse of universalizing his own vocabulary and interpretive redescriptions as *the* authoritative lexicon, narrative and destiny of Western civilization. Derrida makes the same mistake by presenting his early notions of *différance* and 'the myth of presence' as (respectively) the necessary root of all writing and the definitive interpretation of the entire history of metaphysics. Instead, he should recognize that these notions are nothing more than apt new ways to redescribe his own self and thought in relation to the past vocabularies and narratives on which he (like most of us philosophers) was raised.

This error of universalizing one's own preferred vocabulary and story as authoritative for the general public is, for Rorty, a pernicious remnant of the metaphysical claim of reason: the idea that private and public must be united through a rational grounding synthesis, the view that private ideals and beliefs are only truly valid if publicly validated, and that validity and legitimacy involve universalizability. Reason traditionally urged this standard of validity, just as metaphysics had the traditional goal of uniting our words and personal stories with something monumental, eternal and sublime: Truth, Reality, Power, Human Nature, History. But the aesthetic, for Rorty, is different. It can be satisfied with the particular and contingent, even the private, transitory and fictional. For (to use another of Rorty's contrasting pairs), it can seek beauty rather than sublimity (*CIS*, 105–6).

Freedom is thus better served by aesthetic writers who cherish particularity and personal linguistic invention than by philosophers who want to speak for all humanity in the name of universal reason or in terms of something else Big and Basic (like Power or *Dasein*). Such consciously aesthetic creators best realize Rorty's 'liberal ironist' dream 'to overcome authority without claiming authority': overcoming the authority of inherited narratives and vocabularies by creating a strikingly distinctive self and history in one's own terms, but doing so without claiming authority over the language and self-fashioning of others (*CIS*, 105).[10] Proust (in contrast to Nietzsche and Heidegger) proves paradigmatic of the ironist's aesthetic ideal, 'because he had no public ambitions' that his language would determine the true meaning of modern Europe. By unabashedly recounting personal stories rather than offering general theory, such an aesthete displays the humble irony and 'the courage to give up the attempt to unite the private and the public, to stop trying to bring together a quest for private autonomy and an attempt at public resonance and utility' (*CIS*, 118, 125).

The ironist aesthete can likewise escape the performative paradox that both Rorty and Habermas see as the prime stumbling block of postmodern philosophers: the problem of how to displace theory and reason without further theorizing and reasoning. The answer, for Rorty, is simply to circumvent theory's traditional claims of universal, essential truth by instead telling more personal stories for one's own individual emancipation; in short, to privatize philosophy.

Nominalist and historicist, postmodern irony 'thinks nothing has an intrinsic nature, a real essence' (*CIS*, 74). Though privileging language as constitutive of the self and lifeworld, Rorty rejects the idea of 'language in general' as a substantive universal, as some 'entity' or 'unity' 'intervening between self and reality' that constitutes the common core of human experience (*CIS*, 13–15). For such an idea amounts to an essentialism about language that is no better (if indeed different) than an essentialism about reason. Instead Rorty advocates the idea of very particular, contingent, historicized linguistic practices. These are simply tools for coping with experience, and their highest function is not the Habermasian one of cooperative problem-solving to promote mutual understanding and consensus. Instead, this function is aesthetic: individual, original creation, to make things new, 'to make something that never had been dreamed of before'. The most crucial goal is innovative 'self creation': refashioning and mastering oneself and one's structuring world 'by inventing a new language' that redescribes these things in one's 'own terms', 'in words never used before', so as to escape from 'inherited descriptions' and free oneself from the 'horror of finding oneself to be only a copy or replica' (*CIS*, 13, 27–9).

One likely objection to Rorty's aesthetic view of language as a tool for constant novelty and the expression of private individuality is that language requires some stable commonalities and consensus in order to be at all effective. Wittgenstein makes this point in his famous private-language argument, and Habermas similarly urges that language games cannot work (hence sentences cannot 'mean') without a linguistic community sharing to some extent the same vocabulary and *'the presupposition of intersubjectively identical ascriptions of meaning'* (*PDM*, 198).

Rorty has two possible ways of meeting this objection. One is by adopting Donald Davidson's account of metaphoric meaning and his 'passing theory' of language in order to argue that we need no stable shared rules for linguistic understanding. We can simply proceed on intuitive predictions of meaning based on current context and our previous habits of linguistic understanding. The rejoinder is that those habits would be undermined and unprojectible if language were fully aestheticized, privatized and innovationally protean in Rorty's recommended way.

Rorty's preferred response is to separate a private from a public use of language. While the latter is fully shared to serve the needs of consensual social life, the private use need not be fully shared and indeed *should not be*, if the individual is to achieve autonomy. But this private rhetoric of self-creation can remain sufficiently anchored in shared public language so as to be comprehensible to others and thus avoid the problem of the private-language argument. Since effective communication and social functioning require some linguistic consensus and stability, Rorty admits that there can be no 'culture whose public rhetoric is ironist. . . . Irony seems an inherently private matter' and necessarily 'reactive', requiring 'the contrast' of the public as a shared 'inherited' base from which it can assert its novel difference, 'something from which to be alienated'. Here (as elsewhere) Rorty's entire project avowedly 'turns on a firm distinction between the private and the public' (*CIS*, 83, 87–8).

This sharp 'public–private split' (*CIS*, 85) involves not only separating the language of consensus from the language of creation. It also means separating the political realm of 'social organization' from the aesthetic realm of individual autonomy (which Rorty wrongly equates with unique, distinctive self-creation.)[11] Privileging the private and aesthetic as what gives meaning to life, Rorty advocates political liberalism as merely a means to provide the necessary stability and negative liberty for pursuit of our private aims, a framework for 'letting its citizens be as privatistic, "irrationalist", and aestheticist as they please so long as they do ... no harm to others' (*CIS*, xiv).

But, as already noted, Rorty's 'firm distinction between the private and the public' is untenable, because the private self and the language it builds upon in self-creation are always already socially constituted and structured by a public field. Indeed, not only Rorty's particular privatized ethic of linguistic, aestheticist self-styling, but his whole notion of privatizing ethics clearly reflect the particular public and wider society that shape his thinking – the intellectual field and consumerist world of late-capitalist liberalism.[12]

Rorty's very idea of self-constitution and self-creation through language not only confutes his strong public/private dichotomy; it also suggests a lurking linguistic essentialism that differs from the one he repudiates, but seems even more pernicious. His view that the self is nothing but a linguistic web or set of narratives comes uncomfortably close to an essentialist view of human nature as exclusively linguistic. All that matters for selfhood and human being-in-the-world is language: 'human beings are simply incarnated vocabularies'; it is simply 'words which ... made us what we are'. Thus Nietzsche is praised as one who 'by describing himself in his own terms ... created himself', since he 'created the only part of himself that mattered by constructing his own mind. To create one's mind is to create one's own language.' For humans are 'nothing more than sentential attitudes – nothing more than the presence or absence of dispositions toward the use of sentences phrased in some historically-conditioned vocabulary' (*CIS*, 27, 88, 117).[13]

The only nonlinguistic element of experience that Rorty is willing to recognize is brute physical pain. But in contrast to the essentially linguistic *human* pain of 'humiliation', it represents 'the nonhuman, the nonlinguistic', what 'ties us to the nonlanguage-using beasts'. The power of such brute suffering even drives the anti-metaphysical Rorty towards a seemingly metaphysical vision that pits human linguistic creation against a deeper, essentially cruel and inhuman ground-reality of 'just power and pain ... to be found "out there"' (*CIS*, 40, 92, 94).

In arguing that man is essentially mind and that mind is essentially linguistic, Rorty not only violates his antiessentialism but endorses a mentalistic view of human nature against Nietzsche's own emphasis on the body's formative role and value. This linguistic mentalism and somatic neglect is particularly problematic in a philosopher intent on advancing the aesthetic, whose crucial connection with bodily senses and pleasures should be obvious, were it not for the rationalistic bias that has enthralled so much traditional aesthetic theory and still seems to ensnare Rorty's.

Rorty's aesthetic is thus hardly different from Habermas's. He exhibits none of that Dionysian aestheticism of Bataille or Foucault that Habermas condemns as postmodern. Nor does Rorty even affirm the more temperate forms of libidinal somatic aesthetics that I appreciate in certain forms of popular music and 'body work'.[14] He just likes to read books, and those he likes (notably Proust, Nabokov, Orwell and Kundera) all belong to the refined modern canon of serious art rather than to wacky Dadaism, anarchistic postmodernism, or the hedonic works of popular culture. Moreover, he recommends his chosen forms of art not for the wild ecstacies they produce but because they may 'help us become autonomous... [and] less cruel' (*CIS*, 141).

In short, Rorty's aestheticism is rationally melioristic, advocating art to improve the lifeworld by making the individual stronger in himself and more tolerant of others. How different is this from Habermas's strategy for continuing modernity's project of progress while overcoming its cultural fragmentation? Both strategies seek to appropriate the achievements of our progressive, specialized high-art tradition by translating its contents, through expert interpretive criticism, into the language and experience of our lifeworld.

IV

To sum up, Habermas and Rorty see postmodernism as privileging the aesthetic over the Enlightenment tradition of reason, and both supply historico-philosophical narratives to explain this aesthetic turn. Moreover, both cherish the modernist aesthetic tradition of high art in its more formally disciplined and rational forms, prizing it for its useful contributions to the lifeworld. Finally, both identify this lifeworld with language, which thus becomes the essence of human nature and the battleground over which aesthetics and reason struggle for dominance. Here at last, in their contrasting privileging of the linguistic centrality of these terms, Rorty and Habermas exhibit real difference.

But how momentous is it? Habermas clearly affirms language's important aesthetic dimensions: not simply 'the world-creating capacity of language', its special 'poetic-world-disclosive function', but also an 'aesthetic-expressive' dimension that he recognizes in every speech act (*PDM*, 313, 315). Conversely, Rorty readily admits the usefulness of the rational/irrational distinction within 'the interior of a language game' and particularly within the domain of 'public rhetoric' – which Habermas of course would call 'public reason' (*CIS*, 47, 87).

Rorty loves to shock old-fashioned rationalists by advocating aesthetic primacy even in 'the language of theoretical science', which he sees (like Mary Hesse) as 'irreducibly metaphorical'. Metaphor 'is essential to scientific progress', because its innovative aesthetic imagination provides the necessary means to escape the entrenched vocabularies of old scientific paradigms, thus paving the way for more productive new theories (*EHO*, 166; *ORT*, 162). But Habermas also recognizes that 'the specialized languages of science and technology... live off the illuminating power of metaphorical tropes.' He simply insists that these 'rhetorical elements' are eventually submitted to argumentative and experimental disciplines of consensus-oriented discourse in the process of theory justification and in being 'enlisted for the special purposes of problem-solving' (*PDM*, 209; cf. *PT*, 205). So if Rorty portrays the history of scientific progress 'as the history of metaphor' (*CIS*, 16), Habermas is simply objecting that this is not the whole story.

Yet Rorty clearly admits this too. In defending Habermas against Lyotard's postmodern vision of science as pure innovational paralogy, Rorty recognizes the useful regulative role of 'normal science', arguing that science no more aims 'at piling paralogy on paralogy' than politics 'aims at piling revolution on revolution' (*EHO*, 166). Likewise, though preferring to highlight science's revolutionary moment as more interesting and inspiringly heroic through its creative difference, Rorty nonetheless shows great respect for normal science's language of consensus. Celebrating it as the expression of 'unforced agreement' through the discussion of wide-ranging 'suggestions and arguments', he recommends it as an exemplary 'model of human solidarity' (*ORT*, 39). Finally, even the privileged aesthetic moment of novel difference must in some way gain validation through public discourse and its normative (albeit revisable) justificational procedures. This convergence of 'private' fantasy with shared public language and the community's needs is recognized even by Rorty as what distinguishes 'genius' from mad 'eccentricity or perversity' (*CIS*, 37).

The limits of Rortian aesthetic sovereignty become even clearer when we turn to the realm of politics and the public sphere. *There*, as we saw, the 'public rhetoric' of consensus must prevail; there we don't want idiosyncratic metaphors but shared norms, common categories, stable procedures and consistent rules of argument. There, even universalism is affirmed – not in the Habermasian sense of a foundational 'idealizing presupposition of communicative action' (*PDM*, 206), but as the goal of an ever wider, more inclusive community of reasonable, tolerant liberals. The aesthetic and its individualism dominate only in the private sphere, though this is the sphere that Rorty privileges in contrast to Habermas's championing of the public.

We see here another reason why the public/private split is so important to Rorty. It performs his postmodern remapping of modernity's tripartite schema of science, art and the ethico-political into a dualism of *public* discourse based on normalcy and consensus versus a *private* discursive sphere aimed at radical innovation and individual fulfilment. If normal science and politics can be fitted into the former, personal ethics joins art in the latter and becomes aestheticized.

But Rorty's postmodern mapping remains modern and Habermasian in compartmentalizing the aesthetic from the political and normal scientific, even if the aesthetic now includes the ethics of taste in lifestyles. On the other hand, Habermas's ideal of communicative reason is procedural and liberal enough to accept differences of taste in art and aesthetic lifestyles, as long as these differences do not endanger the essential social norms of the public sphere. So if they both insist on the primacy of language and share a taste for aesthetic modernism and liberal politics, why does the Rorty–Habermas debate seem so urgent to us philosophers?

Their question of privileging aesthetics or reason – the private or public – concerns our very conception of philosophy and our self-image as philosophers. For Rorty, philosophy gets aestheticized with ethics and is relegated to the private realm. It becomes an art of living one's own life with greater autonomy and fulfilment, and perhaps inspiring others to do likewise. But it should never pretend to determine general norms for improving the direction of science or the public sphere. For Habermas, in contrast, reason's primacy over the aesthetic means keeping philosophy firmly with science in the public domain of consensus and knowledge. Philosophy remains the unifying discipline of the public sphere, integrating and legitimating its scientific, social, and even aesthetic norms. If no longer the authoritarian arbiter of culture, it remains the crucial 'stand-in [*Platzhalter*] and interpreter', 'the guardian of reason'.[15]

While Habermas presents himself as philosopher of the *polis*, Rorty more often assumes the modest role of campus philosopher, recreating himself through books and inspiring colleagues and students to do the same.[16] It is easy to condemn the retreat from unificational public philosophy to individual aesthetics, particularly from the perspective of European cultures like France and Germany, where organic national publics are still thought to exist and philosophers may still have a visible role in determining their political culture. But current American society neither presents such a *polis* nor grants the philosopher the role of guiding it and securing its unity. In such conditions, which may soon become the conditions of a confederated Europe, one might reasonably concentrate philosophy on what it may do best: help the individual lead a better life. Just as Habermas's fear of noncompartmentalized aesthetics may reflect the horrid national memory of aestheticized Nazism, so Rorty's aesthetic turn may reflect not mere personal taste but recognition of the philosopher's rather limited role in American politics and culture.

Two points, however, must be borne in mind. Between the centre court of the national *polis* and one's private aesthetic theatre, there remains for American philosophers a wide realm for effective political engagement. Besides, political action can be recommended also for its personal aesthetic rewards of self-enrichment through the satisfactions of solidarity and collaborative struggle. Conversely, the aesthetic power of an artwork or a life can be deeply enhanced by its political engagement, even if such aesthetico-political cocktails can have a dangerously blinding power that necessitates an always vigilant philosophical critique. Forcing philosophy to choose narrowly between public reason and private aesthetics therefore makes no sense.

V

In trying to ease the Rorty–Habermas, aesthetic–reason oppositions, I hope to have tempered the opposition between the modern and postmodern. Postmodernity – aesthetically, politically, philosophically, and economically – should be conceived as largely continuous with its modern roots, though conspicuously lacking in modernity's faith in progress, compartmentalization, and in the purity, universality and adequacy of reason.[17] Postmodernism's critique of reason can thus be seen as a continuation of modernity's, while its advocacy of the aesthetic helps highlight dimensions of experience that modern reason could not adequately handle through strategies of compartmentalization and marginalization. The postmodern implosion of aesthetics into ethics and politics shows that modernity's rationalizing differentiation of culture into separate spheres has not been entirely successful.

Rorty's aestheticization of the ethical is a symptom of this post-modern reaction. But his aesthetic remains too constrained by the modern rationalist tradition: not simply in its taste and confinement to the private sphere, but also through its exclusive concern for language, its denial of the somatic which is *alogon* in the sense of nondiscursivity, though not necessarily in the sense of rabid Dionysian excess. The conflation of these two senses, in thinkers like Bataille, Deleuze, and Foucault, comes only by coupling the idea of somatic aesthetics with the avant-garde ideology of radical transgression. One task for postmodern inquiry is to test the limits of reason by probing this nonlinguistic aesthetic realm, which though devoid of discursive rationality is not devoid of intelligent direction. Pervading the experience of our everyday lifeworld but also the activities of expert culture, such nondiscursive *aisthesis* presents a domain whose ameliorative care could enhance our science and politics, not just our ethics and aesthetics. I develop this notion of *somaesthetics* elsewhere,[18] but a sense of its philosophical difficulty (even of its alleged perverse impossibility) should be faced already here.

All theoretical attempts to free the aesthetic from rationalist discursive dominion run against the power of tradition. The very concept of 'aesthetics' was introduced by philosophers (originally by Baumgarten, a Leibnizian rationalist) precisely to rationalize the nonlogical dimension of aesthetic experience. Aesthetics of the nondiscursive must also face the dialectical dilemma that to discourse about the 'other of reason' or 'other of language' is already to inscribe that other within the ambit of reason and language. Habermas sees this as his trump card of performative contradiction against reason's critique by its other, while Rorty's equation of aesthetics with language only suggests a parallel reinforcing argument.

But surely one value of the aesthetic, through the intense pleasures and often overwhelming power of aesthetic experience, is to make us forget for a moment about language and reason, allowing us to revel, however briefly, in nondiscursive sensual joy. This crucial sensual dimension is sadly neglected by Rorty because of his global linguisticism. As its denial makes his aestheticism joylessly eviscerate, his contrasting emphasis on pain is still more discouraging. Despite his emancipatory progress, Rorty remains the product of a puritan America. Ignoring somatic satisfactions, his aesthetic programme is one-sidedly driven by the restless, relentless production of new vocabularies and narrative identities. It is more a toiling poetics, a theory of industrious verbal making, than an aesthetic of embodied delight.

Of course, as Foucault reminds us, the body is not free from the imprint of society's rationalizing practices. But it remains (as he also recognized) a promising place where discursive reason meets its limits, encounters its other, and can be given a therapeutic shock towards redirection. Nor should we heed the objection that somatic aesthetics is impossible because such experience is too subjective and individualistic. We share our bodies and bodily pleasures as much as we share our minds, and they are surely as public as our thoughts.

There remains the ultimate paradox that the very attempt to theorize the body as something outside our linguistic structures self-refutingly inscribes it in those structures. As T. S. Eliot's Sweeney complained, 'I gotta use words when I talk to you.' In one sense, this is a trivial sophism, but in another a deep truth. Discourse about the somatic is not enough, as even Socrates realized in advocating and practising dance for his philosophical life.[19] To understand the body as the 'nondiscursive other', we have to stop pushing words and start moving limbs: stop talking and start dancing. Perhaps I should *say* no more.

Notes

1 Jürgen Habermas, *The Philosophical Discourses of Modernity* (Cambridge, Mass.: MIT Press, 1987), pp. 185–210; henceforth referred to as *PDM*.
2 Richard Rorty, *Contingency, Irony, and Solidarity* (Cambridge: Cambridge University Press, 1989), pp. 44–5, 48, 53; henceforth *CIS*. He glosses the notion of poeticized culture as 'substitut[ing] the hope that chances for equal fulfillment of idiosyncratic fantasies will be equalized for the hope that everyone will replace "passion" or fantasy with "reason"' (p. 53). See also his critique of Habermas's use of communicative reason to answer modern culture's '"need for unification" in order to "regenerate the unifying power of religion in the medium of reason"'; in Richard Rorty, 'Habermas and Lyotard on Postmodernity', in his *Essays on Heidegger and Others, Philosophical Papers*, vol. 2 (Cambridge: Cambridge University Press, 1991), p. 169 (citing *PDM*, 19, 20), henceforth *EHO*. In that volume's introduction, Rorty retrospectively regrets his usage of the contested term 'postmodernism' in defining his position as 'postmodern bourgeois liberalism' and in characterizing other contemporary philosophy. Instead he offers 'post-Nietzschean' as a more precise, uncontroversial label for philosophers (e.g. Heidegger, Derrida, Lyotard) earlier defended under the notion of the postmodern (*EHO*, 1–2). Since Habermas identifies the postmodern with Nietzsche, Rorty's terminological substitution does not affect the sense of their debate. Rorty's 'Postmodern Bourgeois Liberalism' is reprinted in his *Objectivity, Relativism, and Truth, Philosophical Papers*, vol. 1 (Cambridge: Cambridge University Press, 1991), henceforth *ORT*.

3 This essay was originally written for a conference, 'Modernity in Question: Habermas and Rorty', that was held in 1993 at Cerisy-la-Salle with the participation of both philosophers. Its location near the beaches of Normandy only intensified the sense of philosophical conflict that the programme's oppositional facing-off of German and American philosophers (respectively representing modernity and postmodernity) was meant to evoke. Despite the preconference 'hype' of world-historical philosophical conflict, substantive agreement clearly prevailed over difference. So did the philosophical habit of endless paper reading, which provoked this contribution's closing call for alternative expression.

4 The compartmentalization of Habermas's aesthetic of modernity is confirmed in a later, less polemical work. 'The aesthetic experiences are not admitted into forms of *praxis*; they are not referred to cognitive-instrumental skills and moral representations, which are developed from innerworld learning processes; they are tied up [*verwoben*] with the world-constituting, world-disclosing function of language.' From 'Handlungen, Sprechakte, sprachlich vermittelte Interaktionen und Lebenswelt', in Jürgen Habermas, *Post-metaphysisches Denken: Philosophisches Aufsätze* (Frankfurt: Suhrkamp, 1988), pp. 63–104 (quotation from p. 94, my translation). This essay was not included in the book's English version, *Post-metaphysical Thinking: Philosophical Essays* (Cambridge, Mass.: MIT Press, 1992), henceforth *PT*.

5 Jürgen Habermas, 'Modernity: An Incomplete Project', repr. in Hal Foster (ed.), *The Anti-Aesthetic* (Port Townsend, Wash.: Bay Press, 1983), p. 11.

6 For more detailed argument, see Richard Shusterman, *Pragmatist Aesthetics: Living Beauty, Rethinking Art* (Oxford: Blackwell, 1992), pp. 46–9.

7 Habermas's theory of communicative reason does not simplistically limit the connection of validity and meaning to the standard notion of truth as the representation of facts, but concerns also the speech act's dimension of 'rightness' (in the sense of moral normativity) and 'truthfulness' (in the sense of authenticity of expression). This tripartite analysis of validity is explicitly meant to parallel 'the three fundamental functions of language' (representative, appelative-regulative, and expressive), but also clearly suggests modernity's division of spheres into representative science, regulative ethics and politics, and expressive art (*PDM*, 313–15). Earlier, in *The Theory of Communicative Action*, vol. 1 (Boston: Beacon Press, 1984), p. 335, he cites 'works of art' as 'exemplary' of the 'rationality' of 'expressive knowledge' which 'can be criticized as untruthful'. In short, modernity's tripartite differentiation of cultural spheres appears as the rational development of the essential tripartite logic of language itself. Rorty is right to object that our cultural institutions and language are more contingent in origin. But given his own problematically vague and radical sense of contingency, Rorty's contrasting account of all language and culture as 'sheer contingency' should likewise be resisted (*CIS*, 22).

Habermas returns to his tripartite analysis of the validity-dimension of all speech acts in *PT*, 74–9. But the conclusion of that book's essay 'Philosophy and Science as Literature?' presents a seemingly different suggestion for artworks: that validity claims, though still present in fictional texts or utterances, are only binding for the people in the fiction, 'not for the author and the reader' (pp. 223–4). This greatly limits the role of expressive truthfulness for the validity of aesthetic discourse.

8 Through a critical reading of Calvino's experimental novel *If on a Winter's Night a Traveler*, Habermas tries to show how the levelling of the aesthetic-fiction/everyday-real world distinction will not succeed even in aesthetic practice. His central point is that 'Everyday life [with its discourse to solve problems] continues to place limits around literary texts' that are essential for the differentially determined identity and proper functioning of these artworks. See 'Philosophy and Science as Literature?', in *PT*, 205–27, esp. 218, 223.

9 For a critique of this metaphysics, see *Pragmatist Aesthetics*, pp. 79–82.

10 Rorty's plea that philosophy become privatized and avoid all claims to general authority over others can be read as a confession of his own choice not to presume the role of a dominating major philosopher whose views claim to be definitive, preferring instead what he calls a style of 'weak thought' (*EHO*, 6). Such a position dovetails neatly not only with anti-foundationalism but with his liberalist pluralism. Rorty also commends Derrida's later writing as moving in this more personal direction (*CIS*, 135–7).

11 For detailed critique of this conflation, see *Pragmatist Aesthetics* pp. 253–5.

12 For elaboration of this point, see *Pragmatist Aesthetics*, pp. 255–7.

13 Though Rorty always insists on the primacy of the sentential, he is forced by his privileging of the private and the idiosyncratically creative to admit the presence and value of associations and images of words below the level of propositional attitudes. These nevertheless depend for their possibility on sentential meaning (*CIS* 153).

14 See *Pragmatist Aesthetics*, chs. 7, 8, 9; and my 'Die Sorge um den Körper in der heutigen Kultur', in A. Kuhlmann (ed.), *Philosophische Ansichten der Kultur der Moderne* (Frankfurt: Fischer, 1994), pp. 241–77.

15 See Jürgen Habermas, 'Philosophy as Stand-In and Interpreter', in *Moral Consciousness and Communicative Action* (Cambridge, Mass.: MIT Press, 1990), pp. 3, 4. His linking of philosophy with science as opposed to the aesthetic is underlined in 'Philosophy and Science as Literature?', where both the former (as opposed to the latter) cannot 'give up the orientation toward questions of truth' (*PT*, 225).

16 Though Rorty has recently tried to address a wider public by occasionally writing for the general press, these articles remain largely centred on issues of the academy in contrast to Habermas's broader scope.

17 Two substantial and convincing (though very different) cases for the continuity of modernity and postmodernity are found in Albrecht Well mer's *The Persistence of Modernity* (Cambridge, Mass.: MIT Press 1991) and David Harvey, *The Condition of Postmodernity* (Oxford Blackwell, 1989).

18 *Practicing Philosophy: Pragmatism and the Philosophical Life* (New York: Routledge, 1997).

19 See Xenophon's *Symposium*, in his *Conversations on Socrates* (Har mondsworth: Penguin, 1990), pp. 233–4.

Response to Richard Shusterman

Richard Rorty

I am surprised to be told by Richard Shusterman that 'the Rorty–Habermas debate' he describes seems 'urgent to us philosophers'. For, as Shusterman rightly says in section IV of his contribution to this volume, it is hard to find differences between myself and Habermas which concern the role of art and literature in culture. As he notes, we both acknowledge the role of metaphor in making 'world-disclosure' possible. We agree that world-disclosure typically links up with problem-solving, and that the latter typically requires the use of familiar, traditional, literal language.

As I see it, the only serious or interesting disagreement between Habermas and myself is about whether you need notions like 'unconditionality' and 'universal validity' in order to justify social democratic institutions. This disagreement does not put us on opposite sides of what Shusterman calls 'a misleading dualism between reason and aesthetics that seems inconsistent with their [Habermas's and Rorty's] own basic pragmatism.' Granted that each of us has written passages which can be construed as propounding such a dualism, there are many other passages – some of which Shusterman cites in section IV – which are more tempered and less misleading.

Both Habermas and I have, indeed, sometimes spoken of the 'primacy' of reason or of 'the aesthetic', but this locution is particularly unfortunate. Primacy is always primacy in a respect or for a purpose. Once the needed distinctions between different respects or purposes are made, there is little left for the two of us to quarrel about. I entirely agree with Habermas that, as Shusterman summarizes him, 'there is no escaping reason, because there is no escaping language and because language is essentially and necessarily rational.' But saying that is quite compatible with saying that metaphor and fantasy will always be required if the crust of convention is to be broken, and new worlds disclosed. So I do not think it helps to view all the oppositions Shusterman lists at the beginning of section III of his contribution as illustrating a 'reason' vs. 'the aesthetic' dualism.

I doubt that I have ever put forward, nor that Derrida would affirm, the view which Shusterman attributes to us both: that language is 'more fundamentally aesthetic ... more a matter of disseminating creativity, persuasive rhetoric and world-making tropes than of logical validity'. Language has lots of functions – two of which are problem-solving and world-disclosing – but I doubt that there is any need to debate which of its functions is 'fundamental'. That would be like asking whether liberal politics is more fundamental than conservative politics, or whether spending money is more fundamental than saving it, or up more fundamental than down. The most I would say is that the world-disclosing invention of a vocabulary is temporally prior to its use in solving problems, just as fashioning a tool is temporally prior to employing it.

On the other hand people were probably using language to solve problems long before they started disclosing new worlds. Language presumably started out as a way of getting cooperation in projects of basket-weaving, arrow-shaping, antelope-hunting, raising families, propitiating the gods, and the like. That seems reason enough not to say that 'language is ... primarily an aesthetic tool for new creation and self-fashioning.' As civilization has progressed, however, the use of language to create new ways of being human, and to dream up new projects, has become more frequent and prominent. But words have no built-in preference for being used for such purposes rather than for more mundane ones.

Shusterman says that I think that 'particular, contingent, historicized linguistic practices ... are simply tools for coping with experience, and their highest function is not the Habermasian one of cooperative problem-solving.... Instead, this function is aesthetic: individual, original creation'. This is right only if 'highest' is taken in the sense of 'most beautiful, most exciting and most fun'. Orchids are higher than trees in order of phylogenesis, and they strike many of us as more beautiful and more interesting. But without the forests we should not only have no orchids, we should have no oxygen. Without the banal, routine, problem-solving uses of language we should not only lack occasion and motive for inventing orchidaceous language, but would have no economy and no society.

I think there is a reasonably firm distinction between orchids and trees even though all the really showy orchids are epiphytic, and that there is a reasonably firm distinction between the private and public even though, as Shusterman rightly says, 'the private self and the language it builds upon in self-creation are always already socially constituted and structured by a public field.' The private–public distinction I want is between our responsibilities to ourselves and our responsibilities to others. It took many millennia of social cooperation before that hothouse flower, the private self, could blossom. Human beings had been using language for a very long time before anybody had the wealth, leisure and security to develop a private agenda. But that does not detract from the beauty and excitement of such agendas.

Substituting 'responsibilities to oneself alone' for 'freedom' in Hegel's aphorism, one might say that in the beginning only One had such responsibilities (the Emperor, perhaps). Now only Some do (since the vast majority of people now alive cannot afford any such luxury), but eventually (with luck) All will. Political liberalism is not *merely* 'a means to provide the necessary stability and negative liberty for pursuit of our private aims', because it is also a means to minimize suffering. But minimizing suffering and maximizing negative liberty go hand in hand. In most political situations one does not have to choose between these two aims.

There is a sense in which Shusterman is right that I hold 'an essentialist view of human nature as essentially linguistic'. As I say in my response to Norman Geras in this volume, it seems to me that what differentiates us from the brute creation is no more and no less than our ability to use language. But I do not see this claim as any more banefully essentialistic than saying that what differentiates animals from plants is their ability to move around. The only trouble with essentialism is the metaphysical suggestion that some of our classifications, but not others, divide nature at the joints. But one can give up the idea that nature has joints and still remark that we use certain predicates pretty much coextensively with others.

I am a bit at a loss about how to deal with Shusterman's claim that I neglect the fact that beautiful flowers, birds, poems, music and other things 'make us forget for a moment about language and reason, allowing us to revel, however briefly, in nondiscursive sensual joy'. They do indeed. But in what exactly does my 'neglect' consist?

Shusterman goes on to say that because I am the product of a 'puritan America' my 'aesthetic programme' is 'one-sidedly driven by the restless, relentless production of new vocabularies and narrative identities'. What aesthetic programme? I do not know of any

fruitful way to bring nondiscursive sensual joy (of the sort birdwatch-
ers like myself get when kingfishers flash fire) together with the sorts
of non-somatic thrills I enjoy as a person who, as Shusterman puts it,
'just likes to read books'. But neither do I know any interesting
descriptions of the relationship between the somatic pleasures of
food and those of sex, or between the non-somatic delight of reading
Wodehouse and that of reading Hegel. Do we need an aesthetic theory
or an aesthetic 'programme' to exhibit such relationships?

This last rhetorical question expresses my scepticism about 'aesthetics' as a field of inquiry. That has always struck me as another of
Kant's bad ideas – of a piece with the bad idea (to which I think
Habermas unfortunately prone) of splitting culture up into three
spheres, one for each of the three *Critiques*. Some good books have
been written about painting, others about literature, others about
music, others about sex, and still others about birdwatching. But I
have never read a book that succeeded in saying something interesting
about what all these have in common. What Shusterman calls 'the
somatic' typically turns up in all these books, in one form or another.
But I am not sure that we need 'a somatic aesthetics' because I am not
sure that we need an aesthetic theory, or an aesthetic programme, at
all. I doubt that there is much to be said about what unites painting,
literature, music, sex and birdwatching while distinguishing all these
from science, morals, politics, philosophy and religion. (One reason
for my uncertainty on this point is that I entirely agree with Shusterman that 'the aesthetic power of an artwork...can be deeply
enhanced by its political engagement'.)

My doubts about making as much as Shusterman does of the
'reason vs. the aesthetic' distinction are of a piece with my doubts
about his claim that 'the body... remains...a promising place where
discursive reason meets its limits, encounters its other.' For better or
worse – perhaps because of being a product of puritan America, or
perhaps because my views are indeed determined by 'the intellectual
field and consumerist world of late-capitalist liberalism' – Foucault's,
Bataille's and Deleuze's discussions of the body leave me cold. But
even if they turned me on, I would still resist talk about where
'discursive reason meets its limits'. I do not see a difference between
'discursive reason' and talking about things, and I cannot see that
talking about things has either 'limits' or an 'other'.

Talking about things is one of the things we do. Experiencing
moments of sensual joy is another. The two do not stand in a dialectical relationship, get in each others' way, or need synthesis in a
programme or theory. We can agree with Gadamer that 'being that
can be understood is language' while remaining aware that there is

more to life than understanding. Inventing others to reason and then purporting to provide a better discursive understanding of these non-discursive others (a project which stretches from British empiricism through Bergson to existential phenomenology) seems to me a beautiful example of kicking up dust and then complaining that we cannot see.

8
Progress without Foundations?

Norman Geras

While I was writing a book on Richard Rorty published in 1995, I began to work also on the Holocaust.[1] One of the things that soon struck me in the literature was how little attention had been paid to this subject by political philosophers. On the face of it this is rather surprising, given how extensive the literature on the Holocaust has become and how densely populated it is by other sorts of contributors: by historians, theologians, social scientists, novelists, literary critics and so on. There is, so far as I can see, no obvious reason for the gap, for the relative silence about this vast tragedy, within contemporary Anglo-American political thought. Just to anticipate the broad theme that will be central in what follows, political philosophy has been a tradition of normative, critical, sometimes visionary thinking about social and political order. An important strand within it has been the idea of the Good Society, the dream of a just world. As such a critical tradition, political philosophy is linked by a fundamental impulse to an idea that has been very powerful in Western thought since the Enlightenment: I mean the idea of progress. But while many beyond the discipline have come to see the Holocaust as putting a question mark against visions of human progress and so against the Enlightenment project or project of modernity, within mainstream political philosophy there is not much reflection about this, or indeed any other, putative implication of the event.

My own work at the moment involves attempting to make good the gap I perceive, there is no need here to describe how. In making good you take from where you can; you start from what you find. There is not a lot in Rorty's work about the Holocaust, there are only passing comments. Still, there are these passing comments. One of them will enable me to dwell on some of my current preoccupations whilst also referring to more general features of his thinking. This may have the advantage, perhaps, that I do not simply repeat the arguments of my book, although a few of them will figure in condensed form in the later stages of what I have to say. I shall begin by contrasting an observation of Rorty's with the view of another well-known American philosopher – namely Robert Nozick – on the same subject.

In a footnote to his lecture in the Oxford Amnesty series on human rights, Rorty offers the following suggestion:

> [S]ome contemporary intellectuals, especially in France and Germany, take it as obvious that the Holocaust made it clear that the hopes for human freedom which arose in the nineteenth century are obsolete – that at the end of the twentieth century we postmodernists know that the Enlightenment project is doomed...[But] nobody has come up with a better [project]. It does not diminish the memory of the Holocaust to say that our response to it should not be a claim to have gained a new understanding of human nature or of human history, but rather a willingness to pick ourselves up and try again.[2]

By contrast with this, Robert Nozick has written of the Holocaust as 'an event like the Fall in the way traditional Christianity conceived it, something that radically and drastically alters the situation and status of humanity'. With some qualifications and explanations that I shall not here go into, Nozick elaborates on the thought as follows:

> [I]t now would not be a *special* tragedy if humankind ended, if the human species were destroyed in atomic warfare or the earth passed through some cloud that made it impossible for the species to continue reproducing itself...its loss would now be no *special* loss above and beyond the losses to the individuals involved. Humanity has lost its claim to continue.[3]

Now, I find a certain, I don't know, 'depth' in Nozick's sentiment (expressed in a powerful evocation by him of some of the detail of the historical experience he is talking about) that is missing in Rorty's observation; as reflected by the latter thinker's choice of metaphor, the simple image of a pratfall doing duty for him beside the pit of Hell. 'To pick ourselves up and try again' somehow does not quite meet the case. But Rorty's is, as I have already said, a passing comment only, therefore let this pass. I would argue also, contrary to the opinion he puts forward, that in the shadow cast by the Holocaust some further reflection about human nature is very much called for, at least by all those sponsoring a view of human nature as either inherently benign or else more or less completely alterable, to the point where all inner sources of evil could then presumably be subdued.[4] This is a company that includes Rorty himself, in his postmodern, pervasively 'culturalist' persona. In the main substance of his comment, however, in the counsel he gives against any attitude of historical resignation, Rorty's judgement is, I think, the sounder one. At any rate, I hope it is.

The difference which the two philosophers summarily present can be placed upon a spectrum of positions much debated and explored in other conversational modes, other areas of intellectual enquiry. Let me say something, first, about post-Holocaust Jewish theology. In Nozick's view can be seen, perhaps, the death of a certain idea of 'man', of 'humanity' as the foundation of progressive hope, parallel to the death of God as argued for by Richard Rubenstein.

It is an idea, the death of God, that one encounters amongst the survivors themselves. Halina Birenbaum, a woman who went through Majdanek, Auschwitz and other camps, tells how during a forced ten-day fast in one of them she vowed she would never again fast voluntarily, as on Yom Kippur, the Jewish Day of Atonement:

> [V]owing this, I deliberately and with relish declared revenge on that God who had been believed in at the home of my parents, but who had deserted us all in our misery and who, here in the Nazi extermination camps, had proved to be an invention of fraudulent priests who ordered us to love and respect Him, and fear His justice.[5]

Or, as Primo Levi has succinctly put it, 'There is Auschwitz, and so there cannot be God.'[6]

Rubenstein sums up his own viewpoint as follows: 'I have often stated that the idea that a God worthy of human adoration could have inflicted Auschwitz on what was allegedly his people is obscene.'[7] Rubenstein came to this conclusion after a conversation which was to be a turning point for him, the occasion of a crisis of faith. His interlocutor was a German Protestant clergyman with a courageous record of opposition to Nazism, who suggested to him that the Nazi genocide must have been God's will; Hitler was an instrument 'of God's wrath in punishing his sinful people'. Rubenstein found the logic of this compelling: '[G]iven the Judaeo-Christian conception, so strong in Scripture, that God is the ultimate actor in the historical drama, no other theological interpretation of the death of six million Jews is tenable.'[8] But he could not then continue to uphold the idea of 'an omnipotent, beneficent God after Auschwitz':

To see any purpose in the death camps, the traditional believer is forced to regard the most demonic, antihuman explosion in all history as a meaningful expression of God's purposes. The idea is simply too obscene for me to accept.

Rubenstein felt obliged rather to accept the 'death' of the traditional Jewish God of history.[9] He concluded that 'the Cosmos is ultimately absurd in origin and meaningless in purpose'.[10]

Rubenstein's position is opposed to that of other Jewish theologians for whom the destruction of the Jews of Europe is part precisely of a theodicy, in which the ways of God are vindicated. There are different variants of this belief. The Holocaust may be seen as representing a necessary punishment and martyrdom of the Jews for having strayed from God's law, and as a way of trying to bring them back to it. Or it may be seen as part of a wider scheme of progress – brought about through sacrifice – a passage through holy martyrdom to a juster world for the Jews and for all humankind.[11] Either way, the catastrophe is expressive of God's purposes, and this is exactly the type of easy redemptive move which Rubenstein finds repugnant in relation to the scale of barbarity and suffering it is supposed to redeem. He is not alone in finding it so.

In between a justifying theodicy, on the one hand, and the death of God, on the other, there is, however, a third position occupied by a number of post-Holocaust Jewish theologians. I shall take Hans Jonas as one clear representative of it, though I will not be able to do justice to the detail of his argument. Once again here, something similar to the view of the theologian, reflecting after the event, is found amongst the victims of the Shoah themselves. Etty Hillesum, a Dutch Jewish woman who was to perish at Auschwitz, committed these words to the diary she kept in the period leading up to her deportation: 'God is not accountable to us for the senseless harm we cause one another. We are accountable to him!'[12] For Jonas likewise, on the terrain of history good and evil are the responsibility of our kind. In an original act of divestment or 'self-forfeiture' whose reasons we cannot fathom, the Divine (so Jonas proposes) chose to give itself over 'to the chance and risk and endless variety of becoming'. This has led by way of a long evolution, one 'carried by its own momentum', to 'the advent of man', and therewith to 'the advent of knowledge and freedom' and 'the charge of responsibility under the disjunction of good and evil'. Suffering and caring, Jonas contends, God is no longer to be thought of as omnipotent. The image of God, as he puts it, 'passes...into man's precarious trust, to be completed, saved, or spoiled by what he will do to himself and the world'.[13]

In this conception, consequently, humanity is not favoured with a pregiven destiny or end. What we possess in human freedom is only the chance, the possibility, of pursuing and securing good purposes; and what we possess in God is some 'image' of these, the intimation of a world more benign. Darkened by a knowledge of the most terrible events, this is nevertheless the theology of a certain openness: an openness to surviving hope and the possibility of progress.

Parallel differences of perspective are also to be found, I suggest, in the considerable literature there now is of Holocaust testimony and of secondary reflection on the experience of the victims of the Nazi camps. For purposes of economy, I shall focus here on some of the work of secondary reflection. There has been a tendency, understandable in the circumstances, to dwell on the way in which the experience of the concentration and death camps shattered illusions about underlying human decency and mutual sympathy: on how it did this not only through what it revealed in the behaviour of the murderers, torturers, accomplices and bystanders; but also by degrading the victims themselves, reducing them to a bare will to survive at all costs, crushing out of them every humane or other-regarding moral impulse. Such is the message that can be taken, for example, from the work of Bruno Bettelheim on this subject. Bettelheim presents us with a view of the prisoners of the camps as being incapable of self-restraint, lying pathologically, disintegrated as adult moral personalities, regressing to infantile forms of behaviour. They developed, he says, a 'childlike dependency on the guards', came to accept the values of their tormentors and oppressors.[14] For a long time widely influential, Bettelheim's view is regarded more sceptically today: as lacking any real inner sympathy with the situation of the camp prisoners, notwithstanding his own incarceration at Buchenwald and Dachau for a period before the beginning of the war.

This same judgement, however, of a lack of sympathy, could not in fairness be made about the currently more esteemed Lawrence Langer. Langer's embrace of the moral void comes about more subtly. Moved by a quite proper concern to caution against facile myths of heroism and transcendence on this genocidal terrain, he reminds his readers that the victims and survivors of it were faced with impossible, unspeakable, situations and choices. To read their experience through a grid of familiarly uplifting categories is to distort it, seeking comfort merely for ourselves. It is, in Langer's own words, 'introducing some affirmative values to mitigate the gloom'; or 'using language to create value where none exists'.[15]

There is a valid and important proposition here, but (like many another such) it overreaches itself. It does so exactly at the point where it urges upon us, in place of an easy but false redemptive option, the monolithic alternative of gainsaying *all* affirmative value; or, to put the same thing otherwise, where it urges upon us 'the impotence of the humanistic vision in an age of atrocity'.[16] Langer in fact has made himself the unswerving, the relentless, purveyor of unbroken darkness: the unbroken darkness of the experience of other people, even when these other people for their part say different, finding something in their tortured past positively to adhere or to appeal to. But with the more 'refined' appreciation, the 'superior vantage point', the 'careful' approach,[17] of the one who knows how to reinterpret what is put forth by the victims themselves, Langer flattens out the picture, gently redraws its dualities, now accentuates and now downplays, always to the one effect – to purvey the darkness. He shuts out or belittles any saving chink of light which anyone else, including the survivor witnesses themselves, may have witnessed *for* themselves and brought back with them. And the whole exercise is conducted in what is indeed the most refined, the most precious, of literary accents, producing an atmosphere of lugubrious artifice and a mournful, cultured delicacy that are false (for this reader anyway) to the stark nature of the agonies they are meant to address.

Despite all Langer's efforts to the contrary, there *is* another side to this story. From countless direct testimonies we have the evidence of something else than just moral darkness. It does not cancel or 'balance' the enormous darkness that there is. The calamity of the Shoah is irredeemable. Nevertheless, the evidence is there even in the very depths: of surviving human sympathies; of small acts of mutual help and solidarity; of attempts to preserve dignity, to uphold some values, however much reduced; of affirmations of hope and continuity with tradition, people reaching towards a different past or a better future. These traces of another – tenacious – moral universe are duly reflected by an alternative current within the literature. It is best exemplified in a brilliant and necessary book by Terrence Des Pres.[18]

Now I take Rorty, in his own conversational mode, that of the moral and political philosopher (when he is one), as representing the same position of a certain openness, an openness to progressive hope. His comment which I have quoted on the Holocaust already suggests as much. I go on now to elaborate the suggestion by way of a second and rather unlikely comparison: of Rorty's views with those, this time, not of another philosopher, but of the actor Marlon Brando.

In a short, incidental piece, entitled 'Love and Money', Rorty writes about a visit he made to India:

[I]n the course of this trip, I found myself, like most Northerners in the South, not thinking about the beggars in the hot streets once I was back in my pleasantly air-conditioned hotel. My Indian acquaintances – fellow-academics...honorary Northerners – gave the same small percentage of what they had in their pockets to the beggars as I did, and then, like me, forgot about the individual beggars when they got home. As individuals beggars were...unthinkable. [Rorty is referring to a passage from E. M. Forster in which the very poor are said to be 'unthinkable' – NG.][19]

In a moment I shall say something about the wider context of these remarks. But they bring to mind a sentiment expressed by Marlon Brando in the closing pages of his recent autobiography. Brando describes how, having done what he could during most of his adult life to oppose injustice, since he felt he had 'a responsibility to create a better world', he had more lately become resigned. 'I no longer feel that I have a mission to save the world. It can't be done, I've learned.' His attitude began to change one day in Calcutta. He was on the street with the Indian movie director Satyajit Ray, and 'a sea of children in tattered clothing, broken, blinded, twisted and sick, engulfed us...'. Absentmindedly, unconcerned, Ray gently 'swept them aside'. When asked by Brando how he could do this, he replied that there was nothing else he could do. Selling everything he owned would have only an infinitesimal effect: 'some problems are unsolvable'.[20]

There is plainly a common tendency in these two responses to a similar experience. It is a tendency to objectify human suffering and extreme want, to make them part of an objective, as it were *natural* background, emptying them of their subjective content as the lived experience of other human individuals – individuals whose inner world we can share, in conversation, sympathy or solidarity. With what Brando writes, this tendency all but reaches its limit in fatalistic resignation. Broken children become (via Satyajit Ray) an unsolvable problem. Rorty, however, having registered the same sort of sentiment – which, I observe in passing here, is a component element of the bystander mentality, rendering the suffering of others liveable for oneself by making it unthinkable[21] – steps back. He turns away.

Without being very sanguine about this, he nevertheless voices the hope that somehow, whether by way of new 'scientific possibilities', or 'liberal initiatives', or 'bureaucratic-technological' ones, a way out may be found for the 'very poor' of the planet. Marxism, Rorty avers, was right in its thesis that 'the soul of history is economic'; it was wrong, though, in the vision of a revolutionary transformation from below. He himself thinks, instead, in terms of changes guided from the top down, by (I guess) those who can and those who care.[22] For myself I do not share this top-down perspective, but never mind. Within the limits of the occasional piece that this short essay of his obviously is, Rorty puts forward what is his more general moral–political viewpoint, and it is one still receptive to the possibility of progress. It is resistant to the kind of negative teleology that treats vast suffering as humanity's unavoidable fate.

I want to pose the question now of whether this viewpoint, this progressive commitment of his, has what Rorty and too many others today please to refer to pejoratively as a philosophical foundation. He says not. But I say it does have. And good for it that it does, though not that it does not recognize that it does. I shall need to quote at length here, in order to display some representative Rortian arguments. On the one hand, then:

> [Orwell] convinced us that there was a perfectly good chance that the same developments which had made human equality technically possible might make endless slavery possible. He did so by convincing us that nothing in the nature of truth, or man, or history was going to block that scenario...

Again:

> [W]hat our future rulers will be like will not be determined by any large necessary truths about human nature and its relation to truth and justice...

On the other hand:

> [T]he view I am offering says that there is such a thing as moral progress, and that this progress is indeed in the direction of greater human solidarity. But that solidarity is not thought of as recognition of a core self, the human essence, in all human beings. Rather, it is thought of as the ability to see more and more traditional differences (of tribe, religion, race, customs, and the like) as unimportant when compared with similarities with respect to pain and humiliation.[23]

And again:

> [T]his progress [the spread of the culture of human rights] consists in an increasing ability to see the similarities between ourselves and people very unlike us as outweighing the differences... The relevant similarities are not a matter of sharing a deep true self which

instantiates true humanity, but are such little, superficial, similarities as cherishing our parents and our children...[24]

There are, I submit, two different claims conflated in these and other related passages from Rorty's work. The first claim is that human nature does not supply any telos or destiny driving (or 'pulling') historical progress. The second is that there is no tenable idea of human nature at all that could serve us as a ground of solidarity, or of support for progressive change. I agree with the first claim, but I reject the second one. And, indeed, a central thesis of my book on Rorty is that he himself is not faithful to this second claim, despite the many times he affirms it. Against the backdrop of the post-Holocaust debates which I have sketched above, I shall conclude by arguing that Rorty's philosophical position may be summed up as follows: neither the death of the very idea of a common humanity, nor a secularized theodicy with, at its core, some ideal human nature as necessary historical destiny; but rather a notion of certain shared human characteristics and vulnerabilities – in this sense, therefore, *an* idea of human nature – as the guiding principle for a viable ethic and a (merely) possible future.

Before arguing for this conclusion and indicating ways in which I am critical of Rorty's work, I shall first record an area of agreement with him by offering comment on one widely held assumption in progressive thinking. In *Contingency, Irony, and Solidarity* Rorty writes of 'the dimly felt connection between art and torture'. It is a thought, I must say, that I find troubling, repellent. I would prefer not to have to acknowledge, not to know about, the connection between these two orders of human experience. Rorty himself returns to the thought later in the book, in an essay on Orwell. He quotes the statement of O'Brien in *1984* that 'The object of torture is torture', and draws attention to the similarity with the idea of art being for its own sake.[25] One might also bring in Dostoyevsky here. Ivan Karamazov, in the famous conversation with his younger brother Alyosha, says the following:

> [A]ctually, people sometimes talk about man's 'bestial' cruelty, but that is being terribly unjust and offensive to the beasts: a beast can never be as cruel as a human being, so artistically, so picturesquely cruel...It would never enter its head to nail people to fences by their ears and leave them like that all night...Imagine: a mother stands trembling with an infant in her arms...They [the attackers] contrive a merry little act: they fondle the infant, laugh in order to amuse it, they succeed, the infant laughs. At that moment [one of them] points a pistol at it, four inches from its face. The baby boy laughs joyfully,

stretches out his little hands to grab the pistol, and suddenly the artist pulls the trigger right in his face and smashes his little head to smithereens...[26]

Repellent as it may be, the thought is nevertheless difficult to evade: that creativity, gratuitous enjoyment in it, free exercise of the imagination, play, can be expressed in cruel as well as enriching or elevating ways. This thought bore down on me in attempting, on the basis of the experience of the Holocaust, to reconsider utopian projects – and in particular the one to which I am attached, namely the socialist project – that are conceived by many of their supporters in terms of a future end to significant human evil-doing. One standard feature of this sort of thinking has been the vision of a very expansive sphere of human freedom, of a sphere of nearly unlimited creative possibility.

A shadow, however, is thrown across every such vision by the central depravity of our century. Listen to how some of the survivors of it speak. David Rousset: '[N]ormal men do not know that everything is possible. Even if the evidence forces their intelligence to admit it, their muscles do not believe it. The concentrationees do know...' Livia E. Bitton Jackson: '[I]t was before I knew that there are no limits to human cruelty.' Charlotte Delbo: 'Did you know that suffering is limitless/that horror cannot be circumscribed?' Primo Levi: 'I know that in the Lager, and more generally on the human stage, everything happens...' Elie Wiesel: '[E]vil, more than good, suggests infinity.'[27]

If human freedom and an endlessly inventive imagination can generate great evil as well as great beauty, collective enjoyment, great good, most utopians – socialists prominent amongst these – tend to eliminate the problem by envisaging more or less benign future social conditions as the cradle and nursery of changed future people. But is there not a contradiction here: between the notion of human beings acting at last in *freedom*, and the notion of these same human beings as all but the creatures of their now benign social conditions, effectively just conditioned by them? A feasible conception of progress today needs to come to terms with the likely persistence of some of the less pleasant tendencies and potentialities that are lodged within the characteristic make-up of human beings.[28]

Now, Rorty for his part offers a notion of moral progress as being in the direction of greater human solidarity. How does he commend this to us? Not, so he claims, on the basis of appealing to any human universal, since identification with humanity as such is, he says, impossible.[29] He commends it rather via a sense of moral community: as one might have, for example, with one's fellow nationals or co-religionists, and which one can then try to extend to more and more people by progressively expanding the notion of 'one of us'.[30] Moral sentiment in this is more important than moral rationality or principle.[31] And, as one amongst other kinds of universal, the very notion of a common human nature is to be renounced.

In my book I identify three meanings of the concept of human nature to which Rorty's denials purport to apply: human nature as a set of shared, trans-historical characteristics; human nature as a set of shared, trans-historical *and* species-specific characteristics; and human nature as a set of either one sort or the other which serves us as a moral reference point. I show that he relies, in spite of his own repeated denials, on a concept of human nature in all of these three meanings.[32] Here I will limit myself simply to this very condensed explanation: a commitment to progress in Rorty's sense, the sense of a greater (and greater) human solidarity, cannot do without the kind of universalist underpinning he himself wishes to renounce – and nor does he do without it.

Thus, the simplest thing to say about the suggestion that we should start from our fellow Americans – or whoever – and work outwards from there by expanding the notion of 'one of us', is that the suggestion will either work, and thereby it will undo Rorty's own premises, or else it will *not* work. One can move from fellow Americans, for instance, to Mexicans, Brazilians and then others, or from fellow Catholics to all Christians, and then to Muslims and Jews. But either this process stops short somewhere, so as to leave a 'one of them' that can be contrasted with the 'one of us'; and then Africans, say, or atheists, are excluded from the sense of moral community, and they can go hungry or be massacred for all one cares. This is a strange kind of 'human' solidarity. Or, on the other hand, the process need not stop short, and one's sense of moral community can be extended to all human beings. In this case the identification with humanity as such is not impossible after all. Why should it be? Why, for someone who allows that a sense of 'we' might cover all fellow Americans, and then be expanded? Americans are some 250 million people. With only Mexicans and Brazilians added on, 'we' comes to embrace approximately 500 million people. If this scale of identification is feasible, then so is humanity in general. It is not credible that the relevant limit to human compassion lies somewhere beyond several hundred million people.[33]

The fact is that there are other modes of identification than communitarian ones, and Rorty himself knows what they are. They are the very similarities in light of which he says particularist differences can come to be seen as unimportant. They are things like pain and humiliation, cherishing one's loved ones and grieving for them, and then poetry and yet other things besides. In appealing to such similarities, Rorty appeals to nothing other than the idea of a common humanity.

For much of the time and for millions of people the world has been a harsh, sometimes a terrible, place. 'Nobody has come up with a better project' than that of trying to make a world that would be fit for all human beings. It is to Richard Rorty's credit that he remains attached to this project, some misguided philosophical commitments notwithstanding.

Notes

1 This is the revised text of a paper given to the conference 'Richard Rorty, Politics and Postmodernism', held in London on 30 September 1995.
2 R. Rorty, *Truth and Progress, Philosophical Papers*, vol. 3 (Cambridge: Cambridge University Press), p. 175.
3 R. Nozick, *The Examined Life* (New York: Simon & Schuster, 1989), pp. 237–8. I discuss Nozick's view also in the work cited in n. 4 below.
4 On this issue see N. Geras, *The Contract of Mutual Indifference: Political Philosophy after the Holocaust* (London: Verso, 1998), pp. 83–120.
5 H. Birenbaum, *Hope is the Last to Die* (New York: Twayne Publishers, 1971), pp. 227–8.
6 F. Camon, *Conversations with Primo Levi* (Marlboro, Vt.: Marlboro Press, 1989), p. 68.
7 R. Rubenstein, 'Some Perspectives on Religious Faith after Auschwitz', in *Holocaust: Religious and Philosophical Implications*, ed. J. K. Roth and M. Berenbaum (New York: Paragon House, 1989), pp. 349–61, at p. 355.
8 R. L. Rubenstein, *After Auschwitz: Radical Theology and Contemporary Judaism* (Indianapolis: Bobbs-Merrill, 1966), pp. 46, 65.
9 Ibid., pp. 152–3.
10 Rubenstein, 'Some Perspectives on Religious Faith', p. 355.
11 For a brief account and discussion of views of this sort, see D. Cohn-Sherbok, *Holocaust Theology* (London: Lamp Press, 1989), pp. 15–42.
12 Etty Hillesum, *Etty: A Diary 1941–43* (London: Triad Grafton, 1985), p. 169.
13 Hans Jonas, 'The Concept of God after Auschwitz: A Jewish Voice', in *Echoes from the Holocaust: Philosophical Reflections on a Dark Time*, ed. A. Rosenberg and G. E. Myers (Philadelphia: Temple University Press, 1988), pp. 292–305, at pp. 295–9. The essay is reprinted from *Journal of Religion*, 67 (1987), pp. 1–13.
14 For a brief presentation of this view, see B. Bettelheim, 'Individual and Mass Behaviour in Extreme Situations', in *Readings in Social Psychology*,

ed. E. E. Maccoby et al. (New York: Henry Holt, 1961), pp. 300–10, at pp. 302, 305, 308–9. See also B. Bettelheim, *The Informed Heart* (Harmondsworth: Penguin, 1991), pp. 107–235.

15 L. L. Langer, 'The Dilemma of Choice in the Deathcamps', in Roth and Berenbaum, *Holocaust*, pp. 222–32, at pp. 223, 231; also in Rosenberg and Myers, *Echoes from the Holocaust*, pp. 118–27, at pp. 118, 126.

16 L. L. Langer, 'The Writer and the Holocaust Experience', in *The Holocaust: Ideology, Bureaucracy and Genocide*, ed. H. Friedlander and S. Milton (New York: Kraus International, 1980), pp. 309–22, at p. 310.

17 L. L. Langer, *Holocaust Testimonies: The Ruins of Memory* (New Haven and London: Yale University Press, 1991), pp. 139, 143, 146.

18 T. Des Pres, *The Survivor* (New York: Oxford University Press, 1976). See also A. Pawelczynska, *Values and Violence in Auschwitz* (Berkeley: University of California Press, 1979), esp. pp. 135–44.

19 R. Rorty, 'Love and Money', *Common Knowledge*, 1/1 (1992), pp. 12–16, at pp. 14–15.

20 M. Brando, with R. Lindsey, *Brando: Songs My Mother Taught Me* (London: Arrow, 1995), pp. 461–2.

21 For one powerful representation of such a mental process see Ida Fink's story 'A Spring Morning', in I. Fink, *A Scrap of Time* (London: Peter Owen, 1988), pp. 39–47.

22 Rorty, 'Love and Money', pp. 13–16.

23 R. Rorty, *Contingency, Irony, and Solidarity* (Cambridge: Cambridge University Press, 1989), pp. 175, 188, 192.

24 Rorty, *Truth and Progress*, p. 181.

25 Rorty, *Contingency, Irony, and Solidarity*, pp. 146, 180.

26 F. Dostoyevsky, *The Brothers Karamazov*, tr. D. McDuff (Harmondsworth: Penguin, 1993), p. 278. The final ellipsis is in the original.

27 D. Rousset, *The Other Kingdom* (New York: Reynal and Hitchcock, 1947), p. 168; L. E. Bitton Jackson, *Elli: Coming of Age in the Holocaust* (London: Grafton, 1984), p. 120; C. Delbo, *Auschwitz and After* (New Haven and London: Yale University Press, 1995), p. 11; P. Levi, *The Drowned and the Saved* (London: Abacus, 1989), p. 33; E. Wiesel, *One Generation After* (New York: Random House, 1970), p. 47.

28 For a more extensive discussion of these issues, see Geras, *The Contract of Mutual Indifference*, pp. 83–120.

29 Rorty, *Contingency, Irony, and Solidarity*, p. 198.

30 Rorty, *Contingency, Irony, and Solidarity*, p. 189–98.

31 Rorty, *Truth and Progress*, pp. 167–85.

32 N. Geras, *Solidarity in the Conversation of Humankind: The Ungroundable Liberalism of Richard Rorty* (London: Verso, 1995), pp. 47–70.

33 This paragraph summarizes Geras, *Solidarity in the Conversation of Humankind*, pp. 76–8.

Response to Norman Geras

Richard Rorty

Suppose that Bettelheim and Langer were entirely right. Imagine that there is no other side of the story: we find no evidence of human kindness anywhere in the death camps, but only proof that systematic degradation and starvation will invariably remove all concern for other human beings, leaving nothing but animal desires to find food and avoid greater pain. Would this result make any difference to our future actions? To our self-image?

Perhaps, as his concluding paragraph suggests, Norman Geras would agree with me that it would, or at least should, make no difference to our future actions: we should still strive for the same socialist utopia – one in which no one is ever starved or degraded into animality. But presumably Geras thinks that it would make a big difference to our self-image, to our notion of what it is to be a human being. I think that one can envisage a human utopia – a socialist utopia, indeed – without regarding this utopia as somehow corresponding better to the inherent tendencies of human nature than would a fascist dystopia. Geras doubts this.

Because I am a Humean compatibilist when it comes to free will, I do not see the contradiction Geras sees between 'the notion of human beings acting at last [in utopia] in freedom, and the notion of these same human beings as all but the creatures of their now benign social conditions, effectively just conditioned by them'. Human beings can be free, in the relevant sense, only if they do not have to worry constantly about how to get food and avoid pain. Most human beings have had such worries. In a socialist utopia, none of them would have them. The more benign the social conditions, the freer, nicer, kinder and fairer people have a chance of being. I would be glad to help condition everybody into being as much like that as possible. I figure that if you condition in the right ways, freedom takes care of itself.

Since the only distinctive trait I can find in our species is language-use, I take Humanity to be just as malleable as Life. Nothing in the nature of Life tells us that it is better to be a hummingbird than a paramecium, or better to be an anthropoid than a mouse. But it is. Nothing in the nature of Humanity (nor, *pace* Habermas, of Language) tells us that a socialist utopia is better than a vicious oligarchy. But it is. We know that it is as well as we know anything. There are no more certain premises from which this conclusion might be inferred.

Certain contingent causal sequences, unglimpsable by those who look only at the earlier stages of biological evolution, got us from the paramecia to the hummingbirds and the anthropoids. Certain others could get us to a permanent Gulag – a world in which the vast majority of people were reduced to the condition of animals – or to a permanent Brave New World, or to a permanent socialist utopia. I have no certainty that in such a utopia – one in which there was plenty of everything to go around – 'all inner sources of evil [would be] subdued'. But, as Geras and I agree, it's worth trying. Maybe they would be.

At two points in his essay Geras gets me a bit wrong. He suggests that, in saying that we just have to pick ourselves up and try again, I am analogizing the Holocaust to a 'pratfall'. Actually the image I wanted to project was of somebody who has been viciously assaulted, and is left lying on the ground, by a gang of bullies.

Is such an assault too trivial to be compared to the Holocaust? I do not think it is. The Holocaust was unique, in many respects – notably in that it was the work of a literate, educated and apparently civilized nation, a nation whose citizens we (and they) had expected to be less callous, less cowardly, less self-deceptive and less easily persuaded to indulge their sadistic instincts. In many other respects, however, it differs only in scale from, for example, the sort of thing that still goes on in the prisons of many countries – the sort of prison in which the guards steal most of the prisoners' food and leave discipline to the inmates.

Some of the degraded and brutalized prisoners who survive this sort of prison, like some of the half-dead victims of a gang of bullies, may be able to pick themselves up, resume their lives, and join in the task of creating a better world. Or they may not. They may be broken. They may see no point in asking themselves how to stop breeding bullies, how to create more benign social conditions.

Many of us, like Robert Nozick, have read accounts of the Holocaust and wondered if, indeed, there is any such point. Like Geras, I was moved by the passage from Nozick which he quotes. But in Nozick's case such wonderment has proved a passing phase. He has continued to hope for, and work for, a better world. If he really still believed that 'Humanity has lost its claim to continue', presumably he would not be trying, as he still is, to get people to act better.

Though I think that I entirely understand what moved Nozick to write, 'Humanity has lost its claim to continue', I nevertheless believe that he would have done better to write, 'Who cares what happens to a species members of which were guilty of the Holocaust?' The idea that there is something called 'humanity' which makes a 'claim' seems to me a bad one; I am as suspicious of this formulation as of the idea that 'human nature requires' this or that.

It is not a good idea to think of an entity called 'humanity' which claims or demands. It would be better to think of members of a certain biological species having been able, under favourable but contingent conditions, to make something of that species – and of perhaps being capable of making still more of it. The species did not do anything, any more than it demands anything. The species – considered as the biological differences which enable those, and only those, who can interbreed with us to be capable of using language – is simply raw material which some members of that species have put to use in the hope of creating something better.

That a literate, educated, seemingly civilized nation was capable of the Holocaust may be sufficient reason to conclude that the members of our species are not in fact capable of making much more of themselves than they have so far. It may also be sufficient reason to cease to care whether they manage this or not – to just cease to speculate about whether anything better can be made of us.

Nozick, like Geras and myself, has not in fact drawn these inferences. But doing so would not be a stupid or crazy thing to do, any more than it would have been stupid or crazy to have drawn the same inferences after witnessing the enslavement of Melians, the passage of Attila's army, or the rape of Nanjing. The Holocaust is not the first occasion in history to have made such inferences plausible.

The second point at which Geras gets me wrong is when he says that I think of social change as 'guided from the top down, by... those who can and those who care'. He says that he does not share this 'top-down perspective'. But he should not infer from my view that Marxist revolutions did not work out well (in part because they vested control of production and distribution in state agencies rather than the market) to the conclusion that I prefer things to be done from the top down.

Desirable social change sometimes occurs bottom-up, sometimes top-down, and usually from the combination of both sorts of pressure. It is always far more gratifying to see it happening bottom-up. But it does not behove people nearer the top, like Geras and myself, to wait, deferentially, for those nearer the bottom to make their move. (To take one obvious example, the death penalty has rarely if ever been abolished as a result of a popular referendum; it has typically been a measure imposed by an elite, disgusted by the blood-lust of the masses.)

Let me close with a few more words about human nature. I think that it is possible that some day all members of our species will cease to feel exclusionist about any group of their contemporaries. Racism and chauvinism would, I trust, no longer occur among the safe, secure, benevolent citizens of a socialist utopia. They would use the us-vs.-them distinction only to exhibit their disgust with *individual* criminals and villains. The only *groups* they will exclude will be extinct ones (the Nazis, the audiences in the Coliseum, the old-time capitalists, and the like). But, unlike Geras, I would not say that these tolerant and kind people will be displaying an 'identification with humanity as such'.

The latter phrase strikes me as obscuring the difference between general benevolence (a state of mind perhaps capable of being produced by security, wealth and suitable conditioning) and intellectual conviction produced by reflection. Such security, wealth and conditioning seem to me feasible projects, but I do not know how to reflect on whether to identify with humanity as such. I have been, I am happy to say, conditioned into constantly regretting that I am less sensitive and tolerant than I might be. Yet the word 'humanity' leaves me cold, as do arguments that my conditioning was more 'in accordance with reason' than the conditioning received by the Hitler Youth.

I was convinced by the first chapter of Geras's *Solidarity in the Conversation of Mankind* that the opening pages of the last chapter of my *Contingency, Irony, and Solidarity* (about the people who helped the Jews avoid the Gestapo) were misguided. I think I overstated my case in those pages, and now regret them. But I remain unconvinced – either by the remaining chapters of Geras's book or by his contribution to this volume – that there is good use to be made of the notion of 'human nature'.

Once this notion has been cleansed of ahistoricist essentialism, it seems to me to signify little more than 'the ability to use language, either to make things better or to make them worse'. The term 'inhuman', like the term 'irrational' has been used by philosophers in ways that suggest that they somehow know more than most about our species, or about our capacities. I do not think there is much of this sort to be known. Once we have recognized our extraordinary malleability, history has no further lessons to teach us about what sort of beings we are. I see no profit in arguing that the bullies are less, or more, truly human than their victims.

9

Rorty's Neo-pragmatism
Some Implications for International Relations Theory

Molly Cochran

International Relations (IR), a discipline once dominated by positivist approaches, has been transformed in the last ten to fifteen years by powerful criticisms from normative, critical, feminist and postmodern IR theorists who attack the bias in the field towards explanation, objectivity, and facts as separated from values.[1] As a consequence the scope of IR has broadened to incorporate philosophy, political theory and social theory, such that writers previously deemed irrelevant or peripheral to IR theory are now receiving considerable attention. Recently, Richard Rorty was one such theorist favourably invoked in an article by Chris Brown (1994). Brown writes that, although Rorty's work has no explicit international orientation, his writing deserves more attention from IR theorists. This essay takes up Brown's suggestion and evaluates whether there is an important role in IR theory for Rorty and the neo-pragmatism he professes.

It is the contention of this chapter that Rorty's writings *are* relevant to IR. His discussion of each of four issues – liberalism, anti-foundationalism, the implications of liberalism and anti-foundationalism for human rights, and the call to extend our 'we' group – holds significance for IR theory. Moreover, together, their consideration has particular import for a subfield within IR theory, normative IR theory and its two ethical approaches: cosmopolitanism and communitarianism. I believe that it is in relation to the framework of the cosmopolitan/communitarian debate that the significance of Rorty's work may be most strongly developed. There are two reasons for this. First, Rorty has contributed to a debate within political theory between liberals and communitarians, which resonates with the debate in IR theory.[2] Second, through his discussion of an issue central to IR theory, human rights, we may enquire where a liberal, yet anti-foundationalist, ethic might take us and whether it might help to move normative IR theory beyond its cosmopolitan/communitarian impasse. To begin, I want to briefly touch upon the four issues mentioned above, their relevance to IR theory, and their connection to Rorty's work.

Liberalism is a topic much discussed within recent IR theory.[3] Since the events of 1989 the victory of liberalism and liberal democratic institutions has been discussed in tones ranging from the triumphal to the matter-of-fact. Francis Fukuyama's (1992) much-debated 'End of History' thesis draws the finishing line of history, placing liberalism as the political ideology first and last to cross the marker. Rorty writes in a similar vein, pointing to contemporary liberal society and suggesting a conceptual end of history; we in the West have perhaps had our last revolution of concepts within social and political thought (Rorty 1989a: 63). Rorty too is a convinced liberal, yet what is key to Rorty's discussion of liberalism is captured by the way in which he contextualizes this revolution. It is limited to Western thought and does not suggest that the world requires no more political revolutions (Rorty 1989a: 21 n. 63). Rorty's utopian vision of liberalism and its ironic politics is far from conventional and not without controversy, but it is interesting to IR theory because of the way it contextualizes the good offered by liberalism.

A second theme in Rorty's work, anti-foundationalism, is also relevant to IR theory. Richard Bernstein points out that anti-foundationalism has been building steam in political and social theory for the last 150 years (Bernstein 1991: 288). IR has not been able to avoid its momentum. As Steve Smith writes, the debate between foundationalism and anti-foundationalism is 'the fundamental normative issue' in the discipline of IR (Smith 1992: 505). It is also the question which is behind the crisis of modern thought that Chris Brown (1994) identifies as a source of division among contemporary IR theorists. Rorty is a principal contributor to the momentum of anti-foundationalism. For Rorty our starting point should be the recognition that the 'link between truth and justifiability' is broken (Rorty 1991: 176). A closer look at Rorty's anti-foundationalism could offer further insights into whether IR theory should take anti-foundationalism seriously, what the repercussions might be if we do take it seriously, and how IR theory might then proceed.

Rorty espouses the two seemingly contradictory projects of anti-foundationalism and liberalism. It is the aim of his writing to persuade us of their compatibility. In a recent article, 'Human Rights, Rationality, and Sentimentality', the implications of these two projects are played out in his discussion of the third issue mentioned above, human rights (Rorty 1998). Human rights, a tenet of liberal theory valued by Rorty and by the large number of us who participate in what Rorty understands to be a 'human rights culture', cannot be regarded as natural, universal or ahistorical. This represents an interesting turn on how human rights are generally discussed and how they can be defended in IR. It also provides us with a good case for examining the repercussions of such an anti-foundationalist position in world politics. Ultimately the conclusion which results from this piece on human rights is consistent with that drawn in *Contingency, Irony, and Solidarity* (*CIS*) and other articles: an ethic which calls for the extension of our 'we' group, those with whom we have sympathy. This fourth issue, the extension of 'we' feeling, is of particular import to normative IR theory as it is a sentiment which has no regard for boundaries, and thus has implications beyond state borders. Unfortunately Rorty shows no interest in exploring the repercussions of this ethic for IR or its ethical approaches. It is left to IR theorists to evaluate.

It is important that the implications of Rorty's ethic for normative IR theory be developed, particularly for normative IR theory and its two ethical approaches. The cosmopolitan/communitarian debate presently rests in a condition of stasis. The positions taken in the debate are seen to be irreconcilable, with no available means for reaching conclusions. One might regard this impasse as disconcerting, and contend that a resolution must be found, and that grounds or criteria must be settled, in order for any normative judgements or critique of intersocietal relations to be offered. However, Rorty's anti-foundationalism suggests another possible response – that the search for justifiable grounds and the oppositions that this search generates are a non-starter for critique. This essay proceeds in the first section by introducing the cosmopolitan and communitarian positions in normative IR theory. The second section offers an analysis of Rorty's relation to the debate and its three central issues. The third section examines Rorty's discussion of human rights and evaluates the resulting ethic of his work on its own merits and for its significance to normative IR theory.

The cosmopolitan/communitarian debate

The core tension that fuels the cosmopolitan/communitarian debate concerns the nature of ethical relationships in international relations between individuals, of individuals to states, of states to individuals and of states to other states. Should individuals or states be the subject of justice and ethical consideration in normative IR theory? How do we determine ontological priorities regarding individuals and states? This core tension was identified and labelled as the cosmopolitan/communitarian debate by Chris Brown (1992) and Janna Thompson (1992). Brown and Thompson provide a frame of reference for categorizing the ways in which writers such as Michael Walzer (1977), Charles Beitz (1979), Mervyn Frost (1986), Thomas Pogge (1989) and Andrew Linklater (1990), characterize the project of normative theorizing in IR. This framework has taken hold, with the cosmopolitan/communitarian debate informing and constructing the ways in which much of normative theory is thought and written about in IR at present. Cosmopolitans and communitarians offer dissenting views on three central issues: a concept of the person, the moral standing of states and the question of universalism versus particularism.

Regarding the first issue, a concept of the person, this concerns the nature of the individual and how the individual is constituted. Cosmopolitans, like liberals in political theory, attribute to the individual a capacity to choose one's life, unencumbered by social attachments. The person is born with this capacity which, as cosmopolitans stress, constitutes a right *qua* humankind that is essential to the moral development of individuals: that is, their moral personality. The communitarian takes issue with the cosmopolitan's pre-social concept of the person. Instead, the person is constituted by the social matrix of which one is a member. The moral ends chosen by individuals under a cosmopolitan understanding are empty, since they are not grounded in the shared meanings and commitments of community membership. Thus the development of moral personality hinges upon the expression and pursuit of goods within a community.

The question of the moral relevance of states concerns whether states and the present state system promote or impede the individual's personal development. A stance on this issue follows from the ontological assumptions within a concept of the person, because with such a concept comes a notion of the social arrangements required by that understanding. For the political theorist what would follow is a consideration of how the domestic polity is to be arranged; whereas, from the perspective of international relations, an IR theorist is led to ask what intersocietal arrangements are required by this concept of the person. To the cosmopolitan, who regards the person as morally free to choose social attachments, the autonomy of states in world politics has no normative relevance. For the communitarian, it is in the sovereign state that ethical duties are made possible, where the individual may achieve freedom and self-realization in identification with a social totality. Thus, the sovereign state is morally relevant because it is necessary to the development of the individual as a free person.

The universalism versus particularism question concerns whether there is a standard by which ethical judgements can be made across plural conceptions of the good: cosmopolitans seek a standpoint for judging ends offered by morally equal individuals; whereas communitarians focus on the ends of morally equal communities, questioning whether those ends can be evaluated by the same measure. Thus the epistemological question of grounds or foundations for ethical critique in international relations is raised. To mark again the point of difference between the debates in political theory and international relations theory here, the political theorist interested in this issue would limit such a standpoint to judging the plural ends chosen by morally equal individuals within a domestic arrangement and whether they can hold universally or particularly therein; whereas in IR this quite obviously has a global dimension, even for communitarians. Since the cosmopolitan understands each individual to be capable of forming a conception of the good, establishing such a foundation is an obstacle *within* and *between* states because there are no rational means of choosing among the ends of morally equal individuals when they come into political conflict. Thus the cosmopolitan attempts a solution through the construction of a detached standpoint from which we can transcend the particularism of plural goods. This method clears the way for the universal claims to the entitlements of humankind which cosmopolitans are wont to make. For the communitarian, values, ends and goods fostered in the state constitute tradition. Social tradition within the state is the framework which founds and enables ethical discourse. Consequently grounds for ethical critique are not at issue *within* states, but there is a problem *between* them as the world cannot be conceived as a single community whose tradition shapes or constitutes the individual. This raises, for the communitarian, the problem of how a standpoint for judging among states' plural conceptions of the good can be offered.

As with the debate between liberals and communitarians in political theory, possibilities for accommodation are evident across the issues that divide normative IR theorists. However, there remains a structural opposition regarding the correct or proper foundation for justifying ethical claims in international practice. I contend that what often appears to be the most intractable of the three issues of the debate, the tension of the universal (claims for humanity) versus the particular (claims for states on behalf of their citizens), reveals a more important underlying question about *how* to ground the ontological positions at work in cosmopolitan and communitarian argument. Therefore the nature of the impasse is epistemological. In particular, what is at stake in this impasse is not the universal or particular *scope* of moral claims, but *the way they are put forward*: that is how you justify and enforce your claims.

It is for this reason, the epistemological nature of the impasse of the cosmopolitan/communitarian debate, that I find Rorty particularly significant for normative IR theory. The cosmopolitan/communitarian debate is embedded in the context of a wider debate in the social sciences about modernist, foundationalist epistemologies. The social sciences have experienced an onslaught of critiques which challenge the search for foundations or grounds for ethical judgement that hold absolutely and universally. To all intents and purposes, participants in the cosmopolitan/communitarian debate do not seriously acknowledge these critiques or their implications for their own work. In focusing on how to determine ontological priorities regarding individuals and communities, normative IR theory has left undertheorized its own epistemological assumptions, epistemological assumptions that are at the heart of the impasse between cosmopolitans and communitarians. Should normative IR theory shift its attention instead to interrogating whether, in fact, it should be engaged in foundational thinking when offering ethical positions in international relations? Through Rorty, normative IR theory can explore what anti-foundational approaches might suggest for international ethics in contrast to the foundationalism of cosmopolitanism and communitariansim. Rorty can also facilitate important reconsiderations of possibilities for interplay across each of the three issues of the debate.

Reflected through a Rortian lens: the cosmopolitan/ communitarian debate

Rorty does not directly address the cosmopolitan/communitarian debate within normative IR theory, but he does offer commentary on its counterpart in political theory. In particular Rorty, in his article 'The Priority of Democracy to Philosophy', seeks to defend John

Rawls against his communitarian critics (Rorty 1991). Drawing upon this article and other writings, and taking each issue of the debate in turn, I will offer an account of what Rorty contributes to the debate in normative IR theory.

A concept of the self

In line with his anti-foundationalism, Rorty argues that there can be no objective notion of what it is to be human. The self is created. The self and its nature are not out there waiting to be found, existing independently of social practice. The self is no more than a 'centerless web of historically conditioned beliefs and desires' (Rorty 1991: 192), 'constantly reweaving itself . . . not by reference to general criteria . . . but in the hit-or-miss way' of cells reacting to their environment (1991: 199). Historical circumstance shapes the self, and any number of arbitrary things can form identity. A self is a 'contingent web to those with similar tastes and similar identities' (1991: 192). Thus Rorty's position is similar to that of the communitarians who understand the concept of the self to be shaped within the historicity of the social matrix.[4]

Although Rorty shares with communitarians the belief that selves are shaped rather than discovered, he sets himself apart from the communitarians by attributing to them a presupposition that societies are founded upon a concept of the self, and that liberal theory holds an incorrect concept of the self (Rorty 1991: 178). This raises the question of whether liberal society requires justification, which, for Rorty, is a rather modernist, philosophical request. He writes that no idea of the self can serve as a foundation for liberalism, and there is little point in demanding such a theory. He suggests that, should one need such a theory, his picture of the self as a 'centerless web' suffices, but the point is that talk of a self need 'rarely occur' (1991: 192). While Rorty may write that talk of the self is unnecessary to social science, it does make numerous appearances in his work, and not simply in reference to its obsolescence.

Always the pragmatist, Rorty suggests two benefits of understanding the self to be a 'centerless web'. As there is no intrinsic self, one benefit is that there can be no 'natural order of justification of beliefs'. Secondly, questions about to whom we need to justify ourselves are left to public, political deliberation (Rorty 1991: 193). In connection with the benefits of such an understanding, Rorty also raises a practical point. He asks whether a historical understanding of the self makes a better fit with liberal democracy than does the Enlightenment rationalist conception. Again, it is written in the tone of an option; 'if we *want*' to answer such a question, then the communitarians are correct to believe that their concept of the person works well with liberal democracy (1991: 179).

In voluntarily offering a concept of the self, in a 'take if you need it fashion', Rorty maintains his anti-philosophy by refusing to impose a metaphysical ground for a concept of the person. Nonetheless, there is a notion of the self on which Rorty's ideal liberal society is built: the liberal ironist. He attributes to the liberal ironist a will to freedom through self-creation, and the need for the solidarity of a 'we' which implants self-doubt. Thus, in his discussion of a liberal utopia, Rorty is led to draw attention to certain attributes of human nature that he deems integral to this project. Two points with significance for the cosmopolitan/communitarian debate and its epistemological impasse should be noted for the time being. First, it is interesting that Rorty's anti-foundationalism does not prevent him from suggesting a concept of the person, or from constructing a notion of an improved liberal society upon that understanding. The liberal ironist serves as a ground of sorts for his project, despite his protestations against foundation-alism. Second, Rorty's concept of the person is one which bridges cosmopolitan and communitarian understandings. As noted above, his idea of the person as a 'centerless web' has affinities with the communitarian understanding of the social construction of the person. Yet what is also evident, particularly in his discussion of the liberal ironist in *CIS*, is that he attributes to individuals the capacity and the will for their own self-making. He writes that, most import-antly, the ironist wants to be free of 'the metaphysical urge' so that he can say, 'the last of his final vocabularies...really was wholly *his*' (Rorty 1989a: 97). Thus for Rorty persons are socially as well as personally chosen, indicating there is interplay between the two pos-itions on this issue of the debate.

The moral status of states

As noted above, Rorty offers no commentary on states or sovereignty, nor on the morality of states. Nonetheless, he does acknowledge and discuss the dilemma which I take to be the crux of the debate on the issue: 'whether our self-description ought to be constructed around a relation to human nature or around a relation to a particular collec-tion of human beings' (Rorty 1991: 24). The way we describe our-selves is integral to the question of the moral status of states, since those self-descriptions suggest social forms appropriate to such an understanding. For the cosmopolitan, the autonomy of states and/or communities has no normative relevance, because our particular social attachments are not primary to the meaning we accord to our lives. However, the species as a whole is primary, and cosmopolitans claim that communities/states are an obstacle to this moral identification. By contrast, Rorty shares with the communitarians the idea that morality exists only in relation to a community. As discussed earlier, the only form of truth is that which results from social practice. It is the result of conversation which is free and open. Thus the community is morally significant since it is the locus of moral authority, the site where truth is made. Rorty writes that irrationality in ethics 'is a matter of behaviour that leads one to abandon, or be stripped of, membership in some such community' (Rorty 1991: 199). As he argues in 'Solidarity or Objectivity?', he clearly prefers a narrative of one's relation to a community, not to humanity, as the way in which we describe ourselves and make sense of our lives (Rorty 1991).

As it is the aim of the liberal ironist to diminish cruelty, Rorty shares a concern with cosmopolitans for human dignity. Cosmopolitans, like the Kantians discussed by Rorty in 'Postmodernist Bourgeois Liberalism', have a belief in 'intrinsic human dignity, intrinsic human rights'. However, Rorty allies himself with the Hegelians, writing that human dignity is the product of communities, and that human rights can only be born of societal tradition (Rorty 1991: 197, 200). Rorty is careful to distinguish human solidarity from humanity. Solidarity is strongest as an expression of ' "one of us", where "us" means something smaller and more local than the human race' (Rorty 1989a: 191). One's sensitivity to the pain of others is the substance of solidarity for Rorty, but this solidarity cannot extend to the whole of humanity. As Rorty cannot envision the world as a moral community on the basis of our common humanity, he denies the core assumption of cosmopolitanism. Yet, while denying a non-parochial, human solidarity, Rorty does share the cosmopolitan impulse to extend human solidarity as wide as possible. He writes that we are 'profoundly grateful to philosophers like Plato and Kant...because they prophesied cosmopolitan utopias' (Rorty 1998: 173). Although they may have been wrong, they gave us something worthwhile for which to aim. Rorty sees solidarity as 'not discovered by reflection, but created' (1989a: xvi). Thus, with the help of liberal ironists, we can work, through literature, metaphor and imagination, to increase our sensitivity to cruelty, thereby expanding our notion of 'we'.

Rorty has given thought to the central problem behind the moral standing of states issue: whether or not the community is morally significant to the identity of individuals. However, he offers no indications of the institutional repercussions of an expanding 'we'; that is, whether the state will remain or new institutional forms will arise. Nonetheless, we can draw some tentative conclusions regarding Rorty's position on this issue of states. If the liberal democratic institutions we have are all that we need, as Rorty maintains, then we can infer that the state form in which those liberal democratic institutions are housed holds no moral concerns worthy of mention for Rorty.[5] He would concur with communitarians on two points: first, that moral relations can only be constructed within communities; and second, that the state has moral standing as long as it is the conclusion of free and open encounters within liberal culture concerning its status. If not, then the state's moral status is highly questionable.

For Rorty the cosmopolitan contention that humanity is the locus of moral relations is compromised by the fact that 'we' expansion has its limits, since identity as 'we' requires opposition. Yet Rorty cannot necessarily be seen as lending weight to the communitarian position. There is nothing which suggests that his call for 'we' expansion has regard for state boundaries. It is a 'we' that is built around any kind of practice, metaphor or reading that can construct the necessary sympathy, a sympathy which is not limited to the 'we' formed around a state. Thus, this leaves him open to the idea of moral community beyond the institutional form of the state, although this community will never include the whole of humanity. In sum, Rorty is interested in the question of the scope of moral relations, but not necessarily the institutional form which that scope takes.[6] Nonetheless, it can be argued that Rorty falls somewhere in between the two positions. He does not deny the moral standing a state could have, but he does deny the possibility of humanity as a community, and thus its moral standing. However, he does not limit the possibility of moral standing belonging to a community beyond the state. Rorty cannot easily be assigned to either of the poles on this issue, which raises the question of whether the two positions, as they are presented in the framework of the cosmopolitan/communitarian debate, confine the way we can think about the ethical possibilities of forms of community which are smaller than the state, or between the state and humanity.

The universal versus the particular

Rorty does not opt to argue definitely and conclusively for either a universal or particularist justification of knowledge claims, nor does he attempt to reconcile universal and particular epistemological justifications. Instead, he rejects all forms of epistemologically centred philosophy, forms which are replicated in the cosmopolitan/communitarian debate.

Critique of epistemologically centred philosophy and the call for its reconstruction are central themes in American pragmatism. Rorty devotes much attention to surveying past epistemological strategies with the intention to show them wanting of any 'good purpose'. Centuries of speculation on universals, objectivity, truth, and the numerous dualisms which spin off from the mind–body problem have led us nowhere. Philosophy is in a rut of its own making. Rorty writes that the question raised for the pragmatist is not one of the 'necessary and sufficient conditions for a sentence being true, but precisely *whether* the practice which hopes to find a philosophical way of isolating the essence of truth has, in fact, paid off' (Rorty 1982: xxix). For Rorty, the answer is no. Truth-seeking philosophy has not paid off, and what is required, according to Rorty, is a 'new intellectual tradition' which relinquishes epistemological claims and abandons the intellectual obstacles which philosophy has created for itself.

Is the cosmopolitan/communitarian debate a good candidate for a neo-pragmatist interrogation? Does its impasse represent a real problem? Rorty does not directly address this question for the debate in IR theory, but he does interrogate its counterpart in political theory. In justifying claims regarding the self with reference to human nature (a universalist position), or to one's relation to a community (a particularist starting point), Rorty writes that one cannot 'choose between these alternatives by looking more deeply into the nature of knowledge, or of man, or of nature' (Rorty 1991: 24). This is the mistake of both Kantians and communitarians.

Kantians insist upon an 'ahistorical distinction between the demands of morality and those of prudence' (Rorty 1991: 197). As there is no intrinsic self for Rorty, there is no noumenal, rational self laboured with the imperative to fight against his or her inclination and desire. Also, for Rorty, as goods can only be defined within particular, historical communities, there can be no ahistorical truth or moral law that is distinguishable from goods which are seen to be only instrumental in fulfilling one's desire. Thus there can be no distinction between morality and prudence. Kantians search illusively for objectivity upon which to found their claims. Rorty labels 'realists' those who seek knowledge, wanting to distinguish true and false in correspondence with reality (1991: 22). With the Hegelians and communitarians, Rorty agrees that there is 'no appeal beyond the relative merits of various actual or proposed communities to impartial criteria' (1991: 197).

The Kantians are not the only ones accused by Rorty of demanding correspondence. As discussed above, Rorty writes that the communitarians posit a requirement of correspondence by saying that liberal institutions rest upon a false notion of the self. I do not take this to be a fair representation of the communitarian position. That which Rorty understands to be correspondence is not a correspondence with an external, fixed truth, but simply a requirement that notions of the self or anything else be coherent with community practice.[7] Rorty himself has a concern similar to that of the communitarians when he volunteers his agreement with the communitarian account of the self, that Enlightenment rationalism and rights talk is dead, and that the socially and historically constituted self is appropriate to liberal democratic societies (Rorty 1990: 640). Nonetheless, it is correct to say that communitarians are also involved in epistemologically centred philosophy, as they are equally concerned to play the game of knowledge justification, albeit within the shifting, historical grounds of community.

Indeed, debates between liberals and communitarians, and cosmopolitans and communitarians, are subsumed in the kind of philosophy Rorty attacks, at least in terms of seeking forms of weak foundations for knowledge claims. It is also evident that neither the debate in political theory nor that in IR theory has had any success in confirming one or the other position. The debates are without resolution, leaving theorists either to seek reconciliations between the positions or to make technical points about how the debate is misconceived. Rorty's anti-foundationalism offers a radical suggestion as to how the debate is misconceived. Should we be compelled by the pragmatist argument that, if epistemologically centred philosophy cannot definitively settle disputes about claims to knowledge, then we should consider letting such questions go? To proceed without epistemological starting points is a frightening prospect. Relativism ensues. Without such grounds, how are ethical theorists to begin social critique?

Rorty writes that he can offer no more convincing an argument than to say that the intellectual tradition of philosophy 'is more trouble than it is worth', and that what we have is simply a choice between vocabularies: 'one about whether philosophy should try to find natural starting points which are distinct from cultural traditions, or whether all philosophy should do is compare and contrast cultural traditions' (Rorty 1982: xxxvii). Whether we should, with the pragmatist, prefer the second vocabulary is a question of whether a postphilosophical culture is imaginable and desirable. This means a willingness to see ourselves as never 'encountering reality', but only encountering descriptions of reality chosen and made by us (Rorty 1982: xxxix). Rorty recognizes that the effect such a culture has in repressing the urge of philosophy for final vocabularies is, indeed, 'morally humiliating', and, thus, is a good reason for denying the possibility of such a culture (Rorty 1982: xlii). It is humiliating because it means that we have to acknowledge the circularity of our claims, and see that the principles we profess are based on criteria we have made ourselves. Rorty grants that this is a difficult image of ourselves to take on board. Yet, it is less difficult when we understand that post-philosophical culture does not mean the end of social criticism. It only replaces the philosophical aim of finding truth with the pragmatist's aim of acquiring the intellectual habits which best assist us in coping with the social worlds we make. This is the basis of a cultural criticism which aims not to play the justificatory game of foundational thinking.[8]

I will reserve critical analysis of the ethics that results from Rorty's work for the next section. I want to conclude this section by examining what Rorty's writings contribute to the discussion of the universal versus the particular, and the framework of the debate and its impasse as a whole. Rorty demonstrates that relinquishing epistemologically centred philosophy does not result in relinquishing ethics and social critique. Rorty's recognition of the particularity of his claims – his ethnocentrism – does not mean that claims originating from a single community have no reach beyond that community. Rorty's idea of the expansion of 'we' feeling is possible, because Rorty holds that neither cultures nor vocabularies are irreconcilable, making an absolute, universal rationality unnecessary for the possibility of an overlap of values across cultures (Rorty 1991: 26). Thus claims can have legitimacy beyond particular communities, without recourse to epistemological foundations, through, for example, the shared understanding of a metaphor, which allows scope for enlarged moral inclusion. Therefore, in regard to the third issue of the debate, the universal versus the particular, Rorty illuminates the limitations of the cosmopolitan/communitarian framework. It forces an either/or choice between universal and particular epistemological claims that has yielded few solutions. Similarly, one can draw this conclusion for the other either/or positions of the first and second issues of the debate. There is an interplay or a range that can be invoked in thinking about these questions as opposed to the stark dichotomous choices that the cosmopolitan/communitarian framework forces. Alternatively, Rorty directs our attention to the manner in which an anti-foundationalist position *can* yield ethical claims, allowing for the possibility of claims being both particular and something wider, but how wide or universal we cannot be sure. While I am not prepared to suggest that Rorty's ethic, as it stands, is entirely compelling, his neo-pragmatist approach suggests a way of liberating normative IR theory from the stranglehold of foundationalism and its search for universal, ahistorical, transcultural validity.

Ethics, liberal irony and international relations

Looking at Rorty's work against the backdrop of the cosmopolitan/communitarian debate demonstrates that anti-foundationalism and the will to offer an ethics are not mutually exclusive; as Bernstein (1991: 265) writes, Rorty is a 'passionate moralist'. In this section I will give a brief account of Rorty's ethics and his admitted ethnocentrism, developing the implications of his ethical stance for IR theory by working through his recent piece concerning an issue central to IR theory: human rights.[9]

In 'Human Rights, Rationality, and Sentimentality' ('HRS') Rorty begins by explaining how we are able to turn away from the war in Bosnia. We project upon the Serbs an identity as non-human and animal-like. We separate ourselves from such 'borderline cases' of humanity, making human/animal, adult/children or male/non-male types of distinction (Rorty 1998: 167–9). Rorty discusses the attempt by traditional philosophy to counter these sentiments by establishing that which is universally human. He then finishes the story by writing of the progress made in the twentieth century in gradually replacing essentialist questions with those of self-creation: 'What can we make of ourselves?' (Rorty 1998: 169). Rorty claims that we have created in this century a 'human rights culture'.

Rorty borrows the term 'human rights culture' from Eduardo Rabossi, who makes the argument that the search for foundations, or an understanding of human rights as existing naturally, is pointless (Rorty 1998: 170). The post-Holocaust world has changed us, and shaped us into a human rights culture; we should simply welcome it. Rorty agrees with this characterization. Anticipating charges of cultural relativism, Rorty writes that the claim that human rights are morally superior does not have to be backed by universal human attributes (Rorty 1998: 170–1). Human rights need only cohere with our beliefs. For that reason, as long as a *sui generis* understanding of moral obligation based upon human nature is a part of our culture, the argument against human rights foundationalism will be difficult (1998: 175–6). Again the pragmatist, Rorty offers that it is a 'question of efficiency'. The best argument for moving beyond human rights foundationalism is that we need to get on with the task of 'manipulating sentiments' (1998: 176). The human rights culture which we have owes 'nothing to increased moral knowledge, and everything to hearing sad and sentimental stories' (1998: 172).

Rorty suggests the following necessary conditions towards expanding our human rights culture and making it more powerful. First, we must get on with the business of 'sentimental education', acquainting different people with each other 'so that they are less tempted to think of those different from themselves as only quasi-human' (Rorty 1998: 176). Although Rorty does not develop the nature of the means to this education within 'HRS', it flows naturally from Rorty's project outlined in *CIS*, that is, that metaphor, literary criticism and, as he briefly suggests in 'HRS', powerful media images facilitate sentimental education. The goal of this education is the same as that in *CIS*, namely, to expand our 'we' reference, the 'people like us' (Rorty 1998: 176). Second, part of sentimental education involves ridding ourselves of the condescension of traditional philosophy. We must stop labelling those without moral truth as bad people, and replace this practice with an understanding that the violators of human rights are deprived of two things: security in their conditions of life and sympathy bred by sentimental education (Rorty 1998: 180). Finally, we must simply learn to trust that sentimentality is a strong enough glue to bond our human rights culture.

A question for Rorty's readers must be the following: is the ethnocentricity of liberal human rights culture anything more than self-aware domination without the pretty wrapping of moral universals? To answer such a question one would have to examine the nature of encounters between the 'we' of a human rights culture and outsiders. Rorty gives us little indication of their nature in 'HRS', but there are indications in his earlier work. Against the charge of moral irresponsibility for being unable to 'answer Hitler' (that is, prove Hitler wrong), Rorty offers an alternative account of how he might set about converting a Nazi. It would be nothing more than the attempt to show him the contrast of life in free societies, 'how nice things can be'. Even so, one cannot necessarily refute a 'bully'; 'argumentative standoff' is always possible (Rorty 1990: 636–7). It is terribly unsatisfactory that this is all that a free and open encounter can sometimes yield. Yet, for Rorty, it is better than having universals against Fascists and having them 'turn in our hands and bash all of the genial tolerance out of our own heads' (Rorty 1991: 43). Expanding 'we' consciousness is about looking into the detail of lives which are 'marginal' to our own, and examining their fit with us (Rorty 1989b: 202–3). Thus, in answer to the above question, Rorty's account of an expanding 'we' is a matter of consensus rather than power or domination.

Rorty writes that the 'phenomenon' of a human rights culture may just be a 'blip' in human history. He is unwilling to make any suggestions regarding the permanence of liberal democratic culture. We can hope that contingency will work in favour of our valued practices, but Rorty sees no sure way to move from the 'actual world' to our idealized, 'theoretically possible ones' (Rorty 1989a: 182). Nevertheless, there is room for hope. As mentioned above, for Rorty cultures are not irreconcilable. There is enough overlap that conversation can take place. As long as that conversation is possible, Rorty's 'ideal world order' is possible, as an 'intricately-textured collage of private narcissism and public pragmatism' (Rorty 1991: 210).

Is this 'ideal world order' coherent or desirable? As it stands, with a public/private distinction centrally placed in Rorty's work, I want to argue it is neither coherent nor desirable. Rorty replaces the morality/prudence distinction, which he criticizes Kantians for using to 'buttress' liberal institutions, with an equally artificial private/public split. He has replaced one dichotomy with another, and uses it as a methodological prop to bolster his ideal liberal democratic society, now that the floodgates of anti-foundationalism are down.[10] That irony and solidarity can not only coexist but, indeed, together can improve liberal society rests, for Rorty, upon his defence of a public/private split. Rorty writes that we should give up trying to reconcile the private and public in theory and recognize they can both exist, remaining separate in practice (Rorty 1989a: xv). He anticipates the objection that irony and liberalism are unsuited to a degree that the private/public split cannot overcome, and responds that the demand for coherence is an essentialist, rationalist requirement (1989a: 85–9). The 'why' should irony 'be this and be able to do that' kind of questions in regard to liberal institutions are the ones for which we should stop expecting answers. It is asking 'ironist philosophy to do a job which it cannot do, and which it defines itself as unable to do', that is, to offer non-circular justification (Rorty 1989a: 94). Different vocabularies can coexist within communities, as well as within the same person.

Even if we grant that irony and liberalism can coexist in practice, the idea that they can remain separate can only be imagined through the words of Rorty on the page. Rorty writes of the morality/prudence distinction as an appeal to 'two parts of the network that is the self –

parts separated by blurry and constantly shifting boundaries' (Rorty 1991: 200). Why should those boundaries not be equally blurry for the private/public split? This split, too, suggests divisions within the self between one's ends (the private concerns, particularly irony as it can be harmful to the public), and one's means (a detached public self separate from one's ends) operating on practical, seemingly mundane public considerations.[11] It suggests there is a Rawlsian original chooser in a part of all of us, a chooser rejected by Rorty in an earlier article, 'Postmodernist Bourgeois Liberalism' (Rorty 1991: 199). This public/private split required of the self is sure to be blurred and shifting in the face of the contingency Rorty posits.

My second objection asks how we are to be compelled by this distinction when Rorty himself appears to blur the line. He writes that progress, whether poetic, philosophical or political, 'results from the accidental coincidence of a private obsession with a public need' (Rorty 1989a: 37).[12] Coincidence suggests haphazardness, but the underlying point is that the private and public do interact, however randomly, for our benefit. Granted, Rorty does write that irony is not relevant to politics and can in fact be cruel and dangerous when operating within the public realm. Yet Rorty suggests that the benefits of private irony outweigh its harmful effects, benefits which, despite a private/public split, somehow filter down to public liberal institutions. In *CIS* Rorty posits what I would call a 'trickle-down effect': that the growth of poeticized culture can lead to increased solidarity, strengthening and enhancing liberal institutions.[13] The good of the ideal liberal society is in the hands of the liberal ironists; take care of them and liberal institutions will take care of themselves. The question is, how can Rorty put forward this position without blurring the separation of private and public? The coherence of this distinction is undermined by Rorty himself.

One may argue that I am placing too much emphasis on something which, after all, is offered as no more than a tool. My contention, however, is that when used as a tool it has undesirable political repercussions. To be sure, Rorty talks of this split as a tool which is not an accurate representation of reality, yet he regards it as crucial to his defence of irony and solidarity (Rorty 1990: 641). The public/private distinction is drawn in order to provide for the authenticity of social difference,[14] allowing space for genuine self-creation without public interference, as well as space for the public which is free from the interference of the private creator. Thus the private/public distinction is not something which simply fades into the background. As a tool, it has a prominent role for Rorty. Its use is universalized within liberal culture to provide vital support for his project. While it is a universalism of another guise, methodological rather than epistemological, it has a political effect similar to those aspects of traditional philosophy which he labels as dehumanizing. It puts a natural order not necessarily on *what* we speak, but on *where* and *when* we can speak.

Also, a third objection, offered by feminist theorists, is that the private realm is not a realm of freedom for all. For women such space represents a limit on *who* is actually able to speak.[15] Thus a rather shallow form of authenticity results at considerable ethical cost. Using Rorty's own pragmatic approach, in which tools are offered 'experimentally', this tension suggests that the public/private split as a practical tool warrants reconsideration. Rorty also faces the criticism that his public/private split is elitist, closing off the possibility of critical thought except to those ironic intellectuals in their private space (Haber 1994: 52–6). Discarding the public/private split would make social criticism available to a wider audience and would end the pretence that Rorty's ideal liberal society is open to all, even foundationalists and non-intellectuals.[16]

The question of the desirability of Rorty's ideal liberal society remains as long as the public/private split is in place. I would argue that it is a tool he does not need. As discussed above, he believes that irony exercised within the political is dangerous. Is it, however, as dangerous as he suggests? The postmodernist writers he criticizes for trying to use irony for public purposes (Rorty 1982: 83; Rorty 1990: 64) have not exactly sent tremors through the foundations of liberal democratic institutions. My contention is that irony in the public realm is not as destabilizing as Rorty suggests, as long as community membership is valued within liberal democratic society. I think the better defence for irony and solidarity in liberal society is as follows. As he writes, in evaluating a claim, without recourse to transcultural validity, we are left with the question of whether that claim can be made to cohere with a sufficient number of our beliefs (Rorty 1990: 640). Critique and scepticism have long been a part of the liberal ethos. Oddly enough, it is surprising that Rorty should be asking the 'how' or 'why' questions as to whether both vocabularies can exist simultaneously within liberal culture. Public and private concerns can be separated in some instances, and this is a useful goal, given the political aims of liberal societies, but as a tool, the public/private split works as a hindrance to real political engagement on Rorty's part.

As I see it, Rorty's project can stand without the private/public distinction, and without it, his project just might be desirable. After long and unsatisfactory struggles with the search for a transcultural foundation, there is something quite appealing about giving up the fight, examining the consequences, and seeing that we can still say what we want, with no worse effect. For example, by telling a non-liberal government that there are naturally existing universal human rights, we are no better off or more convincing than saying that, 'from the perspective of my liberal culture, your citizens are suffering at the hands of your government, and that is where I stand'. Indeed, by undermining the universal moral authority of our claims about human rights, we may even serve to enhance our powers of persuasion.

One can extrapolate from 'HRS' that the success of efforts to extend our human rights culture rests in demonstrating the potential power that its principles might hold within other cultures as well. This might mean pointing to tensions, or problematic situations internal to those practices outside our human rights culture – perhaps tensions created by economic freedoms unaccompanied by political freedoms – and illustrating how extending certain human liberties can alleviate or mitigate that tension. I also find compelling Rorty's argument that the degree to which this human rights culture can be found to be persuasive hangs on the humility with which it is presented. It is only as persuasive as its grounds are weak. That is, an important element of this process of persuasion is an assumption that any principle offered can be mistaken and is always subject to revision. This assumption of fallibilism, dear to pragmatists, means that conclusions offered as to how the extension of human liberties might mitigate certain tensions within another cultural practice are suggestions to be tried, to be experimented with, and not to be assumed to be instantly workable, or a permanent solution of any kind.

There is much in this anti-foundationalist ethic of Rorty's that is useful to normative theorists of international relations. However, Rorty's light regard for the political and lack of interest in the material, institutional conditions for realizing ethical or cultural critique rear their heads, and present problems for normative IR theorists on this issue of human rights. There are occasions when dialogue hits a concrete wall and can go no further. Situations arise when time is not on one's side, lives are being lost, and the luxury of gentle persuasive dialogue cannot be had. Often power, not dialogue, is the currency of exchange between cultures. How fruitful, then, are the encounters Rorty encourages? As noted above, Rorty acknowledges that it is frustrating that we have no absolutes – and by this I assume he includes violence and its absolutness – to wield when met with such standoffs. That we can only trust in the persuasiveness of our human rights culture is hardly a satisfactory general response.

True, there are instances when violence is used for the purposes of humanitarian assistance such that Rorty's warning about absolutes turning in our hands and bashing all the tolerance out of our heads echoes loudly. One example is Alex de Waal's identification in the international interventions in Somalia and Bosnia of a new doctrine in international relations that he labels 'humanitarian impunity', which sanctions unconscionable violence, often against those who are the object of protection, in order to fulfil the humanitarian missions of international agencies (de Waal 1997). Thus Rorty's warning is one well taken under advisement. However, are there not situations *when violence has to be considered*? It is on the cusp of tough political/ethical choices concerning particular situations such as this that Rorty has a tendency to lose interest.

Like Richard Bernstein, I remain uneasy with the way in which Rorty seems to put discussion of the political on hold; that to whom we justify ourselves, to whom we should listen, and who has the power to enforce claims is left to reflective equilibrium,[17] at the time these issues meet in public conversation (Bernstein 1991: 243). I think Rorty's light regard for the political is reflected in three ways that become issues for normative IR theory. First, it is reflected by the way in which Rorty offers the tool of the public/private split without fully acknowledging its political implications; second, in the lack of development of the potential institutional implications of his expanding 'we' group; and third, in his refusal to consider and engage with problems of power and stalemate when they obstruct the expansion of a human rights culture.[18]

However, it remains that there is much in Rorty's work for normative IR theory to explore and from which it can benefit. Most important, Rorty's anti-foundationalism suggests that the impasse of normative IR theory is an impasse of its own making that need not be in the way of normative theorizing in international relations. International ethics can work free of foundational thinking and, should it choose to do so, it would facilitate thinking in terms of *ranges* rather than oppositions in regard to questions about persons, states and the scope of their claims. Moreover, while it may be alarming to work without a structure of universals or absolutes in international ethics, particularly in situations of power or crisis as discussed above, there is nonetheless reason to believe that Rorty's unique take on the promotion of human rights, free of claims to their naturalness, may be the most workable. Granted, it requires time and a particular context that can afford the slow, plodding process of persuasion and argument, but in casting aside the arrogance of foundational thinking it may work to provide the strongest basis available for long-term efforts in securing a key tenet of international ethics: the expansion of moral inclusion.

Notes

1 A good account of this critique in the discipline of IR is Hollis and Smith (1991). Two earlier critiques of the positivist bias in IR which also make a call for a more central place in the discipline for normative theory are Frost (1986) and Hoffman (1985). Another, and more recent, argument that IR theory must move away from positivism can be found in Neufeld (1995).

2 As will be discussed further below, the debate in political theory shares two central concerns with cosmopolitans and communitarians: a concept of the person and the question of universalism versus particularism. The issue of the moral standing of states sets the two debates apart, as this is an issue for the debate in IR theory only.

3 For a recent sample of IR interest in liberalism, see Hovden and Keene (1995).

4 Communitarians are frequently criticized for failing to offer any account of the substance of the self's social construction, its critical features, or how it takes place. It is interesting to note that one can infer that Rorty would answer that there is no way to account for the social construction of the individual. Borrowing from Sigmund Freud, he writes that 'any seemingly random constellation of such things [sound of a word, colour of a leaf, feel of skin] can set the tone of life' (Rorty 1989a: 37).

5 In the conclusion of 'Rationality and Cultural Difference' (1998: 201), Rorty briefly mentions work undertaken towards building a 'multicultural global utopia'. I do not think that this undermines the inference regarding states that I have made here, since utopias by their nature are unattainable, and like solidarity among humanity, a 'multicultural global utopia' is a good goal, but, according to Rorty, is unrealizable. What *does* possibly undermine this inference is Rorty's 'luck of history' thesis that no vocabularies, cultures or institutions presently valued are guaranteed to be permanent. Thus Rorty would not say that states are a permanent feature of world politics, nor that their moral status is invulnerable.

6 This is one indication of the lack of political engagement on the part of Rorty to be discussed later in the chapter.

7 Rorty also attributes communitarians with the prediction that society cannot survive the end of ahistorical moral truth (Rorty 1991: 177). On the contrary, one liberal communitarian writer, Michael Walzer, often charged with relativism (as is Rorty), employs a particularist method to defend liberal institutions in his book *Spheres of Justice* (1983).

8 However, it cannot help but rely upon a ground, however weak – the liberal ironist self. This, in itself, does not undermine anti-foundationalism. Without some such basis for critique, an ethics would not be possible. More important, and perhaps to the point, is the idea that anti-foundationalism expresses a will to work towards as clean as possible a separation from epistemologically centred thinking as can be made, although it is never regarded as entirely successful.

9 Rorty does invoke Cold War concerns as part of the eight theses shared by his 'we' group. He writes that 'Soviet imperialism is indeed a threat', and there probably will be 'a steady extension of Moscow's empire throughout the Southern Hemisphere' (Rorty 1990: 566). In terms of evaluating what Rorty has to offer IR theory, I do not think that these comments hold much interest. They are indicative of an outmoded liberal rhetoric that can be given the benefit of post-Cold War doubt. It may be that Rorty's personal history strongly influences the strident tone he uses in these passages, as his parents were committed Trotskyites who housed one of Trotsky's secretaries after Trotsky was assassinated in 1940 (see Rorty 1992).

10 It should be noted here that, while Rorty adopts pragmatism as his general framework for philosophical thinking, he does not endorse Dewey's claim to offer a method for a reconstructed, non-epistemological philosophy. Thus he would not agree that his use of the public/private split serves as a methodological tool (see Rorty 1991: 63–77). Nonetheless, I would argue that Rorty *does* offer such a method, however qualified, in his suggestions regarding how new metaphors are created, and in his use of the public/private split to support the project of the liberal ironist.

11 When asked in an interview why he would reassert the public/private distinction, given his praise of Dewey's dismissal of such distinctions, Rorty responded that he does not see it as the kind of distinction Dewey wanted to overcome (Rorty 1989b: 202). I disagree. Dewey, in my view, is attempting to bring the private and public of liberalism closer together, since he sees the reconceptualization of individuality as a socially connected self to be necessary to the organic, participatory democracy he envisions. Dewey writes that his own definitions of the public and private are 'in no sense equivalent to the distinction between individual and social' (Dewey 1927: 13).

12 This is echoed in Rorty (1982: 158).

13 Nancy Fraser (1990) criticizes Rorty for holding the view that irony or radical theorizing is antithetical to politics. She argues that Rorty thereby leaves no place for radical theorizing in the political sphere, and, in effect, 'homogenizes' it. I am arguing that while Rorty sets up the public/private split for the reason Fraser states, he does not consistently maintain this position, and in fact stakes progress on their intermingling. Consequently, radical theorizing is not barred from the public sphere. The improvement of liberal institutions requires, as he writes, that private obsession meets with public need.

14 I want to thank Chris Brown for this point about authenticity. Moussa makes a similar point (see Moussa 1991: 308).

15 For feminist critiques of Rorty's use of the public/private split, see Fraser (1990); Haber (1994). However, in 'Feminism and Pragmatism' (1998) Rorty argues that pragmatism *is* well suited to assisting the agenda of feminism. J. M. Fritzman (1993) writes that since 'Feminism and

Pragmatism', Rorty 'has obviated' most of the feminist critiques, particularly as he makes clear in this piece for the first time (I argue that it is evident in earlier work) that the public and private do meet. Nonetheless, I maintain that as long as the methodological straw man of the public/private split is left in place by Rorty, the feminist critique has force.

16 The problem that remains in Rorty's work is what appears to be a split-level theory of agency. In some inexplicable manner, intellectuals are not socialized all the way down, as are non-intellectuals, and thus only intellectuals are capable of social criticism.

17 Rorty invokes reflective equilibrium, a notion suggested by Rawls (1971), which describes a state reached when 'a person has weighed various proposed conceptions and he has either revised his judgements to accord with one of them or held fast to his initial convictions' (Rawls 1971: 48).

18 On these points, it may be helpful to refer to Dewey. He was deeply engaged in the political and, perhaps, as a consequence: (1) in no way promoted a public/private split, and (2) discussed the implications of his moral concern for growth via the reconstruction of philosophy for the nation-state. However, Dewey represents no vast improvement when it comes to considerations of power. Indeed, it may be said that power is generally undertheorized within pragmatism.

References

Beitz, Charles 1979: *Political Theory and International Relations* (Princeton: Princeton University Press).

Bernstein, Richard 1991: *The New Constellation: The Ethical-Political Horizons of Modernity/Postmodernity* (Cambridge: Polity).

Brown, Chris 1992: *International Relations Theory: New Normative Approaches* (New York: Columbia University Press).

Brown, Chris 1994: '"Turtles All the Way Down": Anti-Foundationalism, Critical Theory and International Relations', *Millennium: Journal of International Studies*, 23/2, pp. 213–38.

de Waal, Alex 1997: 'A Brutal Peace', *Guardian*, 30 October.

Dewey, John 1927: *The Public and its Problems* (Athens, Ohio: Swallow Press).

Fraser, Nancy 1990: 'Solidarity or Singularity? Richard Rorty between Romanticism and Technocracy', in Alan Malachowski (ed.), *Reading Rorty* (Oxford: Basil Blackwell), pp. 303–21.

Fritzman, J. M. 1993: 'Thinking with Fraser about Rorty, Feminism, and Pragmatism', *Praxis International*, 13/2, pp. 113–25.

Frost, Mervyn 1986: *Towards a Normative Theory of International Relations* (Cambridge: Cambridge University Press).

Fukuyam, Francis 1992: *The End of History and the Last Man* (Harmondsworth: Penguin).

Haber, Honi 1994: *Beyond Postmodern Politics* (New York: Routledge).

Hoffman, Mark 1985: 'Normative Approaches', in Margot Light and A. J. R. Groom (eds), *International Relations: A Handbook of Current Theory* (London: Pinter), pp. 27–45.

Hollis, Martin and Smith, Steve 1991: *Explaining and Understanding International Relations* (Oxford: Clarendon Press).

Hovden, Eivind and Keene, Edward (eds) 1995: 'The Globalisation of Liberalism?', Special Issue of *Millennium: Journal of International Studies*, 24/3.

Linklater, Andrew 1990: *Men and Citizens in the Theory of International Relations* (London: Macmillan; first pub. 1982).

Moussa, Mario 1991: 'Misunderstanding the Democratic "We": Richard Rorty's Liberalism and the Radical Urge for a Philosophical Foundation', *Philosophy and Social Criticism*, 17/4, pp. 297–312.

Neufeld, Mark 1995: *The Restructuring of International Relations Theory* (Cambridge: Cambridge University Press).

Pogge, Thomas 1989: *Realizing Rawls* (Ithaca, NY: Cornell University Press).

Rawls, John 1971: *A Theory of Justice* (Cambridge, Mass.: Belknap/Harvard University Press).

Rorty, Richard 1982: *Consequences of Pragmatism* (Minneapolis: University of Minnesota Press).

Rorty, Richard 1989a: *Contingency, Irony, and Solidarity* (Cambridge: Cambridge University Press).

Rorty, Richard 1989b: interview by Danny Postel, 'A Post-Philosophical Politics?', *Philosophy and Social Criticism*, 15/2, pp. 199–204.

Rorty, Richard 1990: 'Truth and Freedom: A Reply to Thomas McCarthy', *Critical Inquiry*, 16/3, pp. 633–43.

Rorty, Richard 1991: *Objectivity, Relativism, and Truth, Philosophical Papers*, vol. 1 (Cambridge: Cambridge University Press).

Rorty, Richard 1992: 'Trotsky and the Wild Orchids', *Common Knowledge*, 1/3, pp. 140–53.

Rorty, Richard 1998: *Truth and Progress, Philosophical Papers*, vol. 3 (Cambridge: Cambridge University Press).

Smith, Steve 1992: 'The Forty Years Detour: The Resurgence of Normative Theory in International Relations', *Millennium: Journal of International Studies*, 21/3, pp. 489–506.

Thompson, Janna 1992: *Justice and World Order: A Philosophical Inquiry* (London: Routledge).

Walzer, Michael 1977: *Just and Unjust Wars* (New York: Basic Books).

Walzer, Michael 1983: *Spheres of Justice* (New York: Basic Books).

Response to Molly Cochran

Richard Rorty

Molly Cochran's essay covers a great many topics, and so I think it best to try to deal with them separately, rather than attempting an integrated discussion.

The cosmopolitan–communitarian issue I am sorry to hear that people working in international relations find this issue of interest. I wish that it would just go away. If a cosmopolitan is one who, as Cochran says, thinks that we are born with a capacity to choose our lives unencumbered by social attachments, then I have never encountered a cosmopolitan. Surely everybody acknowledges that our acculturation limits our choices of lives? Surely everybody also agrees that communities in which these limits are wider are, all other things being equal, better than those in which they are narrow? I have never understood why Rawls, or anybody else, was thought to have denied that the self is a cultural product. The 'Cartesian self' seems to me a philosopher's fiction than nobody has taken seriously for a long time.

The moral status of states Cochran seems to run together 'state' with 'community' when she says that 'for the communitarian, it is in the sovereign state that ethical duties are made possible'. Surely the tribe can play this role as well as can the nation-state? But if the issue is about whether communities have moral status, then I do not see that one needs what Cochran calls 'ontological assumptions within a concept of a person' to figure out whether they do or not. If 'having moral status' means merely 'are such that damage to them may sometimes be morally blameable', then nobody would deny that tribes, sovereign states, families, corporations, interest groups and lots of other associations of human beings have moral status – simply because harming them harms their members. But what more could it mean? Each of these various forms of association has familiar uses and misuses, but I doubt that international relations theory, or any other sort of theory, can say anything general and useful about the 'status' of any of them.

Anti-foundationalism Cochran treats anti-foundationalism as an 'approach' to ethics and to international relations – as a possibly constructive suggestion. I think of it as just a way of setting certain issues aside. Thus when Cochran says that 'it is interesting that Rorty's anti-foundationalism does not prevent him from suggesting a concept of the person', I am inclined to remark that it doesn't prevent anybody from doing anything except trying to answer some bad questions – questions about how to get more conclusive justification than we have ever been able to obtain. There is no such thing as a specifically 'anti-foundationalist ethics'. An ethics is just a set of views about what people should do, and no position within epistemology or ontology or metaphilosophy could, or should, stop anybody from having such views.

Solidarity with humanity as a whole Cochran thinks I think this sort of solidarity is impossible. I do not. I just think it is very difficult, and likely to happen only when, for example, our race is attacked by extraterrestrials, or when competition between human communities for scarce resources has somehow ceased. It's a perfectly good utopian goal, however.

The obsolescence of the nation-state Cochran says that I offer 'no indications of the institutional repercussions of an expanding "we", that is, whether the state will remain or new institutional forms will arise.' Indeed I do not, but who would be fool enough to make predictions in this area? Pretty much everybody agrees that something like a World Federation would be desirable, but what the emergence of such a federation would do to present nation-states is presently as unpredictable as was, in 1790, the effect of the new constitution on the thirteen American colonies.

Truth-seeking Cochran runs together my view that the nature of truth is not a profitable topic for philosophers to discuss with the view that philosophy should not seek truth. Philosophers, like everybody else, should seek to justify their beliefs. 'True' is the commendatory adjective we apply to beliefs we think better justified than their competitors. So in an obvious sense we could not cease to seek for truth as long as we seek to justify our beliefs to one another. I do not want to 'replace the philosophical aim of finding truth with the pragmatist's aim of acquiring the intellectual habits which best assist us in coping'. The pragmatist's point is that 'finding truth' just is, and always was, the process of acquiring such habits. What is to be replaced is a topic of philosophical discussion, not a social practice.

The public–private distinction   As I use the terms, it's private if it affects your responsibilities to yourself but not your responsibilities to other people. It's public if it affects the latter. I don't see that this distinction is artificial, but I quite agree that it is fuzzy. Your private process of self-creation may result in your deciding that you have more, or fewer, responsibilities to others than you had previously thought. The process of dealing with others will often change your sense of who you are and what you want to be. Fuzzy as it is, however, it seems to me a useful distinction, for it permits us to say: the goal of public institutions and socio-political arrangements should be, in addition to the satisfaction of the usual list of basic needs, to facilitate as large a diversity of private selves as possible. Mill's *On Liberty* seems to me the best defence of this view of public affairs.

When is violence justified?   Cochran says that 'it is on the cusp of political/ethical choices such as this [whether the UN should use violence against e.g. Somalian or Serbian warlords and their followers] that Rorty has a tendency to lost interest'. It's not that I lost interest, it's just that I have nothing special to say. I am sorry the UN used violence in Somalia and glad it eventually did so in Kosovo, but I have nothing to offer in the way of advice about what to do in the next international emergency. I doubt that there is anything called 'international relations theory' whose task it is to provide such advice. When intervention by the international community will make things worse and when it will make things better does not seem to me the sort of thing anybody will ever have a useful general theory about.

10
Pragmatism, Social Democracy and Political Argument

Matthew Festenstein

The political meaning of pragmatist tradition in philosophy, and particularly of John Dewey's copious writings, has recently become an intensively researched and vigorously contested topic for historians, philosophers and political theorists. Does a doctrine with a professed bias for practice leave room for a theoretical account of politics? What is the nature of the seemingly robust yet obscure connection between Deweyan philosophy and social democratic politics? Richard Rorty's recent social and political writings provide, among other things, a clear and provocative response to this babble of interpretation. His scepticism about some of the pretensions of grand theory leads him to reject the abstraction he associates with political philosophy. This scepticism has been tethered to a social democratic conception of politics, as Rorty has emphasized from an early stage, albeit in an unusual way: grand theory should be rejected because it adds nothing to the defence of democratic institutions, and there are other ways of thinking about politics which provide a better intellectual armoury. My purpose in this essay is to offer an account of Rorty's conception of political argument and of *Achieving our Country* as a case study in this form of argument. I go on to compare his conception of political argument to Dewey's, less to show that he is an unfaithful disciple than to suggest that there are problems for a transformative politics which Dewey's intellectual style addresses and which Rorty's does not.

I

Rorty is famous for disseminating and defending a 'broad cultural reorientation towards practice and away from theory and structure'.[1] Practice is understood as prior to theory: for example, the practice of political democracy to the theory of it; the latter provides at best an intellectual gloss on the former, not a rational vindication of it.[2] Such practices are intersubjective activities within which reasons, authoritative descriptions, common conceptions of salience and naturalness etc. may be offered and revised; but there is no presumption that there is some realm outside these practices where truly (practice-independent) reasons and descriptions hold true, leaving 'our inheritance from, and our conversation with, our fellow-humans as our only source of guidance'.[3]

At this very general level, the meaning of this reorientation for political theory seems indeterminate. One possibility is suggested by Rorty's own observation that his views parallel Habermas's arguments for a switch from 'subject-centred reason' to 'communicative reason'.[4] For Habermas this switch requires illumination of the rules which are thought to be implicit in conversations with fellow humans, not merely as a descriptive or interpretative but as a regulative enterprise, which sets out to discover the norms underlying all practices of communication; the norms uncovered in turn suggest the adoption of liberal and democratic political arrangements.[5] But this impulse to 'go transcendental' violates Rorty's conception of the primacy of practice. The rules and norms identified by Habermas do no more than articulate some of the elements of the liberal political morality which he hopes to 'ground'; but they do not represent commitments which are prior to or more fundamental than that morality, and which help to explain why people ought to adhere to it. In doing so it upends the relationship between reasons, norms, values etc., and the practices which they purport to 'ground': 'That shift from epistemology to politics, from an explanation of the relation between "reason" and reality to an explanation of how political freedom has changed our sense of what human inquiry is good for, is a shift which Dewey was willing to make but from which Habermas hangs back'.[6]

The alternative may appear to be a more or less subtle fideism about existing practices, and several of Rorty's earlier critics feared that this was what he embraced.[7] If theoretical discourse does not provide a vantage point from which particular practices may be evaluated, then this suggests that the only reason we have for adhering to these practices, rather than some other set, is an unquestioned faith that these practices are best, or best for us, at any rate. Such a view is not only morally complacent but internally unstable, since the 'practices' (say, representative politics) with which political theorists concern themselves trail questions about their appropriate form, demands and rationale, which can be suppressed only at the price of losing sight of what those practices are. Yet as a reading of Rorty this was askew: his views do not imply an unquestioning faith in the existing form of particular practices. Indeed, as he publicly elaborated his social and political views, it became clear that they rubbed against the grain of such moral complacency; with the end of the Cold War, increasingly so.[8] *Achieving our Country*, and some of the associated political essays and occasional writings, try to carve out a political position which does not rest content with the pieties or drift of contemporary American economic, political and intellectual life.

How, if at all, is the philosophical doctrine of the primacy of practice to be reconciled to a transformative conception of political practice? The interpretation of Rorty as a fideist about existing practices may be mistaken, but it offers an intelligible account of the relation between the scepticism about theory and the practices of political democracy which Rorty claims should be considered prior to any mere theoretical gloss on them. An alternative response says that there is no relationship to be explored: the primacy doctrine has no implications for our understanding of politics at all. Yet this is not Rorty's view either. Instead, he argues for what may be called anti-neutralism, that social and political criticism should not appeal to criteria which try to stand above the fray of ethical disagreement. There is no space outside evaluative schemes in order to make a judgement about the superiority of one or other of them, from some putatively neutral standpoint.[9] Such judgements are necessarily made within some or other scheme. The absence of a 'largest possible framework' or 'permanent ahistorical matrix' which supplies neutral criteria for the ranking of all schemes does not imply that it is illegitimate to assess one scheme from the standpoint of another, and to arrive at valid appraisals: for example, to assess a theistic outlook from the standpoint of an atheistic one.[10] Indeed, part of what it would mean to have an outlook would be that one is committed to appraising others in a particular way, as in the case of the theistic and atheistic outlooks, or liberal and, say, fascist schemes. But these appraisals are necessarily the product of one's own particular, historically conditioned standpoint: 'To accept the claim that there is no standpoint outside the particular, historically conditioned and temporary vocabulary we are presently using from which to judge this vocabulary is to give up on the idea that there can be reasons for using languages as well as reasons within languages for believing statements.'[11]

To this claim Rorty attaches what may (for want of a better word) be called methodological advice, antipathetic though he is to the idea that a methodology can be ascribed *a priori* to some path of inquiry. Negatively, this advice is to reject any appeal to putatively ahistorical standards, but it also has some positive injunctions:

> The import of Dewey's pragmatism for movements such as feminism can be seen if we paraphrase Dewey as follows: do not charge a currently spoken language with being unfaithful to reality, with getting things wrong. Do not criticize it as a result of ideology or prejudice, where these are tacitly contrasted with your own employment of a truth-tracking faculty called 'reason' or a neutral method called 'disinterested observation'. Do not criticize it as 'unjust' if 'unjust' is supposed to mean more than 'sometimes incoherent even on its own terms'. Instead of appealing from transitory appearances to the permanent reality, appeal to a still only dimly imagined future practice. Drop the appeal to neutral criteria, and the claim that something large like Nature or Reason or History or the Moral Law is on the side of the oppressed. Instead, just make invidious comparisons between the actual present and a possible, if inchoate future... pragmatism allows for expanding logical space, and thereby for an appeal to courage and imagination rather than to putatively neutral criteria.[12]

Narrative, redescription and sad and sentimental stories are viewed as the means to achieve a particular moral end, namely, the reconstruction of people's view of their identity, so that the previously repugnant and incontrovertibly other may be accepted as a fellow citizen, comrade or human being: 'The process of coming to see other human beings as "one of us" rather than as "them" is a matter of detailed description of what unfamiliar people are like and of redescription of what we ourselves are like.' But, he goes on, this is a goal most effectively accomplished not by 'theory' but by 'genres such as ethnography, the journalist's report, the comic book, docudrama, and, especially, the novel.'[13]

Achieving our Country exemplifies the attempt to yoke a narrative to the reformation of practical identity. As Rorty puts it, 'the appropriate intellectual background to political deliberation is historical narrative rather than philosophical or quasi-philosophical theory.'[14] It constitutes a sentimental narrative redescribing twentieth-century American leftist thought in the service of Rorty's conception of social hope: that is, it is an attempt to find in the resources of a narrative of this tradition, rather than an attempt to start from a general account of the human good etc., the impulse for a renewed 'moral identity'. The central claim of *Achieving our Country* is that, in order to revive a progressive project, it is necessary to revive a sense of national pride on the American left: it is not only the case that 'only a rhetoric of commonality can forge a winning majority in national elections'.[15] More generally, it motivates policies and campaigns for social justice within the nation-state, which require a renewed sense of national identity as the basis for social solidarity. Rorty of course does not rely on the thought that he is offering an uncontentious description of American nationality. In part, this is because he is not offering a description, in the ordinary sense, at all. *Achieving our Country* embodies an attempt to recapture and to recreate a self-understanding of the national identity of the United States which in Rorty's opinion mobilized the reformist left. This attempt is not descriptive but a project of practical reorientation:

> Stories about what a nation has been and should try to be are not attempts at accurate representation, but rather attempts to forge a moral identity. The argument between Left and Right about which episodes in our history we Americans should pride ourselves on will never be a contest between a true and false account of our country's history and its identity. It is better described as an argument about which hopes to allow ourselves and which to forgo.[16]

Such an account ought not to abandon a sense of 'shame' at some aspects of American history, but it should not be overwhelmed by the sense of shame to the point where it becomes merely 'spectatorial and retrospective', undermining the sense of agency required for a transformative politics.[17] The reformist left of the first half of the twentieth century successfully joined a sense of national pride to a project of social redistribution through political institutions. This claim is made easier to justify by the breadth of the definition: the term 'reformist left' covers 'all those Americans who, between 1900 and 1964, struggled within the framework of constitutional democracy to protect the weak from the strong'; its success lies in the achieved armature of the welfare state.[18] This was challenged and actively undermined by the New Left for whom its predecessor was insufficiently oppositional. In turn, one of the offshoots of this rejection of reformism was what Rorty calls the cultural left, which has shifted the focus of socialism from redistribution to recognition: this takes a wholly justified sense of the hidden injuries which accompany some social identities but exaggerates this into an obsession with identity which ignores growing economic fragmentation and polarization in a simple-minded celebration of 'difference'. The cultural left is variously charged with an obsession with 'identity', an obsession with difference rather than commonality, excessive theoretical abstraction, a 'Gothic' and pessimistic conception of social power, which sees it as omnipresent darkness, a correspondingly magical view of social change as total systemic transformation occurring through unspecified social agencies, and a misguided faith in participatory democracy (the latter shared, as Rorty concedes, with Dewey).[19] Against this Rorty enjoins a blend of utopianism, in the moral project of American national identity, and practicality, understood as a more respectful treatment of the quotidian politics of 'step by step reform'.

Rorty's argument can be seen as part of a broader renewal of patriotic discourse on the part of the left.[20] This renewal is partially influenced by the sense that the tensions between the democratic welfare nation-state and global capitalism are becoming increasingly acute, and that national identity may be mobilized as a force against the 'Brazilianization' of welfare states. The latter is a tendency toward a society in which fluid global and capital markets produce

> a world economy in which an attempt by any one country to prevent the immiseration of its workers may result only in depriving them of employment. This world economy will soon be owned by a cosmopolitan upper class which has no more sense of community with any workers anywhere than the great American capitalists of the year 1900 had with the immigrants who manned their enterprises.[21]

Rorty wishes to re-establish the legitimacy of arguing in terms of the interests of fellow nationals in the face of an instinctive cosmopolitanism on the part of the left (or cultural left), partially because he finds persuasive the thought that in its absence such a discourse may be potently and viciously perverted by a neo-fascist right. Nationalism or patriotism in this form of left argument is thought to help define those bonds of solidarity which have been considered vital in democratic socialist thought: patriotism resolves the question of with whom solidarity should be felt, and is conveniently aligned with an institution which offers the possibility of collective agency against social fragmentation, the nation-state. The picture of Rorty which emerges is far from the complacent bourgeois or frivolous ironist which he is often painted as. Instead, his is plainly an argument on familiar, if now hotly contested, political terrain: how to understand

and assess the relationship of social justice, the nation-state and the global economy.

II

Now Dewey is properly viewed as an anti-neutralist, as is Rorty, but does not follow the latter's positive or negative methodological injunctions. For Dewey any helpful account of political morality cannot start *ex nihilo* but must build from the commitments and beliefs of those to whom it is taken to apply. Philosophy as 'reconstruction' or 'criticism' consists in 'criticism of the influential beliefs that underlie culture ... which considers the mutual compatibility of the elements of the total structure of beliefs'.[22] His claims are meant to be truths of and for modern agents, where 'modern' is seen as a fairly thickly constituted social and ethical identity; one which, for example, embraces the value of individual freedom, even if it does not wholly prescribe what freedom means. But this is not a value which is available or compelling for anyone except those who are appropriately positioned in historical or cultural terms.

At the same time there is a structure to the modern self, which Dewey attempts to describe accurately. In 'The Priority of Democracy to Philosophy', Rorty rejects this project, as 'the claim that political institutions "presuppose" a doctrine about the nature of human beings and that such a doctrine must, unlike Enlightenment rationalism, make clear the essentially historical character of the self.'[23] Yet this is precisely one of the tasks which Dewey saw as necessary and fundamental. For example, in *Reconstruction in Philosophy*, he argues that the 'individualistic school' of England and France in the eighteenth century errs in conceiving of the individual as 'something *given*, something already there', outside of society, and in seeing social institutions as instruments for advancing the interests of pre-social individuals. This form of individualism fails to grasp the constitutive role of the institutional and social environment in shaping individual identity. Social arrangements are not 'means for obtaining something for individuals ... They are means for *creating* individuals'.[24]

Since this is an area where there seems to be a clear opposition of Dewey's practice with Rorty's methodological advice, it is worth examining the latter's grounds for banning the mode of discourse. There are two principal negative claims. The first is that this kind of metaphysical assertion enjoys no priority in practical deliberation; to argue in terms of the self, historically conditioned or otherwise, is to presuppose that there is a 'natural order of premises' in practical deliberation, leading from statements about the self to statements about political action.[25] The presumption of this natural order of premises is nonsensical, Rorty insists: political institutions and actions are not reducible to the philosophical back up which one can ascribe to them. Yet Dewey need not be committed to such a project of reduction, or to the assumption that political values must be derived from a prior account of the self. As Charles Taylor argues, distinguishing advocacy arguments, which urge a political position, from ontological arguments:

> Taking an ontological position does not amount to advocating something; but at the same time, the ontological does help to define the options which it is meaningful to support by advocacy... Your ontological proposition, if true, can show that your neighbor's favorite social order is an impossibility or carries a price that he or she did not count with. But this should not induce us to think that the proposition *amounts* to the advocacy of some alternative.[26]

In other words, arguing in these terms does not presuppose according priority to this mode of argument in the sense that moral and political positions are derived from conceptions of the self, etc. But it does presuppose that the account of the self presupposed by a political position furnishes one dimension in which to assess its coherence.

Rorty's second negative claim is that such conceptions of the self are in any case dispensable in the elaboration of a political theory, adding nothing to the latter.[27] But it is possible to agree that one may eschew articulating any such philosophical anthropology when elaborating a political position while acknowledging that those principles may nevertheless be assessed in terms of the view of human beings, their interests and their capabilities, which they imply. It does not seem to have occurred to Dewey that one could dispense with this kind of discourse. In the absence of this kind of critical scrutiny of conceptions of the individual, freedom etc., there would still exist the conceptions acquired from the surrounding cultural and intellectual environment. His belief was that these conceptions are in fact often incoherent (as he thought the common separation of self-interest and altruism was, for example). Furthermore, prevalent conceptions of the self and freedom often served to bolster existing unjust practices: for example, the view of the self as a repository for desires and interests which are held to be immune from rational criticism; or the idea of freedom as consisting solely in the absence of intentional interference.

This was a dimension of argument which was crucially important for Dewey's articulation of his own liberal socialism. For it allowed him to replace a negative conception of freedom understood in purely legal or formal terms, which connoted 'a capacity to act without being exposed to direct obstructions or interference by others'.[28] This 'negative view of freedom is at the root of the defects of our so-called individualism'.[29] A richer account of the self allowed him to claim that freedom in its 'total' sense consisted not merely in the absence of interference but in 'the power to be an individualized self', a power which may be more effectively realized with the appropriate social conditions.[30] This is why (to return to the argument laid out in *Reconstruction in Philosophy*), once we understand the constitutive role of social environment, it becomes possible to see how 'the interest in individual moral improvement and the social interest in the objective reform of economic and political conditions are identified'.[31] This was found to be 'appalling jugglery' with the concept of freedom by, for example, F. A. Hayek, who was clear as to what was driving Dewey's deviousness: the attempt to locate socialist and democratic commitments at the heart of a political culture which prided itself on individualism.[32] Subsequent neglect of this dimension of Dewey's thinking led later commentators to see in his work, variously, a hazy utopianism or a submersion of questions of principle in an unreflective concern with practical considerations. Neither interpretation survives much scrutiny, but the models of pragmatic social thought which they embody are oddly reproduced in Rorty's own prescriptions for the left.

It was through making central a rich account of the self, then, that Dewey attempted to outflank hard-boiled accounts of the social responsibilities of the American liberal by arguing that the value of individual freedom requires the appropriate social circumstances (and hence welfare and democratic arrangements) for its flourishing. The realization of this idea involves a cultural transformation, rather than merely a redirection in social policy (although the latter may be involved too, of course). The 'problem of freedom and of democratic institutions is tied up with the question of what kind of culture exists; with the necessity of free culture for free institutions.'[33] Democracy does not consist merely in institutional 'machinery', but in the prevalence of habits of tolerance and participation, which may be suppressed in other social spheres: education and (less famously) the workplace were his favourite examples of sites where habits of individuality may be successfully or unsuccessfully shaped.

Rorty's methodological preference for a narrative and utopian style of political argument raises an obvious question, of why this style should be adopted. One answer is that these forms of argument fit better with their subject matter, the nature of moral and political value: there are no neutral philosophical standards with which to judge different political goals and public cultures. This is not only a *non sequitur*; it also allows the ideal of neutrality back in, as it suggests that there is a reason for adopting this methodological outlook which is independent of particular ethical commitments, breaking with the injunction not to 'charge a current social practice or a currently spoken language with being unfaithful to reality, with getting things wrong'. Instead, Rorty's own preference is that anti-neutralism be assessed in terms of expediency, that is, its capacity to furnish desirable consequences. Such expediency may be apparent only in the very long run and not to those who first employ a new vocabulary; but if this vocabulary is to be judged superior to an old one, this superiority consists not in its better picturing the underlying reality but in supplying a way of thinking which improves human life. Dewey concurs: for example, in the essay 'Pragmatic America', having poured scorn on Russell's idea that pragmatism is only an intellectual reflection of commercialism, he suggests that the American 'spiritual estate' has contributed to pragmatist epistemology the conviction (itself much maligned) that the consequences for human welfare are the test of the worth of beliefs. Such an attitude is itself a 'faith', can 'be demonstrated only in *its* works, its fruits'.[34] In both Rorty's and Dewey's formulations this idea is vague in crucial respects: whose judgements count when it comes to assessing the new vocabulary's superiority? And whose interests count, when judgements are made about the improvement of life?

In Dewey's case, his developed account of individuality supplies the relevant standards: 'liberation of the potentialities of members of a group in harmony with the interests and goods which are common' provides the formal notion which is given more specific content in the development of his liberal socialism. For Rorty, dispensing with this sort of discourse, the beginnings of an answer may be found in the thought that it is the utopian dimension of American national identity which suggests responses to these questions, however contested that identity may be. It is striking that Rorty shares with the maligned cultural left an emphasis on the reformation of identity as the underlying and general locus (as opposed to the many practical and specific sites) of social and political change. Rorty's patriotic politics offers not an alternative to identity politics but a particular form of it, based upon the privileging of national identity over those other identities which have also animated the politics of recognition, such as race, economic class, gender and sexuality. This privilege hardly needs unmasking: Rorty's appeal to the necessary conditions for the continued survival of a democratic welfare state explicitly provides the argument for it. What does require more consideration is whether or not this is a form of identity which provides the appropriate grounds for social justice, even if it is invoked only as a more or less rhetorical flourish. Rorty seems to share with the most optimistic cultural leftist the presumption that to assign an identity to someone is to present her with a set of concerns, interests and obligations, which she will find transparently relevant to her. But to impress on someone that she is American is only to initiate an exploration of what that identity means, and means for her: plainly there are many different ideas of what American national identity entails, including (as Dewey was conscious) hard-boiled conceptions, which leave no room for generous social provision. The strategic advantage of Dewey's project in this respect was that it tried to work from – to outflank or undermine – this hard-boiled understanding in order to show that it is only one possible understanding of the individual and of freedom, and that there is an alternative which better reconciles the superficially conflicting claims of individuality and community – better from a liberal perspective, but, as Rorty and Dewey agree, there is no neutral perspective from which this judgement can otherwise be made.

My understanding is that Rorty disagrees with Dewey not merely in his views of the appropriate idiom for political argument but in ethical doctrine, a disagreement which is concealed precisely by the former's refusal to engage in argument at this level of discourse. For Rorty a fundamental question is how to articulate the relationship between individual self-realization and solidarity, once the Platonic and Christian belief that 'the springs of private fulfilment and of human solidarity are the same' is rejected.[35] This is the problem for which the 'liberal utopia' sketched in *Contingency, Irony, and Solidarity* is put forward as a solution. Dewey's presumption is precisely the opposite: that possession of a sense of the common good is required for individual self-realization, and that the task of moral theory is to clear away those social and personal confusions which lead individuals to view self-realization and the common good as necessarily presenting conflicting demands. Unlike Rorty, Dewey did not see his task as to offer a contingent reconciliation of two fundamentally conflicting sources of value, but to show how this apparent conflict between self-interest and altruism was based on a false metaphysical separation of individual and society, and obscured the relationship between more authentic sources of self-fulfilment and the common good.[36]

This is not the place for a ground–up argument (if a successful one can be made) for this Deweyan outlook. But an observation about the disagreement between Dewey and Rorty can be made. What is passed off by Rorty as common sense, once the lumber of the Platonic and Christian error is cleared away, itself turns out to be one contentious ethical position – certainly from Dewey's standpoint. It is an ethical position which is not obviously favourable for the construction of the sort of solidarity which Rorty wishes citizens to acquire: on the face of it, an ethical stance which conjoins individual self-realization and the collective good, rather than one which drives a wedge between them, would better promote this solidarity. Rorty's social hopes seem to be led here by a philosophical presupposition about the relationship between self-interest and solidarity, where his explicit methodological advice enjoins just the opposite. Dewey's ethical stance seems to play an ineliminable strategic role in articulating the content of his liberal socialism, and its difference from the hard-boiled individualism which he thought gripped American political culture.

III

I have explored Rorty's relationship to Dewey not in order to bela-bour him with being at odds with the tradition with which he aligns himself (he is a confessedly opportunist pragmatist) but in order to bring out some of the difficulties in his conception of political argument. Dewey's work shows that what has been called anti-neutralism does not imply the kind of dialectical tactics which Rorty favours, and there is a rationale, grounded in the liberal socialist politics which Rorty and Dewey share, for embracing more 'theoretical' forms of political argument. Indeed, on these strategic grounds, it would be a mistake to identify the idea of 'theory' with that of the Gothic cultural left: it is hard to see how an extensive and optimistic conception of social obligation can be helped by simply eschewing the 'criticism of the influential beliefs that underlie' the public cultures of modern democracies. The meaning of individualism seems to me just as much a question in Rorty's epoch of globalization as it was for Dewey.

Even if one can accept that there is no plausible account of progress which can now unproblematically rest on appeal to 'deep underlying forces – forces that determine the fates of human communities', the forces themselves remain as potent as ever, as in the phenomena of globalization and the apparently evaporating sovereignty of nation-states which provoke Rorty.[37] Rorty has done as much as any other thinker to undermine the epistemological certitude behind grand narratives of social progress. In the face of this, one response for political thinking which hopes to extend what is vital in socialism is to find in politics a greater source of value than socialism has often assigned it. This requires the abandonment of the view of politics as an ultimately eliminable symptom of class rule, due ultimately to be folded back into society. For if social forces are not to underwrite the promise of human amelioration, then politics remains the sphere, however flawed, through which some control, however partial, may be exercised. In broad terms, this vague commendation is in keeping with some of Rorty's emphases, notably his exasperation with what he views as the cultural left's vision of a total and angelic transfiguration of power relations,[38] but not with others.

For, first, this emphasis on politics carries with it a wariness about utopianism, while Rorty happily embraces the construction of such visions. It is not only a *non sequitur* but a mistake to identify the optimism of the will or ethical confidence needed for social improvement with a utopian impulse (as Habermas does too, here adhering to an unreconstructed fragment of Frankfurt School discourse). Utopianism characteristically envisages societies without conflict, from which the need to engage in politics has been expunged.[39] A second point is that there is a difference between viewing political activity instrumentally as a channel for specific social reforms (as does Rorty) and viewing it as the source of collectivity or solidarity. Facile jibes at the fonder hopes of participatory democrats obscure an important question which they raise about whether an instrumental conception of politics can provide any sense of the collectivity which Rorty's own social democratic hopes surely require.[40] In Dewey's case, this is supplied (optimistically) in a naturalist teleology which yokes the self-fulfilment of moderns to democratic forms of action, and which he believed was immanent in existing social and industrial practices. Even if Dewey's optimism is not shared, proponents of a progressive form of politics need some language such as the one he provides in which to articulate forms of collectivity which do not entirely depend on the discretion of participants. But it seems to me that proponents of this politics are not strategically wise to deprive themselves of the theoretical language that allows such an articulation, or to invest their social hopes in a utopia which exists only on the far side of all political conflict.

Notes

1 James Tully, 'The Agonic Freedom of Citizens', *Economy and Society*, 28 (1999), p. 163.
2 Richard Rorty, 'The Priority of Democracy to Philosophy', *Objectivity, Relativism, and Truth* (Cambridge University Press, Cambridge, 1991), pp. 175–96.
3 Richard Rorty, *Consequences of Pragmatism* (University of Minnesota Press, Minneapolis), p. 166.
4 e.g. Richard Rorty, *Truth and Progress* (Cambridge University Press, Cambridge, 1998), pp. 12, 308–10; Richard Rorty, *Contingency, Irony, and Solidarity* (Cambridge University Press, Cambridge, 1989), p. 84.
5 Compare Jürgen Habermas, *Moral Consciousness and Communicative Action*, tr. Christian Lenhardt and Shierry Weber Nicholson (Polity, Cambridge, 1990).
6 Rorty, *Contingency, Irony, and Solidarity*, p. 68.
7 e.g. William Connolly, 'The Mirror of America', *Raritan*, 3 (1983), pp. 124–35; Frank Lentricchia, *Criticism and Social Change* (University of Chicago Press, Chicago, 1983), pp. 15–19; Milton Fisk, 'The Instability of Pragmatism', *New Literary History*, 17 (1985), pp. 23–30.
8 Richard Rorty, *Philosophy and Social Hope* (Penguin, Harmondsworth, 1999).
9 e.g. Rorty, *Truth and Progress*, p. 217.
10 Rorty, *Consequences of Pragmatism*, p. 161.
11 Rorty, *Contingency, Irony, and Solidarity*, p. 48.
12 Rorty, *Truth and Progress*, pp. 217–18.
13 Rorty, *Contingency, Irony, and Solidarity*, p. xvi.
14 Rorty, 'Globalization, the Politics of Identity and Social Hope', *Philosophy and Social Hope*, p. 231.
15 Richard Rorty, *Achieving our Country: Leftist Thought in Twentieth Century America* (Harvard University Press, Cambridge, Mass., 1998), p. 101.
16 Ibid., pp. 13–14.
17 Ibid., pp. 9, 14, 105–6.
18 Ibid., p. 43. Compare James Kloppenberg, *The Virtues of Liberalism* (Oxford University Press, New York, 1998), esp. chs. 7, 8.
19 It is not part of the purpose of this essay to consider the fairness of this representation. Exemplary texts cited by Rorty include Fredric Jameson, *Postmodernism, or the Cultural Logic of Late Capitalism* (Verso, London, 1991); Bill Readings, *The University in Ruins* (Harvard University Press, Cambridge, Mass., 1996), Fred M. Dolan, *Allegories of America* (Cornell University Press, Ithaca, NY, 1994).
20 See David Miller, *On Nationality* (Oxford University Press, Oxford, 1995); Maurizio Viroli, *For Love of Country: An Essay on Patriotism and Nationalism* (Clarendon Press, Oxford, 1995); Martha Nussbaum

et al., in Joshua Cohen (ed), *For Love of Country: Debating the Limits of Patriotism*, (Beacon, Boston, 1996).

21 Rorty, *Achieving our Country*, p. 85.

22 John Dewey, 'Context and Thought', *Later Works of John Dewey, 1925–1953*, ed. Jo Ann Boydston (17 vols; Southern Illinois University Press, Carbondale, 1981–92), vol. 6, p. 7.

23 Rorty, *Objectivity Relativism, and Truth*, p. 178.

24 John Dewey, *Reconstruction in Philosophy*, vol. 12, *Middle Works of John Dewey*, ed. Jo Ann Boydston (15 vols; Southern Illinois University Press, Carbondale, 1976–83), p. 190.

25 Rorty, *Objectivity, Relativism, and Truth*, pp. 178, 190.

26 Charles Taylor, 'Cross-Purposes: The Liberal–Communitarian Debate', in *Liberalism and the Moral Life*, ed. Nancy Rosenblum (Harvard University Press, Cambridge, Mass., 1989), pp. 159–82, at p. 160. And compare Dewey's presumption here (emphasis added): 'Is democracy a comparatively superficial human expedient, a device of petty manipulation, or does nature itself, as that is uncovered and understood by our best contemporaneous knowledge, sustain and support our democratic hopes and aspirations? Or, *if we choose to begin arbitrarily at the other end, if to construct democratic institutions is our aim, how then shall we construe and interpret our natural environment and the natural history of humanity in order to get an intellectual warrant for our endeavours...?*', Dewey, 'Philosophy and Democracy', *Middle Works*, vol. 11, p. 48.

27 Rorty, *Objectivity, Relativism, and Truth*, pp. 179, 197–8.

28 John Dewey, *Ethics*, 1st edn, *Middle Works*, vol. 5, p. 392.

29 John Dewey, 'Religion and Morality in a Free Society', *Later Works*, vol. 15, p. 181.

30 John Dewey, *The Public and its Problems, Later Works*, vol. 2, p. 329.

31 Dewey, *Reconstruction in Philosophy*, p. 192.

32 F. A. Hayek, *The Constitution of Liberty* (Routledge and Kegan Paul, London, 1960), p. 424. the *fons et origo* of Hayek's critique of Dewey is Dorothy Fosdick, *What is Liberty? A Study in Political Theory* (Harper, New York, 1939), esp. pp. 28–9, 50, 91, from whom Hayek drew both his quotations and his criticisms of Dewey. Both Fosdick and Hayek represent a political difference as a semantic mistake, while polemicizing against the political position that issues in the alleged error.

33 John Dewey, *Freedom and Culture, Later Works*, vol. 13, p. 72.

34 John Dewey, 'Pragmatic America', *Middle Works*, vol. 13, p. 307.

35 Rorty, *Contingency, Irony, and Solidarity*, p. xiii.

36 See Jennifer Welchman, *Dewey's Ethical Thought* (Cornell University Press, Ithaca, NY, 1995); this point is monotonously drummed home, with fuller references, in Festenstein, *Pragmatism and Political Theory* (Polity, Cambridge, 1997), chs. 1–3.

37 Rorty, 'The End of Leninism, Havel, and Social Hope', *Truth and Progress*, p. 228.

38 Rorty, *Achieving our Country*, p. 104.
39 Cf. Festenstein, *Pragmatism and Political Theory*, pp. 131–2.
40 Compare, for example, Jon Elster, *Sour Grapes* (Cambridge University Press, Cambridge, 1983); David Miller, *Market Socialism* (Clarendon Press, Oxford, 1989); Joshua Cohen and Joel Rogers, *Associations and Democracy* (Verso, London, 1995).

Response to Matthew Festenstein

Richard Rorty

I am grateful for the sympathetic and accurate account of the relation between my philosophical writings and *Achieving our Country* that Matthew Festenstein offers in the first section of his essay. That book was, just as he says, 'a sentimental narrative redescribing twentieth-century American leftist thought in the service of Rorty's conception of social hope'. I should be very glad indeed if readers of that book were persuaded, as Festenstein suggests they should be, that whatever its author's other faults, he is neither complacent nor frivolous – two adjectives which are still frequently applied.

In the second section of his essay, Festenstein detects a 'clear opposition' between Dewey and me on the question of what modes of argument and discourse are best suited for the defence of promotion of social democracy. I find the opposition less clear than he does.

It is certainly true that I do not see much point in writing about the nature of freedom or the nature of individualism, or about the structure of the modern self, and that Dewey did. But I am not sure that this is more than a reflection of a difference in intellectual environment, or of a difference in skills, or perhaps of both of these differences. 'Opposition' seems too strong.

Festenstein says that I reject 'the claim that political institutions "presuppose" a doctrine about the nature of human beings and that such a doctrine must, unlike Enlightenment rationalism, make clear the essentially historical character of the self'. The words in quotes are taken from my essay 'The Priority of Democracy to Philosophy'. In that essay I did not reject this claim, though I did raise two questions about it.

The first question was about whether the word 'presuppose' suggested, wrongly, that you should first get the self straight and then figure out what politics to have. I argued in my 1984 essay that we should, as I said there, 'put politics first and tailor a philosophy to suit'. I take this suggestion to be in the spirit of the italicized sentence in the passage from Dewey that Festenstein quotes in his note 26. When Dewey uses the word 'arbitrarily' in that passage, he seems to be saying that it does not make much difference whether we say 'this is what the self is, so these should be our political goals' or 'these are our political goals, and here is a theory of the self which might serve those goals'. If that is what he meant, then I quite agree – though I suspect that the first formula encourages an undesirable sort of *chutzpah* among theorists.

The second question I raised about the claim formulated above was whether a 'conception of the self that, as [Charles] Taylor says, makes "the community constitutive of the individual"...comports better with liberal democracy than an Enlightenment conception of the self' (Richard Rorty, *Objectivity, Relativism and Truth, Philosophical Papers*, vol. 1 (Cambridge University Press, Cambridge, 1991), p. 178). I answered 'yes' to that latter question, as Dewey also would have. So the only difference between Dewey and me in this area is whether formulating the former conception of the self is 'necessary and fundamental' – Festenstein's description of Dewey's view.

Dewey is unlikely to have held that such a formulation was necessary always and for everybody, though he might well have held that it was just what was needed in the socio-intellectual environment in which he was writing. Did he think it 'fundamental'? Well, 'fundamental' was not really one of Dewey's favourite words. But these are quibbles. I am happy to admit Festenstein's larger point: that Dewey saw more of a use for formulating systematic theories about traditional topics of theoretical debate than I do.

I am also happy to concede to Festenstein that there is no harm, and possibly some benefit, in having such theories. I never intended to do what he calls 'banning [this kind of] discourse'. At most, I have optimistically suggested that someday, in a better socio-intellectual environment, there will be no market for this kind of discourse.

I do, however, think that it is easy to overestimate the practical value of philosophical theories, as when Taylor (in a passage cited, with apparent agreement, by Festenstein) says that 'your ontological proposition, if true, can show that your neighbor's favorite social order is an impossibility.' Believing as I do that the only way to find out whether an imagined social order is an impossibility is to try it out and see, I doubt that ontology, sociobiology, cognitive psychology, or any other theoretical discipline is going to show anything like that. We theorists can summarize the results of past social experiments and offer suggestions about which new experiments it might pay to try and which would be too dangerous to try, but when we start attempting to prove *impossibility* we lose credibility.

Festenstein treats Dewey as having a 'developed account of individuality' which tells us that we should judge political alternatives by reference to their ability to liberate 'the potentialities of members of a group in harmony with the interests and goods which are common [to them]'. He says that I, in contrast, do not have such a developed account but merely a proposal for American 'identity'. I cannot see a big difference here, but merely the sort of difference in style and tactics which is not worth quarrelling over.

That standard for judging political alternatives is one which all admirers of Mill's *On Liberty* would happily adopt. I cannot see that it matters much whether one backs it up with an 'account of individuality' or with a suggestion about what sense of identity is appropriate for citizens of present-day America. Anybody who doesn't like the standard is going to reject both the account and the identity.

Towards the end of his paper, Festenstein claims that Dewey and I disagree in 'ethical doctrine'. I do not see the disagreements he cites as very great or very significant. Dewey, Festenstein says, thinks that 'possession of a sense of the common good is required for individual self-realization'. Well, it certainly is for most people's self-realization, but was it for Nietzsche's? Emerson's? Kierkegaard's? Would Dewey have said that it was? Would he have insisted on the point?

Maybe he would, but if so I think he would have overstated his case. It is one thing to say that, for most of us, our sense of what makes our life worth living is bound up with our sense of responsibility towards others. It is another thing to say that no human being can succeed in separating his project of individual self-realization from such responsibilities. Some people, not all of them sociopaths, have succeeded in doing so. Maybe such separation usually produces pretty nasty selves, but that is another question.

Did Dewey really think that 'the apparent conflict between self-interest and altruism was based on a false metaphysical separation of individual and society'? At most, it seems to me, he would have said that the claim that there is a *necessary* conflict of this sort is based on bad metaphysics. He had no need to deny that such conflicts were both real and common, nor that one form this conflict took was between responsibilities to others and responsibilities to oneself (as in the case of Gauguin, made vivid in Bernard Williams's famous discussion of 'moral luck').

I do not think that my discussion of the private and the public 'drives a wedge between' individual self-realization and the collective good. All I need say is that for many people – more and more people, to the extent that wealth, leisure and high culture become more equably distributed – these two may well conflict. There is no pre-established harmony here. I admit that Dewey sometimes talks as if there were such a harmony, and at those passages I do indeed disagree with him. But I do not think that these passages are central to his ethical views.

At the very end of his paper Festenstein says that Habermas and I should beware of utopianism because 'utopianism characteristically envisages societies without conflict'. This is a point which has recently been urged by Chantal Mouffe, and perhaps a survey of the literature of utopianism would support it. If so, then I think we should take greater pains to dream up utopias which, though filled with conflict, are nonetheless greatly preferable to the socio-economic setup we have at present.

Many such utopias can be found in science fiction, which seems to me to have become the most widely read, most imaginative and most fruitful genre of long-range political deliberation. (Think of the difference having read *Brave New World* makes to our students, for example – how tempted we are to tell students in courses in moral and political theory who have not read it to do so before the next class.) Some of these science-fiction utopias and dystopias envisage what Festenstein calls 'forms of collectivity which do not entirely depend on the discretion of the participants', and some do not. Deliberation about the virtues and vices of these forms is facilitated by narratives that recount the fortunes of an ever greater variety of possible human societies.

11

Justice as a Larger Loyalty

Richard Rorty

All of us would expect help if, pursued by the police, we asked our family to hide us. Most of us would extend such help even when we know our child or our parent to be guilty of a sordid crime. Many of us would be willing to perjure ourselves in order to supply such a child or parent with a false alibi. But if an innocent person is wrongly convicted as a result of our perjury, most of us will be torn by a conflict between loyalty and justice.

Such a conflict will be felt, however, only to the extent to which we can identify with the innocent person whom we have harmed. If the person is a neighbour, the conflict will probably be intense. If a stranger, especially one of a different race, class or nation, it may be considerably weaker. There has to be *some* sense in which he or she is 'one of us', before we start to be tormented by the question of whether or not we did the right thing when we committed perjury. So it may be equally appropriate to describe us as torn between conflicting loyalties – loyalty to our family and to a group large enough to include the victim of our perjury – rather than between loyalty and justice.

Our loyalty to such larger groups will, however, weaken, or even vanish altogether, when things get really tough. Then people whom we once thought of as like ourselves will be excluded. Sharing food with impoverished people down the street is natural and right in normal times, but perhaps not in a famine, when doing so amounts to disloyalty to one's family. The tougher things get, the more ties of loyalty to those near at hand tighten, and the more those to everyone else slacken.

Consider another example of expanding and contracting loyalties: our attitude towards other species. Most of us today are at least half-convinced that the vegetarians have a point, and that animals do have some sort of rights. But suppose that the cows, or the kangaroos, turn out to be carriers of a newly mutated virus, which, though harmless to them, is invariably fatal to humans. I suspect that we would then shrug off accusations of 'speciesism' and participate in the necessary massacre. The idea of justice between species will suddenly become irrelevant, because things have gotten very tough indeed, and our loyalty to our own species must come first. Loyalty to a larger community – that of all living creatures on our home planet – would, under such circumstances, quickly fade away.

As a final example, consider the tough situation created by the accelerating export of jobs from the First World to the Third. There is likely to be a continuing decline in the average real income of most American families. Much of this decline can plausibly be attributed to the fact that you can hire a factory worker in Thailand for a tenth of what you would have to pay a worker in Ohio. It has become the conventional wisdom of the rich that American and European labour is overpriced on the world market. When American business people are told that they are being disloyal to the United States by leaving whole cities in our Rust Belt without work or hope, they sometimes reply that they place justice over loyalty.[1] They argue that the needs of humanity as a whole take moral precedence over those of their fellow citizens and override national loyalties. Justice requires that they act as citizens of the world.

Consider now the plausible hypothesis that democratic institutions and freedoms are viable only when supported by an economic affluence that is achievable regionally but impossible globally. If this hypothesis is correct, democracy and freedom in the First World will not be able to survive a thoroughgoing globalization of the labour market. So the rich democracies face a choice between perpetuating their own democratic institutions and traditions and dealing justly with the Third World. Doing justice to the Third World would require exporting capital and jobs until everything is levelled out – until an honest day's work, in a ditch or at a computer, earns no higher a wage in Cincinnati or Paris than in a small town in Botswana. But then, it can plausibly be argued, there will be no money to support free public libraries, competing newspapers and networks, widely available liberal arts education, and all the other institutions that are necessary to produce enlightened public opinion, and thus to keep governments more or less democratic.

What, on this hypothesis, is the right thing for the rich democracies to do? Be loyal to themselves and each other? Keep free societies going for a third of mankind at the expense of the remaining two-thirds? Or sacrifice the blessings of political liberty for the sake of egalitarian economic justice?

These questions parallel those confronted by the parents of a large family after a nuclear holocaust. Do they share the food supply they have stored in the basement with their neighbours, even though the stores will then only last a day or two? Or do they fend those neighbours off with guns? Both moral dilemmas bring up the same question: Should we contract the circle for the sake of loyalty, or expand it for the sake of justice?

I have no idea of the right answer to these questions, neither about the right thing for these parents to do, nor about the right thing for the First World to do. I have posed them simply to bring a more abstract, and merely philosophical, question into focus. That question is: Should we describe such moral dilemmas as conflicts between loyalty and justice, or rather, as I have suggested, between loyalties to smaller groups and loyalties to larger groups?

This amounts to asking: Would it be a good idea to treat 'justice' as the name for loyalty to a certain very large group, the name for our largest current loyalty, rather than the name of something distinct from loyalty? Could we replace the notion of 'justice' with that of loyalty to that group – for example, one's fellow citizens, or the human species, or all living things? Would anything be lost by this replacement?

Moral philosophers who remain loyal to Kant are likely to think that a *lot* would be lost. Kantians typically insist that justice springs from reason, and loyalty from sentiment. Only reason, they say, can impose universal and unconditional moral obligations, and our obligation to be just is of this sort. It is on another level from the sort of affectional relations that create loyalty. Jürgen Habermas is the most prominent contemporary philosopher to insist on this Kantian way of looking at things: the thinker least willing to blur either the line between reason and sentiment, or the line between universal validity and historical consensus. But contemporary philosophers who depart from Kant, either in the direction of Hume (like Annette Baier) or in the direction of Hegel (like Charles Taylor) or in that of Aristotle (like Alasdair MacIntyre), are not so sure.

Michael Walzer is at the other extreme from Habermas. He is wary of terms like 'reason' and 'universal moral obligation'. The heart of his book, *Thick and Thin*, is the claim that we should reject the intuition that Kant took as central: the intuition that 'men and women everywhere begin with some common idea or principle or set of ideas and principles, which they then work up in many different ways.'

Walzer thinks that this picture of morality 'starting thin' and 'thickening with age' should be inverted. He says that, 'Morality is thick from the beginning, culturally integrated, fully resonant, and it reveals itself thinly only on special occasions, when moral language is turned to special purposes'.[2] Walzer's inversion suggests, though it does not entail, the neo-Humean picture of morality sketched by Annette Baier in her book *Moral Prejudices*. On Baier's account, morality starts out not as an obligation but as a relation of reciprocal trust among a closely knit group, such as a family or clan. To behave morally is to do what comes naturally in your dealings with your parents and children or your fellow clan members. It amounts to respecting the trust they place in you. Obligation, as opposed to trust, enters the picture only when your loyalty to a smaller group conflicts with your loyalty to a larger group.[3]

When, for example, the families confederate into tribes, or the tribes into nations, you may feel obliged to do what does not come naturally: to leave your parents in the lurch by going off to fight in the wars, or to rule against your own village in your capacity as a federal administrator or judge. What Kant would describe as the resulting conflict between moral obligation and sentiment, or between reason and sentiment, is, on a non-Kantian account of the matter, a conflict between one set of loyalties and another set of loyalties. The idea of a *universal* moral obligation to respect human dignity gets replaced by the idea of loyalty to a very large group – the human species. The idea that moral obligation extends beyond that species to an even larger group becomes the idea of loyalty to all those who, like yourself, can experience pain – even the cows and the kangaroos – or perhaps even to all living things, even the trees.

This non-Kantian view of morality can be rephrased as the claim that one's moral identity is determined by the group or groups with which one identifies – the group or groups to which one cannot be disloyal and still like oneself. Moral dilemmas are not, in this view, the result of a conflict between reason and sentiment but between alternative selves, alternative self-descriptions, alternative ways of giving a meaning to one's life. Non-Kantians do not think that we have a central, true self by virtue of our membership in the human species – a self that responds to the call of reason. They can, instead, agree with Daniel Dennett that a self is a centre of narrative gravity. In nontraditional societies most people have several such narratives at their disposal, and thus several different moral identities. It is this plurality of identities that accounts for the number and variety of moral dilemmas, moral philosophers and psychological novels in such societies.

Walzer's contrast between thick and thin morality is, among other things, a contrast between the detailed and concrete stories you can tell about yourself as a member of a smaller group and the relatively abstract and sketchy story you can tell about yourself as a citizen of the world. You know more about your family than about your village, more about your village than about your nation, more about your nation than about humanity as a whole, more about being human than about simply being a living creature. You are in a better position to decide what differences between individuals are morally relevant when dealing with those whom you can describe thickly, and in a worse position when dealing with those whom you can describe thinly. This is why, as groups get larger, law has to replace custom, and abstract principles have to replace *phronēsis*. So Kantians are wrong to see *phronēsis* as a thickening up of thin abstract principles. Plato and Kant were misled by the fact that abstract principles are designed to trump parochial loyalties into thinking that the principles are somehow prior to the loyalties – that the thin is somehow prior to the thick.

Walzer's thick–thin distinction can be aligned with Rawls's contrast between a shared *concept* of justice and various conflicting *conceptions* of justice. Rawls sets out that contrast as follows:

> the concept of justice, applied to an institution, means, say, that the institution makes no arbitrary distinctions between persons in assigning basic rights and duties, and that its rules establish a proper balance between competing claims.... [A] conception includes, besides this, principles and criteria for deciding which distinctions are arbitrary and when a balance between competing claims is proper. People can agree on the meaning of justice and still be at odds, since they affirm different principles and standards for deciding these matters.[4]

Phrased in Rawls's terms, Walzer's point is that thick 'fully resonant' *conceptions* of justice, complete with distinctions between the people who matter most and the people who matter less, come first. The thin concept, and its maxim 'do not make arbitrary distinctions between moral subjects', is articulated only on special occasions. On those occasions the thin concept can often be turned against any of the thick conceptions from which it emerged, in the form of critical questions about whether it may not be merely arbitrary to think that certain people matter more than others.

Neither Rawls nor Walzer think, however, that unpacking the thin concept of justice will, by itself, resolve such critical questions by supplying a criterion of arbitrariness. They do not think that we can do what Kant hoped to do – derive solutions to moral dilemmas from the analysis of moral concepts. To put the point in the terminology I am suggesting: we cannot resolve conflicting loyalties by turning away from them all towards something categorically distinct from loyalty – the universal moral obligation to act justly. So we have to drop the Kantian idea that the moral law starts off pure but is always in danger of being contaminated by irrational feelings that introduce arbitrary discriminations among persons. We have to substitute the Hegelian–Marxist idea that the so-called moral law is, at best, a handy abbreviation for a concrete web of social practices. This means dropping Habermas's claim that his 'discourse ethics' articulates a transcendental presupposition of the use of language, and accepting his critics' claim that it articulates only the customs of contemporary liberal societies.[5]

Now I want to raise the question of whether to describe the various moral dilemmas with which I began as conflicts between loyalty and justice, or rather as conflicting loyalties to particular groups, in a more concrete form. Consider the question of whether the demands for reform made on the rest of the world by Western liberal societies are made in the name of something not merely Western – something like morality, or humanity, or rationality – or are simply expressions of loyalty to local, Western, conceptions of justice. Habermas would say that they are the former. I would say that they are the latter, but are none the worse for that. I think it is better not to say that the liberal West is better informed about rationality and justice, and instead to say that, in making demands on non-liberal societies, it is simply being true to itself.

In a paper called 'The Law of Peoples', Rawls discusses the question of whether the conception of justice he has developed in his books is something peculiarly Western and liberal or rather something universal. He would like to be able to claim universality. He says that it is important to avoid 'historicism', and believes that he can do this if he can show that the conception of justice suited to a liberal society can be extended beyond such societies through formulating what he calls 'the law of peoples'.[6] He outlines, in that paper, an extension of the constructivist procedure proposed in his *A Theory of Justice* – an extension which, by continuing to separate the right from the good, lets us encompass liberal and non-liberal societies under the same law.

As Rawls develops this constructivist proposal, however, it emerges that this law applies only to *reasonable* peoples, in a quite specific sense of the term 'reasonable'. The conditions that non-liberal societies must honour in order to be 'accepted by liberal societies as members in good standing of a society of peoples' include the following: 'its system of law must be guided by a common good conception of justice... that takes impartially into account what it sees not unreasonably as the fundamental interests of all members of society.'[7]

Rawls takes the fulfilment of that condition to rule out violation of basic human rights. These rights include 'at least certain minimum rights to means of subsistence and security (the right to life), to liberty (freedom from slavery, serfdom, and forced occupations) and (personal) property, as well as to formal equality as expressed by the rules of natural justice (for example, that similar cases be treated similarly)'.[8] When Rawls spells out what he means by saying that the admissible non-liberal societies must not have unreasonable philosophical or religious doctrines, he glosses 'unreasonable' by saying that these societies must 'admit a measure of liberty of conscience and freedom of thought, even if these freedoms are not in general equal for all members of society'. Rawls's notion of what is reasonable, in short, confines membership of the society of peoples to societies whose institutions encompass most of the hard-won achievements of the West in the two centuries since the Enlightenment.

It seems to me that Rawls cannot both reject historicism and invoke this notion of reasonableness. For the effect of that invocation is to build most of the West's recent decisions about which distinctions between persons are arbitrary into the conception of justice that is implicit in the law of peoples. The differences between different *conceptions* of justice, remember, are differences between what features of people are seen as relevant to the adjudication of their competing claims. There is obviously enough wriggle room in phrases like 'similar cases should be treated similarly' to allow for arguments that believers and infidels, men and women, blacks and whites, gays and straights should be treated as relevantly *dis*similar. So there is room to argue that discrimination on the basis of such differences is *not* arbitrary. If we are going to exclude from the society of peoples societies in which infidel homosexuals are not permitted to engage in certain occupations, those societies can quite reasonably say that we are, in excluding them, appealing not to something universal, but to very recent developments in Europe and America.

I agree with Habermas when he says, 'What Rawls in fact prejudges with the concept of an "overlapping consensus" is the distinction between modern and premodern forms of consciousness, between "reasonable" and "dogmatic" world interpretations.' But I disagree with Habermas, as I think Walzer also would, when he goes on to say that Rawls can defend the primacy of the right over the good with the concept of an overlapping consensus only if it is true that post-metaphysical worldviews that have become reflexive under modern conditions are epistemically superior to dogmatically fixed, fundamentalistic world-views – indeed, only if such a distinction can be made with absolute clarity.

Habermas's point is that Rawls needs an argument from transcultur-ally valid premises for the superiority of the liberal West. Without such an argument, he says, 'the disqualification of "unreasonable" doctrines that cannot be brought into harmony with the proposed "political" concept of justice is inadmissible.'[9]

Such passages make clear why Habermas and Walzer are at oppos-ite poles. Walzer is taking for granted that there can be no such thing as a non-question-begging demonstration of the epistemic superiority of the Western idea of reasonableness. There is, for Walzer, no tribu-nal of transcultural reason before which to try the question of super-iority. Walzer is presupposing what Habermas calls 'a strong contextualism for which there is no single "rationality"'. On this conception, Habermas continues, 'individual "rationalities" are cor-related with different cultures, worldviews, traditions, or forms of life. Each of them is viewed as internally interwoven with a particular understanding of the world.'[10]

I think that Rawls's constructivist approach to the law of peoples can work if he adopts what Habermas calls a 'strong contextualism'. Doing so would mean giving up the attempt to escape historicism, as well as the attempt to supply a universalistic argument for the West's most recent views about which differences between persons are arbi-trary. The strength of Walzer's *Thick and Thin* seems to me to be its explictness about the need to do this. The weakness of Rawls's account of what he is doing lies in an ambiguity between two senses of universalism. When Rawls says that 'a constructivist liberal doc-trine is universal in its reach, once it is extended to . . . a law of peoples',[11] he is not saying that it is universal in its validity. Universal reach is a notion that sits well with constructivism, but universal validity is not. It is the latter that Habermas requires. That is why Habermas thinks that we need really heavy philosophical weaponry, modelled on Kant's – why he insists that only transcendental presup-positions of any possible communicative practice will do the job.[12] To be faithful to his own constructivism, I think, Rawls has to agree with Walzer that this job does not need to be done.

Rawls and Habermas often invoke, and Walzer almost never invokes, the notion of 'reason'. In Habermas this notion is always bound up with that of context-free validity. In Rawls things are more complicated. Rawls distinguishes the reasonable from the rational, using the latter to mean simply the sort of means–end rationality that is employed in engineering, or in working out a Hobbesian *modus vivendi*. But he often invokes a third notion, that of 'practical reason', as when he says that the authority of a constructivist liberal doctrine 'rests on the principles and conceptions of practical reason'.[13] Rawls's use of this Kantian term may make it sound as if he agreed with Kant and Habermas that there is a universally distributed human faculty called practical reason (existing prior to, and working quite independently of, the recent history of the West), a faculty that tells us what counts as an arbitrary distinction between persons and what does not. Such a faculty would do the job Habermas thinks needs doing: detecting transcultural moral validity.

But this cannot, I think, be what Rawls intends. For he also says that his own constructivism differs from all philosophical views that appeal to a source of authority, and in which 'the universality of the doctrine is the direct consequence of its source of authority.' As examples of sources of authority, he cites '(human) reason, or an independent realm of moral values, or some other proposed basis of universal validity'.[14] So I think we have to construe his phrase 'the principles and conceptions of practical reason' as referring to *whatever* principles and conceptions are in fact arrived at in the course of creating a community.

Rawls emphasizes that creating a community is not the same thing as working out a *modus vivendi* – a task which requires only means–end rationality, not practical reason. A principle or conception belongs to practical reason, in Rawls's sense, if it emerged in the course of people starting thick and getting thin, thereby developing an overlapping consensus and setting up a more inclusive moral community. It would not so belong if it had emerged under the threat of force. Practical reason for Rawls is, so to speak, a matter of procedure rather than of substance – of how we agree on what to do rather than of what we agree on.

This definition of practical reason suggests that there may be only a verbal difference between Rawls's and Habermas's positions. For Habermas's own attempt to substitute 'communicative reason' for 'subject-centred reason' is itself a move towards substituting 'how' for 'what'. The first sort of reason is a source of truth, truth somehow coeval with the human mind. The second sort of reason is not a source of anything, but simply the activity of justifying claims by offering arguments rather than threats. Like Rawls, Habermas focuses on the difference between persuasion and force, rather than, as Plato and

Kant did, on the difference between two parts of the human person – the good rational part and the dubious passionate or sensual part. Both would like to de-emphasize the notion of the *authority* of reason – the idea of reason as a faculty which issues decrees – and substitute the notion of rationality as what is present whenever people communicate, whenever they try to justify their claims to one another, rather than threatening each other.

The similarities between Rawls and Habermas seem even greater in the light of Rawls's endorsement of Thomas Scanlon's answer to the 'fundamental question why anyone should care about morality at all', namely that 'we have a basic desire to be able to justify our actions to others on grounds that they could not reasonably reject – reasonably, that is, given the desire to find principles that others similarly motivated could not reasonably reject.'[15] This suggests that the two philosophers might agree on the following claim: The only notion of rationality we need, at least in moral and social philosophy, is that of a situation in which people do not say 'your own current interests dictate that you agree to our proposal', but rather 'your own central beliefs, the ones which are central to your own moral identity, suggest that you should agree to our proposal.'

This notion of rationality can be delimited using Walzer's terminology by saying that rationality is found wherever people envisage the possibility of getting from different thicks to the same thin. To appeal to interests rather than beliefs is to urge a *modus vivendi*. Such an appeal is exemplified by the speech of the Athenian ambassadors to the unfortunate Melians, as reported by Thucydides. To appeal to your enduring beliefs as well as to your current interests is to suggest that what gives you your *present* moral identity – your thick and resonant complex of beliefs – may make it possible for you to develop a new, supplementary, moral identity.[16] It is to suggest that what makes you loyal to a smaller group may give you reason to cooperate in constructing a larger group, a group to which you may in time become equally loyal or perhaps even more loyal. The difference between the absence and the presence of rationality, on this account, is the difference between a threat and an offer – the offer of a new moral identity and thus a new and larger loyalty, a loyalty to a group formed by an unforced agreement between smaller groups.

In the hope of minimizing the contrast between Habermas and Rawls still further, and of rapprochement between both and Walzer, I want to suggest a way of thinking of rationality that might help to resolve the problem I posed earlier: the problem of whether justice and loyalty are different sorts of things, or whether the demands of justice are simply the demands of a larger loyalty. I said that question seemed to boil down to the question of whether justice and loyalty had different sources – reason and sentiment, respectively. If the latter distinction disappears, the former one will not seem particularly useful. But if by rationality we mean simply the sort of activity that Walzer thinks of as a thinning-out process – the sort that, with luck, achieves the formulation and utilization of an overlapping consensus – then the idea that justice has a different source than loyalty no longer seems plausible.[17]

For, on this account of rationality, being rational and acquiring a larger loyalty are two descriptions of the same activity. This is because *any* unforced agreement between individuals and groups about what to do creates a form of community, and will, with luck, be the initial stage in expanding the circles of those whom each party to the agreement had previously taken to be 'people like ourselves'. The opposition between rational argument and fellow-feeling thus begins to dissolve. For fellow-feeling may, and often does, arise from the realization that the people whom one thought one might have to go to war with, use force on, are, in Rawls's sense, 'reasonable'. They are, it turns out, enough like us to see the point of compromising differences in order to live in peace, and of abiding by the agreement that has been hammered out. They are, to some degree at least, trustworthy.

From this point of view, Habermas's distinction between a strategic use of language and a genuinely communicative use of language begins to look like a difference between positions on a spectrum – a spectrum of degrees of trust. Baier's suggestion that we take trust rather than obligation to be our fundamental moral concept would thus produce a blurring of the line between rhetorical manipulation and genuine validity-seeking argument – a line that I think Habermas draws too sharply. If we cease to think of reason as a source of authority, and think of it simply as the process of reaching agreement by persuasion, then the standard Platonic and Kantian dichotomy of reason and feeling begins to fade away. That dichotomy can be replaced by a continuum of degrees of overlap of beliefs and desires.[18] When people whose beliefs and desires do not overlap very much disagree, they tend to think of each other as crazy or, more politely, as irrational. When there is considerable overlap, on the other hand, they may agree to differ and regard each other as the sort of people one can live with – and eventually, perhaps, the sort one can be friends with, intermarry with, and so on.[19]

To advise people to be rational is, on the view I am offering, simply to suggest that somewhere among their shared beliefs and desires there may be enough resources to permit agreement on how to coexist without violence. To conclude that someone is irredeemably *irrational* is not to realize that she is not making proper use of her God-given faculties. It is rather to realize that she does not seem to share enough relevant beliefs and desires with us to make possible fruitful conversation about the issue in dispute. So, we reluctantly conclude, we have to give up on the attempt to get her to enlarge her moral identity, and settle for working out a *modus vivendi* – one which may involve the threat, or even the use, of force.

A stronger, more Kantian, notion of rationality would be invoked if one said that being rational guarantees a peaceful resolution of conflicts – that if people are willing to reason together long enough, what Habermas calls 'the force of the better argument' will lead them to concur.[20] This stronger notion strikes me as pretty useless. I see no point in saying that it is more rational to prefer one's neighbours to one's family in the event of a nuclear holocaust, or more rational to prefer levelling off incomes around the world to preserving the institutions of liberal Western societies. To use the word 'rational' to commend one's chosen solution to such dilemmas, or to use the term 'yielding to the force of the better argument' to characterize one's way of making up one's mind, is to pay oneself an empty compliment.

More generally, the idea of 'the better argument' makes sense only if one can identify a natural, transcultural relation of relevance, which connects propositions with one another so as to form something like Descartes's 'natural order of reasons'. Without such a natural order, one can only evaluate arguments by their efficacy in producing agreement among particular persons or groups. But the required notion of natural, intrinsic relevance – relevance dictated not by the needs of any given community but by human reason as such – seems no more plausible or useful than that of a God whose will can be appealed to in order to resolve conflicts between communities. It is, I think, merely a secularized version of that earlier notion.

Non-Western societies in the past were rightly sceptical of Western conquerors who explained that they were invading in obedience to divine commands. More recently, they have been sceptical of Westerners who suggest that they should adopt Western ways in order to become more rational. (This suggestion has been abbreviated by Ian Hacking as 'Me rational, you Jane'.) On the account of rationality I am recommending, both forms of scepticism are equally justified. But this is not to deny that these societies *should* adopt recent Western ways by, for example, abandoning slavery, practising religious toleration, educating women, permitting mixed marriages, tolerating homosexuality and conscientious objection to war, and so on. As a loyal Westerner, I think they should indeed do all these things. I agree with Rawls about what it takes to count as reasonable, and about what kind of societies we Westerners should accept as members of a global moral community.

But I think that the rhetoric we Westerners use in trying to get everyone to be more like us would be improved if we were more frankly ethnocentric, and less professedly universalist. It would be better to say: Here is what we in the West look like as a result of ceasing to hold slaves, beginning to educate women, separating church and state, and so on. Here is what happened after we started treating certain distinctions between people as arbitrary rather than fraught with moral significance. If you would try treating them that way, you might like the results. Saying that sort of thing seems preferable to saying: Look at how much better we are at knowing what differences between persons are arbitrary and which not – how much more *rational* we are.

If we Westerners could get rid of the notion of universal moral obligations created by membership in the species, and substitute the idea of building a community of trust between ourselves and others, we might be in a better position to persuade non-Westerners of the advantages of joining in that community. We might be better able to construct the sort of global moral community that Rawls describes in 'The Law of Peoples'. In making this suggestion, I am urging, as I have on earlier occasions, that we need to peel apart Enlightenment liberalism from Enlightenment rationalism.

I think that discarding the residual rationalism that we inherit from the Enlightenment is advisable for many reasons. Some of these are theoretical and of interest only to philosophy professors, such as the apparent incompatibility of the correspondence theory of truth with a naturalistic account of the origin of human minds.[21] Others are more practical. One practical reason is that getting rid of rationalistic rhetoric would permit the West to approach the non-West in the role of someone with an instructive story to tell, rather than in the role of someone purporting to be making better use of a universal human capacity.

Notes

1 Donald Fites, the CEO of the Caterpillar tractor company, explained his company's policy of relocation abroad by saying that 'as a human being, I think what is going on is positive. I don't think it is realistic for 250 million Americans to control so much of the world's GNP.' Quoted in

Edward Luttwak, *The Endangered American Dream* (New York: Simon & Schuster, 1993), p. 184.

2   Michael Walzer, *Thick and Thin: Moral Argument at Home and Abroad* (Notre Dame Ind.: Notre Dame University Press, 1994), p. 4.

3   Baier's picture is quite close to that sketched by Wilfrid Sellars and Robert Brandom in their quasi-Hegelian accounts of moral progress as the expansion of the circle of beings who count as 'us'.

4   John Rawls, *Political Liberalism* (New York: Columbia University Press, 1993), p. 14n.

5   This sort of debate runs through a lot of contemporary philosophy. Compare, for example, Walzer's contrast between starting thin and starting thick with that between the Platonic–Chomskian notion that we start with meanings and descend to use, and the Wittgensteinian–Davidsonian notion that we start with use and then skim off meaning as needed for lexicographical or philosophical purposes.

6   John Rawls, 'The Law of Peoples', in *On Human Rights: The Oxford Amnesty Lectures, 1993*, ed. Stephen Shute and Susan Hurley (New York: Basic Books, 1993), p. 44. I am not sure why Rawls thinks historicism is undesirable, and there are passages, both early and recent, in which he seems to throw in his lot with the historicists. (See the passage quoted in n. 9 below from his recent 'Reply to Habermas'.) Some years ago I argued for the plausibility of a historicist interpretation of the meta-philosophy of Rawls's *A Theory of Justice* in my 'The Priority of Democracy to Philosophy', reprinted in my *Objectivity, Relativism, and Truth* (Cambridge: Cambridge University Press, 1991).

7   'The Law of Peoples', pp. 81, 61.

8   Ibid., p. 62.

9   All quotations in this paragraph are from Jürgen Habermas, *Justification and Application: Remarks on Discourse Ethics* (Cambridge, Mass.: MIT Press, 1993), p. 95. Habermas is here commenting on Rawls's use of 'reasonable' in writings earlier than 'The Law of Peoples', since the latter appeared subsequent to Habermas's book.

When I wrote the present essay, the exchange between Rawls and Habermas published in the *Journal of Philosophy* (92/3, March 1995) had not yet appeared. This exchange rarely touches on the question of historicism versus universalism. But one passage in which this question emerges explicitly is to be found on p. 179 of Rawls's 'Reply to Habermas': 'Justice as fairness is substantive ... in the sense that it springs from and belongs to the tradition of liberal thought and the larger community of political culture of democratic societies. It fails then to be properly formal and truly universal, and thus to be part of the quasi-transcendental presuppositions (as Habermas sometimes says) established by the theory of communicative action.'

10   Habermas, *Justification*, p. 95.

11   Rawls, 'The Law of Peoples', p. 46.

12 My own view is that we do not need, either in epistemology or in moral philosophy, the notion of universal validity. I argue for this in 'Sind Aussagen universelle Geltungsansprüche?' *Deutsche Zeitschrift für Philosophie*, 42/6 (1994), pp. 975–88. Habermas and Apel find my view paradoxical and likely to produce performative self-contradiction.

13 Rawls, 'The Law of Peoples', p. 46.

14 Both quotations, ibid., p. 45.

15 I quote here from Rawls's summary of Scanlon's view at *Political Liberalism*, p. 49n.

16 Walzer thinks it is a good idea for people to have lots of different moral identities. '[T]hick, divided selves are the characteristic products of, and in turn require, a thick, differentiated, and pluralistic society' (*Thick and Thin*, p. 101).

17 Note that in Rawls's semi-technical sense an overlapping consensus is not the result of discovering that various comprehensive views already share common doctrines, but rather something that might never have emerged had the proponents of these views not started trying to cooperate.

18 Davidson has, I think, demonstrated that any two beings that use language to communicate with one another necessarily share an enormous number of beliefs and desires. He has thereby shown the incoherence of the idea that people can live in separate worlds created by differences in culture or status or fortune. There is always an immense overlap – an immense reserve army of common beliefs and desires to be drawn on at need. But this immense overlap does not, of course, prevent accusations of craziness or diabolical wickedness. For only a tiny amount of non-overlap about certain particularly touchy subjects (the border between two territories, the name of the One True God) may lead to such accusations, and eventually to violence.

19 I owe this line of thought about how to reconcile Habermas and Baier to Mary Rorty.

20 This notion of 'the better argument' is central to Habermas's and Apel's understanding of rationality. I criticize it in the article cited above in n. 12.

21 For a claim that such a theory of truth is essential to 'the Western Rationalist Tradition', see John Searle, 'Rationality and Realism: What Difference does it Make?', *Daedalus*, 122/4 (Fall 1992), pp. 55–84. See also my reply to Searle in 'Does Academic Freedom have Philosophical Presuppositions?', *Academe*, 80/6 (November/December 1994), pp. 52–63. I argue there that we should be better off without the notion of 'getting something right', and that writers such as Dewey and Davidson have shown us how to keep the benefits of Western rationalism without the philosophical hangups caused by the attempt to explicate this notion.

Index